WHERE THE LAW IS:

AN INTRODUCTION TO ADVANCED LEGAL RESEARCH

Second Edition

By

J.D.S. Armstrong

Associate Director for Educational and Research Services
Arthur W. Diamond Law Library
Columbia University School of Law

Christopher A. Knott

Associate Law Librarian for Patron Services
Georgetown University Law Library
Georgetown University Law Center

AMERICAN CASEBOOK SERIES®

THOMSON

WEST

Mat # 40396696

© West, a Thomson business, 2004
© 2006 Thomson/West
      610 Opperman Drive
      P.O. Box 64526
      St. Paul, MN 55164–0526
      1–800–328–9352

ISBN–13: 978–0–314–16296–0
ISBN–10: 0–314–16296–8

TEXT IS PRINTED ON 10% POST CONSUMER RECYCLED PAPER

Acknowledgements for the Second Edition

To the acknowledgements made in our first edition, I would like to add gratitude to my esteemed library colleagues Aslihan Bulut, Karin Johnsrud, Andrew Larrick, Dana Neacsu, and Beth Williams (Columbia), Ronald E. Day (University of Pennsylvania), and Candice Spurlin (University of South Dakota), and to my helpful and inspiring students at Columbia Law School, especially Raymond Cho, Paul Cosmovici, Kati Daffan, Ryan Fahey, David Finkelstein, Brett Kingsbury, and Jeffrey Meriggi.

–JDSA

In addition to those I singled out in the first edition, I would like to thank my terrific colleagues at Georgetown Law who have made these past six years so enjoyable. I shall miss them very much. Also, I would like to acknowledge the contributions of the hundreds of students at Georgetown Law who have taught me at least as much as I have taught them. Their curiosity is infectious, their energy inspiring.

–CAK

*

Acknowledgements for the First Edition

I would like to express my indebtedness to the members, past and present, of the Reference Department of the Columbia Law School Library. I would also like to thank Kent McKeever and Simon Canick for their gracious assistance and valuable input, and Ian Armstrong for his graphical contribution. To my parents, to whom I dedicate this book, I offer my loving gratitude for their inspiration and encouragement in this as in so many things. And, above all, to Matthew, Angus, and Ian: as you well know, I couldn't have done it without you.

–JDSA

I would like to acknowledge the debt I owe to Bob Oakley, Director of the Georgetown University Law Library, for all his support and encouragement. Also, I want to thank a group of great librarians and even better friends who have taught me and guided me along the way: Kent McKeever, Jody Armstrong, Kris Gilliland, Marci Hoffman, and Bob Oakley. Thanks also to Uncle Bill for encouraging me to join the family business. Finally, I want to thank my wife Maggi and my daughter Acy for making life so happy and so fun.

–CAK

*

For Matthew, always.

— JDSA

For Maggi, Acy, and baby Alexander, as ever.

— CAK

*

Table of Contents

_____

Location of Tables

*

WHERE THE LAW IS:

AN INTRODUCTION TO ADVANCED LEGAL RESEARCH

Second Edition

*

Chapter 1

ADVANCED LEGAL RESEARCH: GETTING STARTED

1.1 WHAT THIS BOOK IS ABOUT

As a lawyer, an important part of your job is to advise your client on the law and on its implications for your client's affairs, both prospectively and within the context of litigation. Your responsibility encompasses being as sure as possible about what the law is *not*, as well as what the law is, on any particular subject. Establishing a negative proposition through research, an exigency which arises constantly in legal practice, requires a very sure hand. In order to answer questions from your client or from the court about the law authoritatively and confidently, you must know that you have looked for the law in all the right places. Hence, the title of this book.

As a student of advanced legal research, you are already familiar with the nuts and bolts of legal information. Cases and statutes are no longer alien or frightening creatures to you, but rather the eagerly-sought tools which you know you need for your daily work. But as you shoulder more and greater research responsibilities, as you graduate from canned research exercises to the real world, you will want to ensure that you know where you have to look to do your job competently and reliably. This book, we hope, will help you learn to do just that.

In the old days, finding the law was a jumpy sort of process, involving the use of multiple sources, some of which were interconnected, which had grown up as historical fruits of the evolution of American legal publishing. Legal research instruction focused on how to use each of these legal publications, most of which were either unique or had rival publications which were essentially the same in structure. Many of the great research treatises, such as Cohen, Berring and Olson's *How to Find the Law* and Price, Bitner and Bysiewicz's *Effective Legal Research*, concern themselves primarily with the description and illumination of these discrete publications.

Today, on the other hand, the information which emanates from the sources of legal authority is available from many suppliers, packaged in many different formats and combinations. Accordingly, today's legal researchers need to focus more on the information they are looking for, and less on any particular publication. In today's arena, you can no longer rely on any one publisher to have covered the field for you. The scope and coverage handled by a given publisher is influenced by competing licensing agreements, distribution networks, and both economic and political pressures that go beyond what the legal research market would seem logically to dictate. Researchers need to navigate through the shifting sands of the legal publishing world to locate all the information that they, as a matter of their own professional competency, deem necessary to the task at hand.

1.2   WHAT THIS BOOK IS NOT ABOUT

This book is about legal research, not about general research conducted by lawyers, which of course also happens all the time. Today's lawyer is called upon to argue from statistics, from marketing data out of the business world, from medical arcana, and from most other fields of human endeavor that furnish the background of discord. In order to construct their arguments and to master those anticipated from their opponents, lawyers may need to research facts or background in areas far afield from the law. Such research, since it is not specifically legal research, falls outside the scope of this book.

This book is also not about current awareness. All practicing lawyers have the responsibility of keeping up to date on legal developments in their areas of expertise, so as to be able to spot issues and recognize emerging problems or opportunities for their clients. Many of the sources discussed in this book arrive in the law practitioner's establishment fairly bristling with aids to maintaining such current awareness. Each volume of West's National Reporter System, for example, is chockablock with goodies intended for this purpose, e.g., tables of rules of procedure cited in that volume, words and phrases judicially construed in that volume, and so forth. These may, indeed, furnish the conscientious attorney with passingly interesting reading. However, they rarely figure in the process of active legal research, limited as they are to the tiny subset of materials (albeit recent materials) included in the selfsame volume. While we will occasionally mention some of these sources, we will focus instead on those elements that contribute usefully to research on a specific legal question rather than to speculative and abstract consideration of a legal authority's recent output.

1.3   WHY YOU MUST MAKE
A RESEARCH PLAN

As advanced legal research students, it is you who are advanced. You are already somewhat versed in the law and know a bit about what you are looking for and about what problems you might encounter in finding it. Perhaps the most common problem expressed by students beginning a course in advanced legal research is the difficulty of knowing when to stop searching. We have already mentioned the frequent and demanding obligation to prove a negative through research. Yet the opposite, seemingly simpler and more inviting task of establishing a positive legal proposition is actually more fraught with peril because of this very problem of not knowing when to stop. When looking for legal authority for a proposition, the inexperienced legal researcher all too often falls prey to the *"EUREKA!"* syndrome, i.e., he finds something which supports his claim, and calls it quits right there. In trying to prove a negative, on the other hand, there is no treacherous *"EUREKA!* I have found it!"* moment. There are only slowly mounting indications that you have, in fact, done enough: you start to see no new authorities cited, you have made a rational research plan and you have carried it out.

The importance of making a rational and informed research plan cannot be overemphasized. By making such a plan (in writing, please, since this is tantamount to a contract with yourself!), you can avoid the pitfall of settling for the first (or fifth) plausible answer you encounter, when your conclusion is based on still incomplete research. This pitfall yawns all the larger in the electronic world. The speed and facility of flitting from one source to another in the multitasking environment makes it easy to fall into the trap of basically random research stabs at each new source; this leads to sketchy results, inviting error and defeat.

The research plan can save you from this all too common fate. Basically, the purpose of the research plan is twofold. First, it ensures that you have built checks into your research that will keep you from reaching unwarranted conclusions. Second, once carried out, it provides the structure for logical and orderly documentation of what you have done. This documentation is particularly important when you do not find anything that satisfies the requested conditions, since the worth of your negative findings lies wholly in your testimony of where you looked. This also applies when you <u>did</u> find something, your document trail serving to validate its appropriateness.

1.4 DOCUMENTING WHAT
YOU FIND: CITATIONS

Documenting the fulfillment of your research plan should be done in such a way as to allow both today's and tomorrow's researchers to follow your trail easily. Such is the principle behind the sometimes irritating but nonetheless monumentally helpful rules of legal citation, such as (pre-eminently) those enshrined in the *Bluebook*. But in your own personal research writeups, you need not restrict yourself to leaving a trail universally legible to any and all researchers wherever they may be. You can and should feel free to enrich your paper trail with additional comments and details that pertain to your local environment. To be sure, you should always give full and correct cites to all references, so there is no possibility of error later. But you can also benefit by noting additional location information such as page numbers that are not part of the cite, hints on getting to a particular URL, volume numbers, shelf locations, even color or other physical characteristics of volumes. The key here is to give such additional information in an easily strippable form, so that it can be removed at a stroke when adapting your research for a more generic reader.

At the other end of the spectrum from such private notes about exactly where the information you have found is enshrined, you need to be aware of the developing trend of universal citation systems. These systems derive from the star pagination schemes of yesteryear, which directed readers of a subsequent edition of a legal text, by means of graphical symbols interposed in that text, to the original location of the same text in an earlier edition. The "star pagination" concept was widely used during the last century to enable researchers to move back and forth between the West editions of published cases and their counterparts published by the government or by competing commercial publishers.

Today's universal citation systems, such as those adopted by the American Bar Association, the American Association of Law Libraries, and by some federal and many state courts since the early 1990's, seek to remove the "pagination" from the star pagination idea. Rather, the text itself gets divided up and labelled in manageable chunks (typically a paragraph), each of which is assigned an identifying number which is associated with the larger document and set of documents of which it is a part. One purpose of this graphically ungainly exercise is to remove the systemic preference which the traditional page-bound citation systems afforded to established print publishers of legal authorities. But by so doing, the new systems undercut one of the basic functions of citation: i.e., the referral of the researcher to an unchangeable physical reference standard, a tangible and yet distributed text of record. The world is grappling with this issue in a wide variety of contexts; suffice it for now to remember that, as of this writing, the *Bluebook* requires the legal writer to cite to physically inscribed texts when they exist.

1.5 DOCUMENTING WHAT
YOU FIND: FORMATS

Such physically inscribed texts need not be consulted in paper format in order to furnish the desired unchangeable physical reference standard. The tangible reality of a book page is preserved for the researcher's purposes when it is reproduced in any analog-based format: thus, the longstanding acceptance of microformats (microfilm, microcard, microfiche) as reliably equivalent to the volumes they enshrined. To be sure, a manufacturing error can render an individual page illegible or misleading, and this has certainly created problems for individual researchers dependent on microformats for their information. But when it works, it works great. Even better for some purposes are the new generation of image-based reproductions of print pages: digital graphic versions of the documents, such as .pdf files, that capture the reality of the page content for digital reproduction and distribution. Since the publisher can see instantly that an error in image capture has occurred, the image can be redone on the spot, preserving the integrity of the document.

Thus .pdf files and microfiche can be said to function as proxies, full equivalents of their print originals for citation purposes. Yet no analog-based format can approach the flexibility, penetrability, and manipulability of text-based resources such as the full-text databases of Lexis and Westlaw. When a choice exists, the researcher needs to identify the proper source for each stage of research. In many cases, the electronic text-based resources will be the sources of choice for location of information, while the print-origin sources (whether distributed in paper, fiche, or electronically) will still be relied upon for text verification and authentication.

1.6 WHAT SOURCE TO USE?

Although *The Bluebook* is now beating around the bush a bit on this matter of physical format, no such shyness is in evidence in preferring one source to another within format. The general principle in play is that the preferred citation is to the source authorized by the legal authority in question, even when that is not really the source that most researchers use in everyday life. Thus, *The Bluebook* commands the writer to "cite the official code whenever possible" (Rule 12.3), compelling the researcher who has done all the leg work via, e.g., the USCA, to cross check the text found there against the official text, the US government-produced but comparatively unwieldy United States Code. All sources are clearly not created equal, and to avoid getting tripped up by a discrepancy, you need to keep strict track of which ones you actually perused with your own eyes. Looking at a reprint source may be the best you can do, or even the best thing that anyone could do, but you must acknowledge that you looked at that reprint source rather than at the original on which it was based. This comes up frequently in the case of the *United States Code Congressional and Administrative News*, the indispensable USCCAN, frequently the first (and therefore for a while the only) widely distributed print source for United States federal statutes. You are specifically required to cite to USCCAN if that is all that is available, rather than to use the Statutes at Large pagination indicated in USCCAN to construct a hypothetical Stat. cite. To maximize usefulness to the subsequent researcher, you are to include the Stat. pagination as a parenthetical part of your USCCAN cite, but you are not to omit mention of your USCCAN source (Rule 12.5(b)).

This principle is generalized in *Bluebook* Rule 1.6 (a)(ii), governing the use of material conveniently reprinted in a non-official source. The third example given, citation of a USCCAN reprint of a Congressional committee report, comes up frequently. Moreover, the notion of using a USCCAN reprint of a committee report without indicating USCCAN as its source vividly demonstrates the dangers of not acknowledging your true source. The USCCAN versions of the reports are generally excerpts, and even though the precise text quoted may have survived the transplant intact, the context in which it appears may be different enough to affect how it is read and understood. The same dangers are posed by using materials culled from casebooks, treatises, or looseleaf services. You should always either go the extra mile of referring back to the original source for the reprint material, or acknowledge what you have done and either take the rap or accept the praise for having engaged in such a shortcut.

1.7 FOLLOWING TANGENTS: HOW MUCH IS TOO MUCH?

Don't let your research plan keep you from doing *more*. You must be prepared to recognize new opportunities for investigation as they present themselves in the course of your research. You cannot allow the plan (your own or any canned instructions or checklists for legal research) to turn you into an automaton. Grappling with the implications of the legal authorities you uncover is the heart of your professional function, and you cannot abdicate this responsibility. That said, you need to be able to decide when to stop.

You can and should stop a line of research when you get to a point where the facts you are encountering, the law you are finding, or both, are no longer relevant to your research question. This is a judgment call that will become easier to make as you become more familiar with the subject at hand. More straightforwardly, you should stop when you come full circle and are back at your familiar core of material again. Once you are in a closed system of this type, you need to step back and consider whether it would be prudent to take a fresh approach.

On the other hand, you should not stop when you get to a point where you continue to find new cases but they are all similar. The temptation here is to get overwhelmed by the multiplicity of similar cases, and to stop reading. Instead, you can spot-check them for relevant variables such as similar facts or analogous law, and then narrow them down by applying combinations of criteria that make them ever closer to your situation. Another way to narrow down a potentially overwhelming array of seemingly similar cases is to run them through a citator to see which ones are of lasting importance. Which ones have been recently cited? Which ones have been voluminously cited, cited in law review articles, cited by higher courts, or in other jurisdictions? These are the cases that are likely to be the bases for the next stage of your research.

Another factor to consider in deciding when your research is finished is what kind of assignment you received. Different types of research are called for at different times. "Get me a case" means something very different from "what is the law on x". The former is clearly calling for a more abbreviated research foray than the latter. But beware! "A case" doesn't mean any old case relevant to the matter, but one <u>good</u> case. A "good case" ideally means one with a desirable interpretation of the law from the client's point of view, especially when it explicitly criticizes undesirable interpretations. As compared with the client's situation, the ideal "good case" will involve similar facts, a relevant jurisdiction (maybe even the same judge!), and still be valid, i.e., still "good law." Obviously this latter point, if explored in detail, takes you over into the other sort of research, the more exhaustive "find me the law on x". It is all a matter of degree.

1.8   HOW TO MAKE A RESEARCH PLAN

As you start to make a research plan you will need to determine first who it is that has authority to speak on your issue. Often more than one legal authority has legitimate claim to speak to an issue, so you should plan to address them in descending order of authority. As a simple example, if one legislative body, e.g., the United States Congress, has preemptive authority over a particular subject matter, you should research its output before considering the output of other lesser, probably more local, authorities. As a less simple example, if there is reason to anticipate that a normally higher authority would afford deference to the opinion of a nominally subordinate one, you should start with the output of the latter. Thus, for matters of local court rule interpretation, you would start with the opinions of the local court involved, rather than go straight to the Supreme Court to see what it has to say. Similarly for substantive issues of state law.

Once you have decided upon the authority in whom you are interested, you next need to consider what are the different places where you could look for its output. As you will see in the following chapters, the output of most legal authorities is now available in many different places and formats. You will need to consider the differences between the options and whether there is anything to be gained by looking in multiple places.

Finally, you should consider whether somebody has done this work before. Other attorneys in your workplace may have considered this same issue last week, and you will want to find out how that work may be accessible to you. The armies of law students, law professors, and practitioners toiling away to produce law journals may have done a lot of the leg work on your subject already. And of course, librarians and other legal writers sustain a whole industry of publications aimed at distilling and distributing legal research to the profession. Make sure you are not reinventing the wheel, at least where an appropriate wheel already exists!

When you have considered all the factors above, you are ready to set down a logically ordered and thorough plan. Your plan should account for all the elements in our diagram on page 12 below. It should specify where and how you are going to look for each of the following: the primary source which determines the legal issue, its history, its commentary, and its progeny or applications. Although each of these should be accounted for, elements that may not be necessary should not be sketched out in detail unless they prove to be so, e.g., mention "legislative history to be investigated if necessary," but only plan legislative history out if you, the courts, or commentators find some ambiguity, error, or omission in the governing statute.

Writing out a research plan will probably prove discomfiting to many at first, since it calls for an assertion of researcher control over the process that may seem unfamiliar. The untutored legal researcher of today first dives instinctively into exploratory full-text searching of legal databases. This may or may not be a good idea, depending on the problem at hand. Whether it is a good idea or not can become apparent to the researcher in the course of writing out the research plan. You will need to consider the best uses of full-text searching, and what is its optimal place or places in your plan. You do not usually want to be in the situation of having full-text searching as the only arrow in your quiver.

1.9   BEST USES OF FULL–TEXT SEARCHING

That said, the full–text searching of large legal databases is understandably a mainstay of legal researchers today, and the unique functionalities which such searching entails should be exploited in almost every research plan. When doing case law research, full–text searches can be used by the clueless to mount fishing expeditions to figure out what the blazes is going on. Plugging terms from your situation's fact pattern into a query put to a large case law database without any constraining knowledge of the law will usually retrieve other cases from similar situations; these can illuminate for you broadly what the legal issue in the case might actually be. The simplest form of this kind of search would include distinctive keywords from the facts, especially in combination with each other. Terms of art, either factual or legal, are particularly powerful used in this way. Another approach would be to combine such keywords with the names of attorneys involved in the current matter, since they may have been called in to deal with familiar, i.e., similar, legal issues. More complex exploratory searches could include terms associated with particular procedural postures in combination with a judge's name, to see how a judge handles particular kinds of requests.

At the other end of the process, full–text searching should always be employed as a check on the completeness and validity of index-based research. Once you are approaching the end of research through other means, you should do a full–text search to see whether completely different indexing terms come up on cases retrieved via the full-text search, and, if so, figure out why. This use of full–text searching allows you to reap the benefits of indexing without subjecting you to its limitations.

Beyond fishing expeditions, and beyond checking up on your other research, full–text searching can be especially effective in areas with which you are already quite familiar. In such cases you are really using it as an updating and current awareness tool to supplement your own knowledge of the area, and it is a powerful tool indeed. However, as a beginning lawyer, such areas will take a while to accumulate.

Finally, full–text searching can be the best way to go in areas of the law that are poorly or unsuitably indexed. This is an example of how the elimination of the middleman (the indexer) can pay off in certain circumstances. Indexing has necessarily focused on areas of greater industry demand, usually as a result of the economic or political environment. But cases of all types come to trial and get published, even ones that do not have a powerful economic or political constituency behind them. For finding these kinds of cases, the full–text database search can be the best way to go.

1.10 BEST USES OF FIELD– LIMITED SEARCHING

While full–text searching offers some indispensable capabilities, the more focused results offered by field–limited searching are usually what the researcher wants and needs. While many fields offered in the large legal databases are specific to certain types of document and will be handled in the appropriate later chapters, some general observations are in order at the outset. The concept of fields, that is, particular categories of information about or from documents that can be searched in isolation from other categories, is not limited to the electronic environment. Highly developed print indexes of field–limited information have long been available in American law. Some of the most important field-limited searching in law is done in indexing documents which are also available in print in the West digest system. However, the electronic environment does uniquely offer both newly created fields and the ability to combine field–limited searching with full–text searching.

Newly created fields, i.e., fields that are only accessible in the electronic databases, allow searching by judge's name, by date of decision, and by submerged party names (i.e., parties not included in the short title of the case). The essence of focused and effective searching consists of combining fields effectively in a number of ways. One field-combining technique that speeds case location is to combine a distinctive word in the title field with a range of dates in the date field.

Many field-combining techniques boost the effectiveness of subject-oriented research. One such technique is to require multiple key numbers that must all be present. Another is to focus the subject search by limiting it to the headnote/summary field. The language in the headnotes is extracted for the most part directly from the language in the case, but since the headnotes refer only to the significant legal points made by the court in the opinion, a search limited to the headnotes field will only pick up cases where the search terms relate to the main thrust of the case, not to passing asides.

1.11 BEST USES OF SEARCHING INDEXED/EDITED DATA

American common law is a huge edifice and its key is the indexing that has developed over the last hundred and fifty years. A principal branch of that indexing, the West key number system, dates back to 1907, and continues to evolve (conservatively) to this day. The enormous utility of the West key number indexing has prompted competing publishers to develop analogous indexing systems, such as the "core concept" terms added to case law documents in the Lexis database. Whichever indexing scheme is used, there are several common circumstances in which resort to searching the indexing fields is strongly indicated.

First, the use of indexes is invaluable to the researcher who is learning about the structure and development of the law in a particular area. While the area may have been preliminarily identified via a full-text fishing expedition, mapping it out in a coherent fashion will be expedited by use of indexed information. The indexing schemes are built on hierarchical subject arrangements, so incorporation of that structure into your search will present you with the case law arranged in a meaningful order.

This meaningful order means that you don't need to hit the bullseye every time. Because of the structure of the index, if you don't come up with just the right legal authority on your first try, the material adjacent to, above or below what you found might well be better for you than what you came looking for. This serendipity factor, made possible by the ability to rummage around in the subject-structure of the indexed resource, can help you get your bearings in a new subject.

Indexing can also enable the researcher to narrow down a large body of case law to a specific point, especially when few or no distinctive key words are anticipated in the judicial language. Again, the hierarchical structure of the indexing system enables you to progress from general areas of law to highly specialized points of legal doctrine, based on the refinements of the subject headings assigned to each case by specialized indexers. The difficulty of doing similarly refined searching in an unindexed data base is compounded when the researcher is not sufficiently familiar with the language used in a particular area to distinguish between apparently minute or inconsistent variations in terminology.

When, on the other hand, the range of vocabulary that can be used in a given legal situation is unusually varied, indexing again comes to the rescue. Even though the judge in one case wrote "lawyer" and "dereliction" and the judge in another similar case wrote "counselor" and "misfeasance", both cases can be found through the good offices of the indexer who put them both (as well as many others) under the rubric of "attorney" and "misconduct". This collocation function of indexing is particularly important in our country, with its fifty-one principal jurisdictions, each of which can develop its own strain of terminology for the same legal reality.

Finally, indexing collocates cases not only across jurisdictions, but also over time. The language of indexers needs to be responsive to new developments in the law, but it also needs to enable us to reach across the generations to understand the foundations of today's law in the cases of yesterday. Indexes change slowly, in order to facilitate the comparison of cases from different stages of the law's development. While context and, especially, language change in response to the life of the world outside the courtroom, the indexing terms provide enough continuity to enable the researcher to recognize the legal identity of issues considered.

1.12   WHAT YOU ARE GOING TO LOOK FOR

Please be forewarned that this book is not about checklists or flow charts. Such cookbook instructions may have their place, but they will not teach you how to think about doing legal research. You must yourself be able to generate the checklist, the flow chart, the research plan since this process contributes to your professional work product.

The unique opportunities in case law research provided by full-text database searching have led us to address case law in many of these opening remarks. However, the point about being able to understand the law's development across a span of time can usefully be extended to all sources of legal authority. You will always want to be armed with an understanding not only of the applicable legal authorities, but of the antecedents, the commentary on, and the applications of those authorities. In order to emphasize this injunction, we are willing, despite our aforementioned aversion to formulae for the researcher, to present one simple diagram **(see Table 1.A)**.

This diagram, which represents graphically the elements you need to account for in your research plan, can be adapted to the different types of legal authority which you will be using. The elements represented in it are conceptual and general enough that they will not relieve any researcher from the burden of thought about what they are doing. Rather, it is hoped that the diagram will stimulate thought about how the law you are researching has developed over time, and where it is likely to develop in the future.

Table 1.A

Historical Background

Legal Authority

interpretation

Subsidiary implementing authority

Chapter 2

STATUTES

2.1 STATUTES FIRST

American legal research today starts with statutes. The first step in deciding legal obligations and rights is to determine whether there is a statute that governs the situation. A statute is a decree by the sovereign establishing a legal requirement of those subject to its authority. In the United States we have many kinds of statutes, and many sorts of legal requirements, but ultimately their authority can all be traced to the granting of legislative powers by "we, the People of the United States," in our Constitution. The humblest parking ordinance passed by a one stop-light hamlet gets its teeth from the nation's consent to be so governed.

How that consent gets translated into the myriad levels of legislating and regulating is treated later in the chapters on Legislative History and Administrative Law. But its most direct and unalloyed product is the legislation that emanates from our sovereign political body, the United States Congress. In the following discussion of statutory law, we will focus primarily on the statutory output of the federal legislature, as exemplar of the legislative function in this country, and comment only secondarily on state statutory research as differences require. Be aware, however, that the code/session law structure is typical of state law as well as federal. Be aware also that it is frequently better to get your hooks into statutory law via the use of secondary sources. Nonetheless, you will always need to know how to work with the primary sources so you can absolutely scour them for every relevant provision, once you have found a way in to the statute via your chosen secondary source.

2.2 CODES

As legal researchers, our work with statutes usually begins (and often ends, as well) with a by-product of legislation: the statutory code.

The United States Code is a confection based on the legislative output of Congress, but infinitely easier to digest. Since the Code takes the raw federal statutes and incorporates them into a subject arrangement of the law, it is the usual starting point for federal legal research. The researcher needs, of course, to concern herself as well with the statutory sources of the code, and with statutes that are not incorporated into the code, but those concerns should usually be addressed after thorough exploration of what the Code has to offer.

Three different publishers produce versions of the United States Code, and each of them offers it both in print and electronically. Additionally, archival editions of each version are available on microfiche, and various convenience products (e.g., CD–ROM and PDA versions) are also marketed. The most useful and most frequently consulted versions of the Code are the annotated versions, which are commercially published and continually updated. The *United States Code Annotated (U.S.C.A.),* published by West since 1927, was for many years the most widely used tool in American legal research. It now appears on Westlaw as well. The *United States Code Service (U.S.C.S.),* currently published by Lexis in paper and as part of its database, offers a variety of different features. Finally, the *United States Code* itself (*U.S.C.*), as published by the U.S. Government, is produced in print and also distributed electronically by a number of different entities **(see Table 2.A)**. It appears in a new edition every six years, and is supplemented several times between editions.

2.3 WORKING WITH A STATUTORY CODE INDEX

The researcher seeking to identify a statute which will control the legal situation she confronts must choose whether to start looking from the bottom up—i.e., from the details of the situation—or from the top down, i.e., working through the logic of the hierarchical structure of the code. In most instances, the researcher will start from the bottom up, working from the salient details of the situation at hand. The most efficient way to locate statutes pertaining to a particular set of circumstances is through a code index. Thus, the very first step in most legal research using primary materials is to consult the index of the appropriate statutory code.

What does the index do for you? It pulls together all the code sections on a given topic from wherever they may appear in the Code.

Since the Code is a subject arrangement, this may seem redundant. However, a quick examination of the Code's structure will reveal the reason for the considerable utility of its index. The Code is built on the basis of fifty "titles," or broad subjects. These fifty titles are ordered alphabetically and each is assigned a number. Within each title, the code sections are to some extent arranged hierarchically and thematically. General provisions on a given subject come before more specific ones, and new sections are jammed in between existing ones where necessary to preserve thematic continuity. Thus, browsing the Code will play an important part in statutory research, as sections proximate to a retrieved section will quite probably also be relevant to a researcher's concerns.

However, not all code sections with bearing on a particular topic will necessarily be found proximate to each other, nor even within the same title. The process by which new statutes are incorporated into the Code requires each statute to be worked in to the Code sections and areas it most clearly affects. A statute can be chopped up and incorporated into a number of different titles if necessary. But if the subject of interest to the researcher is one that does not fit wholly within the boundaries of a given title, a tool is required to launch the researcher into all the different titles which have incorporated statutes on said subject. That tool is the index.

Typically, statutory codes like the United States Code will have a General Index which covers the whole edifice. Thus, the *U.S.C.A.*, the *U.S.C.S.*, and the *U.S.C.* all have multiple volume General Indexes that direct the researcher to particular titles and sections. The commercial versions (the *U.S.C.A.* and *U.S.C.S.* indexes) are republished annually; the *U.S.C.*'s periodic updating supplements get their own indexes. In addition to the General Indexes, the *U.S.C.A.* and *U.S.C.S.* have indexes at the end of each Title in the main volumes. Since each of these individual Title indexes is only updated when the main volume containing it is updated, the General Index is usually more up to date. Changes to the code which appear in a pocket part are therefore usually indexed only in the General Index, the exception being Title 42, whose "length and complexity" have led the *U.S.C.A.* to issue a revised index to that title annually.

Code indexes cannot be mere concordances: they need to do more than just register and sort the actual language of the statute. They need to include or omit a section in which a particular term is used from an index heading depending on whether the section is really *about* that subject or, on the contrary, just mentions the term. The best indexes also use alternate language so that a researcher without prior knowledge of the statutory terminology can find some way in to the code's content.

Table 2.A: Sources for the United States Code

1. Office of the Law Revision Counsel, United States House of Representatives

    http://uscode.house.gov/search/criteria.shtml

2. United States Government Printing Office

    http://www.gpoaccess.gov/uscode/index.html

3. Cornell Legal Information Institute

    http://www4.law.cornell.edu/uscode/

4. *United States Code: containing the general and permanent laws of the United States, in force on January 2, 2001 / prepared and published under the authority of Title 2, U.S. code, section 285b, by the Office of the Law Revision Counsel of the House of Representatives.* Washington, D.C.: U.S.G.P.O., 2001–. (This is the "2000 Edition." Editions appear every six years. The third supplement to the 2000 edition was distributed at the end of 2005 and contained laws in effect on January 19, 2004.)

5. *United States Code Annotated.* St. Paul: Thomson/West, 1996 –.

6. Westlaw:

    Database = USCA (United States Code Annotated)

    Database = USC (United States Code Annotated without annotations)

    Database = USCA–IDX (United States Code Annotated General Index)

    Database = USCA–POP (a hybrid document, combining some features of the print Popular Name Table with some features of the Tables volume, but not all of either. Notably, the entries in this database for acts by popular name refer only to the original acts, without listing those acts' subsequent amendments as does the print Popular Name Table.)

    Database = USCA–TABLES (United States Code Annotated Tables)

    Databases = USCA90 through USCA05 (Historical versions of the USCA)

    There are also practice area files which include subject-specific subsets of the USCA.

7. *United States Code Service.* Charlottesville, Va.: Lexis Law Publishing, 1998 –.

8. Lexis:

File = USCS (United States Code Service)

File = USNAME (Table of Acts by Popular Name: unlike the Westlaw USCA–POP, this is the real thing, offering all the functionality of the USCS Popular Name Table, plus click-through to the cited code sections (although not to the session laws)).

File = USSALT (United States Code Service—Statutes at Large Table)

File = USREVT (USCS—Revised Title Table)

Files = US1992 through US2004 (Historical versions of the USCS)

9. Lois: United States Code, with Popular Name Table Quick Links (as with Westlaw, the online Popular Name Table on Lois does not list amendments to the named acts).

2.4   TERMS TO LOOK UP IN CODE INDEXES

First and foremost, you should be looking for terms that you anticipate finding in the code language itself. Distinctive terms from the code language are almost always picked up in the code indexes. Abstract legal concepts are sometimes picked up, but by no means always. Moreover, the language you seek may only be represented in the index by a subheading, without an alphabetical main entry of its own. If you can't find the term you seek, think more generally about what larger subject headings should contain your term as a subheading. If the language that you expect to find in the code is not turning up in the index at all, try looking for synonymous terms.

Occasionally interpretive, analytic or synthesizing terms are used to draw terms together. For example, in the *U.S.C.S.* index the entry for the insanity defense is a subhead under the MENTAL HEALTH heading, with a referring reference leading there from the heading INSANITY DEFENSE REFORM ACT OF 1984. Unfortunately this helpful drawing together of code sections pertaining to all manner of mental health-related topics points up a big drawback with indexed materials: the potential for editorial error. The researcher who duly proceeds to "MENTAL HEALTH—Defense of insanity.—Generally, 18 sec. 20" is left dangling: 18 sec. 20 proves to be titled "Financial institutions defined," and contains nary a mention of the insanity defense. Depending on your opinion of the institutions of capitalism, this index heading may or may not have a certain poetic resonance, but it probably does not accomplish the task you had in mind. Somehow, the current number of the section of the Code, Title 18 sec. 17 (changed to this from sec. 20 in 1986 by an act of Congress), was not updated by the index compilers. Happily, we have the opportunity to do an end run around the sloppy indexer by searching in the full text of the code database when the index lets us down (if not before).

2.5   DISTINCTIONS BETWEEN CODE INDEXES

As mentioned above, the most important distinction between the General Indexes and the Title indexes is the potential difference in currency. The General Index is updated annually, and therefore will cover additions and revisions to the Code that appear in the pocket parts to the main volumes. The Title indexes, however, are only as recent as the main volume that they appear in, and the pocket parts do not contain their own indexing. The Title indexes also contain listings only for code sections within the confines of that one title. For example, the General Index to the *U.S.C.A.* lists Copyrights—Civil Air Patrol, Title 36 sec. 40306. There is no cross reference to this section within the Title index to Title 17, Copyrights, because it falls outside of Title 17.

The Title indexes do offer some entry points that are absent from the General Index. Despite the claim in the General Index's prefatory matter that "it incorporates index references for . . . selected Code of Federal Regulations' promulgations and other materials set out in the Code," the Title indexes contain many more references to CFR sections reprinted in the Code volumes than does the General Index. For example, the Title index to Title 17, Copyright, contains numerous subject subheadings which lead to CFR sections; these entries do not appear in the General Index. And, of course, the Title index offers easy portability! Despite these Title index features, however, the more up-to-date coverage of the General Index makes use of the latter indispensable.

It is important to note that the index is not itself a legal document, but a separate and independent work of authorship. Different indexes can use different terms to point researchers to the same code sections. For example, compare these entries from the indexes of the different publications of the Code: *U.S.C.A.*: WEAPONS—Look-alike firearms, definitions, penalties for entering into commerce, exceptions, 15 sec. 5001; *U.S.C.S.*: WEAPONS AND FIREARMS—Replicas or imitations, 15 sec. 5001. On the other hand, the same (or equivalent) terms can point to different sections according to different indexes. For example, *U.S.C.A.*: WEAPONS—Silencers, fines, penalties and forfeitures, 18 sec. 924; *U.S.C.S.*: WEAPONS AND FIREARMS—Silencers, 18 sec. 921; *U.S.C.*: same as *U.S.C.A.*; no other entry in any of the three under weapons/silencers.

The order of the index headings is different in the different sets: *U.S.C.A.* and *U.S.C.* put the general sections first, out of subordinate alphabetical order, beneath a given subject heading. The *U.S.C.S.* does not separate out general sections conceptually, but puts "—generally" where that term would fit, alphabetically, as a subheading. Hierarchical structuring of the subjects varies as well. For example, *U.S.C.S.*: WEAPONS AND FIREARMS—Nonmailable matter, 18 sec. 921 note, 922, 1715, 1716; 39 sec. 3001; *U.S.C.A.*: WEAPONS—nothing under "Nonmailable matter" directly, but "Mail and mailing" subjects include all of those sections EXCEPT 18 sec. 1716, and there is a subheading under "Mail and mailing" for "Nonmailable" matter, 39 sec. 3001.

The indexes also differ in the granularity with which different subjects are handled, although not consistently: each of the three indexes contains a different combination of headings. For example, the *U.S.C.A.* and *U.S.C.* both contain entries for "WAX", but the *U.S.C.S.* contains no equivalent entry. On the other hand, the *U.S.C.S.* and *U.S.C.* both contain entries under their WEAPONS heading for some variation on "Congressional findings and policy;" the *U.S.C.A.* does not. The point to remember here is that while, as you would expect, the index language does closely track the statutory language to which it refers, the indexes of different code versions still differ. If you are not finding what you need in one version, it may prove fruitful to try another. Do note that the indexes to the *U.S.C.A.* and the *U.S.C.* are far more similar than are any other pair of indexes; there is an overlap, as will be seen, between the production process of the two publications. Since the *U.S.C.S.* index is more different from the other two than they are from each other, combining a *U.S.C.S.* index search with one of the other two is more likely to add something to your search than searching the other two would do.

2.6   USING A CODE INDEX ONLINE

The only electronic version of the Code that offers an online index is the USCA on Westlaw (database = USCA–IDX; a different presentation of this information is available through the Index view of the USCA database). When using the Index view of the USCA online, you first see only main subject headings, not the subheadings that break down the subjects into detail and actually lead you to Code sections. The browsing feature of the index only allows you to scan the already visible alphabetical list of main subject headings, not the underlying subheadings. In order to get to the subheadings and Code references, you have to choose a main heading and click on it. If it doesn't turn out to have anything of use to you, you have to go back to the main subject heading screen and look again. This inability to scan subheadings from the start makes use of the online index clunkier and more time-consuming than it would be to sweep your eye over the equivalent amount of material in the print indexes.

However, there are some offsetting advantages to the online version. If you only have a very specific phrase, and do not know its context, searching the online USCA Index database (identifier = USCA–IDX), rather than browsing the index feature of the USCA database itself, will take you directly to the appropriate section of the index, assuming you have the phrase exactly right. Thus, entering "involuntary transfers" takes you (among other places) to the index section for "copyright", whereupon you can proceed via term locator to the sections of the copyright index that pertain to involuntary transfers. And once you have found an entry that looks good, you can simply click on it to go to it. By contrast, the print index leaves you dangling if all you know is "involuntary transfers" and not the copyright context.

Once you get to the pertinent section of the electronic index, however, there is a problem. The print version of the *U.S.C.A.* Index carefully indicates hierarchical relationships between several layers of subject headings by means of indentation. The graphical arrangement of the entries in the electronic index database does not allow for hierarchical indentation, so the clear presentation of those relationships is lost.

Most importantly, the number of index headings and subheadings viewable at a glance is significantly smaller than with the print index. The print index offers the ability to sweep over large portions of subject matter, capsulized in the form of index subject headings and subheadings, and thus to see your sought-after topic in context. Here, in our very first research tool encountered, we meet up with the issue of serendipity versus targeted searching discussed in the first chapter, and see the different problems and opportunities offered by each. In this case, the balance is unusually skewed in favor of serendipity, since in statutory searching, the language being searched is typically so taut and precise that the structure of the index adds more value than does the ability to zero in on particular language used in the statute but not in the index.

2.7 FINDING THE STATUTE BY FINDING A CASE

The other principal way to figure out what statute may be applicable to the facts of your particular situation is to find cases in which the facts are close to yours, and then ascertain what statute or statutes were found applicable or at least discussed in those cases. Finding a case with good fact pattern resemblance is discussed in Chapter Five below. Once you find such a case, in Westlaw and Lexis you will be able to click through to the statutes cited, but remember that you should not restrict yourself to those precise sections alone. As ever with code-based research, you should take advantage of the subject arrangement and peruse both all the proximate sections and the larger structure of the code to make sure that you are finding every relevant portion.

2.8   WORKING WITH THE STRUCTURE
OF THE CODE

You can think of both the similar case method and the code index method as being "from the bottom up" techniques for finding relevant statutory law. These methods are definitely the way to go when you are unfamiliar with the law in a given area. But once you are reasonably well-versed in some area of the law, you will probably feel the urge to use a more "top down" method when working with statutory codes. This would mean working from the structure within the code itself to arrive at the sections you need.

As mentioned above, the U.S. Code is arranged in fifty named titles, which are alphabetically arranged and then numbered. The numbers and, for the most part, the names of titles have remained fixed since the Code was created in 1926, at which time it fit into one physical volume! Some of the titles have become enormous and complex since that time, necessitating elaborate elongated section numbering schemes to accommodate burgeoning legislative developments within particular portions of the Code.

Title 42, Public Health and Welfare, for example, has seen lots of growth and has a correspondingly complex structure: 42 U.S.C. sec. 1395i–2a has a subsection 1395i–2a (d)(1)(B)(i), and 42 U.S.C. sec. 1320a–7a has a subsection 1320a–7a(i)(6)(A)(iii)(I). Title 15, Commerce and Trade (which covers securities) also fairly bristles with letters and numbers, as in 15 U.S.C. sec. 77bbbb, which is preceded by sec. 77aaaa, which is in turn preceded by sections 77aaa through 77zzz, sections 77aa through 77zz, sections 77a through 77z, and plain old section 77. Some of these fancier section numbers pose more of a problem than others: considerable care is needed to make sure, e.g., that section 77lll is not misrendered somewhere along the line of transmission as simply a five digit number!

Some titles of the Code make up in variety of subject matter (each covered in a separate section) what they lack in organizational complexity: Title 36, Patriotic and National Observances, Ceremonies, and Organizations marches straight up to sec. 300,111. On the other hand, some titles, rooted in a different historical world, are almost moribund. Title 27, Intoxicating Liquors, has seen few changes since its inception, as can be seen by its current iteration in one slim volume of the *U.S.C.A.*, with a copyright date of 1927, accompanied by a slim current pocket part.

This unassuming volume of the *U.S.C.A.* illustrates the difficulties of pinning down authority in an immutable form. Although the latest printing of this volume consulted during the preparation of this book, the 1927 edition in its 1987 (25th) reprint, retains the original copyright date and, therefore, one would assume, the original content, it has a reset title page and has dropped one of the publishers both from the title page and from the copyright page. Nowhere in the formal citation to this source would the distinction between this printing and the earlier printings be evident. This points up a very practical reason the official code is preferred for authentication purposes: no reprinting is involved, since each edition is published separately.

Title 34, Navy, is completely defunct: Congress repealed it in 1956 and distributed its provisions within Title 10, Armed Forces (formerly Army). A similar fate befell Title 6, Surety Bonds, in 1947. After many years, that title number has now been reassigned to Domestic Security. Changes to the Title arrangement are infrequent; when they occur, tables are published showing the distribution of the code material to new sections, or its other disposition (see **section 2.13**, below).

When working from the top down, the first step is to pick which Title to examine. Electronically, this is just a matter of consulting a menu in whichever U.S. Code database you have selected to use. In print, the commercial publishers make title location easier by putting the names of the titles on the spine. *U.S.C.A.* puts no more than one title in a volume, except for the foundational Titles 1–4; both *U.S.C.S.* and *U.S.C.* include some mixed-title volumes throughout the Code.

If you are really at a loss for which Title to examine, you can do a full-text search of the Code database as a fishing expedition for suggested Titles. But searching the entire Code for most terms is an awkward, confusing, and frustrating enterprise which—except for this limited preliminary step—we counsel against.

Having selected a Title of the Code, the structurally-oriented researcher turns next to that Title's table of contents. In print, the table of contents appears at the beginning of the Title, and (in the commercially published versions) any changes to the table of contents appear in an updated version at the beginning of the pocket part for the Title's first volume. In the electronic versions, the table of contents is a separate file: as with the print tables of contents, the entries are descriptively-named groupings of sections. You can drill down from these groupings to an array of individual sections and thence to the text of those sections. In order to see which numbered sections are in which file, you will usually need to expand several groupings at a time. At any point in your drilling down below the Title level, you can try a full-text search of the resulting data subset. This can help you pick the right subgroupings below on which to focus. In addition to the drilling down, in Lexis you can search all levels of the USCS Table of Contents from the top level. Entering a search in the box on the screen that lists the fifty titles of the Code will search for those terms at all levels of the Table of Contents, down to the section name (or further, if you select to "search the full-text of source documents" at any point).

The groupings listed in the first level of the Table of Contents are called "Chapters," with a capital "C". They appear in the official Code and are uniform throughout the different publications. The original Chapters were devised by the codifiers. Sometimes changes and additions are devised by the Code editors, but more often they are included in the legislation which is changing or adding to the text of the Title. The Chapters tend to be very broad in scope. Sometimes, as in the new Title 6, Domestic Security, they are further divided into subchapters. The numbering of some chapters occasionally furnishes the beginning of the section numbers that fall within them, but more usually they are unrelated.

But while the chapter structure is crucial for "top-down" research, it does not comprise part of the citation scheme for any section. Nor are Chapters themselves usually cited formally as a unit, although they can be used as informal shorthand: think of "Chapter 11 reorganization" as a term in bankruptcy discourse. Instead, if you want to discuss the group of code sections that make up Chapter 4 of Title 17, Copyright, you would cite to Title 17 U.S.C. sects. 401–412. This is in order to provide maximum precision in what you are telling the reader. The Chapter 4 of today is not necessarily the Chapter 4 that existed last week, and by specifying the sections under discussion you eliminate the need for the reader laboriously to reconstruct what Chapter 4 looked like at the moment you were writing. Note also that the Table of Contents of the print code does not send you from a Chapter number and name to a page number, but rather to a starting section number for that Chapter. The fluid and dynamic nature of the Code, subject to constant revision, addition, amendment, and deletion, means that page numbers would be more confusing than helpful. Instead, the section numbers themselves form the basis for locating text within the volume or the database, and thus constitute necessary elements for citation to the text.

This multi-level structure accounts for an irritating flaw in using the table of contents locating function in the electronic codes. Suppose you want to look at a known section in the context of other sections. Since your citation tells you nothing about the chapter number, and since drilling down through the table of contents requires you to go through a level comprised of chapter headings, and since in addition you have no way to know in which chapter your section will be, you end up throwing balls at a screened off bullseye, opening up chapter after chapter until you hit the one that has your section in it. This could be corrected by the publishers putting the corresponding section numbers in parentheses after the chapter headings—another level of data that would have to be kept up to date in real time—or, less conveniently for the researcher, by adding a separate document equivalent to the list of chapter numbers with corresponding initial section numbers that appears at the beginning of each chapter in the print codes. Note that on Westlaw you can expand the Table of Contents of a Title with one click to show all subdivisions, down to the section level, but this is an all or nothing affair. In a lengthy or complicated title you will have lots of screens to scroll through if you go this route.

Having found the right Chapter or Chapters, the structurally-oriented researcher skims the individual section names for likely looking ones, reads those, and then reads outward from them in an expanding circle. The subject-hierarchical structure of a statutory code means that linear proximity is usually a good indicator of relevance. This is one reason why working with statutory codes is easier in print than electronically. Having the whole Chapter physically before you as you work through it gives you a tangible sense of where you are in relation to the section you started from, and thus how all the bits that you are finding fit together. By contrast, the item by item reading style necessitated by screen formats can make it hard to keep each section you read squarely in its appropriate context. Moreover, the order in which things are stated in a code can be significant when construing the statute, and that sense of order is harder to perceive and keep track of in the electronic text.

2.9 CODE CURRENCY

Both the "top-down" and the "from the bottom up" researcher will eventually arrive at the sections they want to use. The text of those sections, however, may vary depending on which version of the Code you have chosen to look at. Electronic versions may already have incorporated changes to the code text effected by statutes that were enacted after the most recent print versions went to press. Thus, the electronic version of the U.S. Code incorporates changes made by Supplements to the current edition before those supplements have been distributed in print. The as-yet electronic-only content added to the USC database at the website of its creator, the Law Revision Counsel, gets incorporated there into the structure of the code. Later statutory developments affecting the code are noted in the file for the affected section, and a link is provided to a list of relevant citations. Meanwhile, the electronic versions of the commercially published codes include statutory material that is even more recent than that on the Federal government's Code website.

The code updating structure online can be less streamlined in the state law context. For example, while Lexis offers a New York statutory database that integrates the code with recent statutes up through a date that is considerably later than the date of the last printed pocket part to the code, Westlaw puts even newer statutory enactments, unedited, into a separate database from the code. You are then alerted via KeyCite graphical symbols (on the Web version of Westlaw) or an instruction to update (on the proprietary software version) when that separate database contains material that affects the code section you have retrieved. We shall return to this point in the section on how to find session laws.

Although updating code text online is obviously a more seamless process, some researchers prefer to go as far as possible with the paper sources before resorting to electronic databases for final updating. When you have a series of paper sources in front of you, each containing an updating change to a code section, it makes the timing and interrelationship of the changes graphically clear, and facilitates comparison of the different evolving versions of the text. How, then, to go about updating the Code using paper sources? We will assume, for this purpose, that you will use a commercially produced version of the Code, since the official U.S. Code has so much more of a publication lag (the annual supplements usually cover laws enacted two or three years earlier).

Before you begin, make sure that the version of the Code that you are using is the most recent one. This can be ascertained by referring to the website of the publisher. As soon as you think you have found a relevant section or sections, you should check for updates. Do not get caught up in spending too much time parsing a section that has perhaps already been superseded. The first step in updating is to consult the pocket part, the unbound supplement tucked into the slot at the back of the book. Every volume of the commercially-published codes has such a slot to accommodate pocket parts. Every such slot must either (a) be filled with a current pocket part, (b) be filled with a cardboard tag alerting you to the existence of a freestanding paperback supplement for the volume, a "proxy pocket part," if you will, or (c) be in a main volume that was published within the current year. You must ascertain which of these alternatives is in play and consult the appropriate material because the next step, supplementation *beyond* the pocket part (or its proxy, the freestanding paperback supplement to the volume), does not cumulate the contents thereof.

The process of going "beyond the pocket part" in print varies slightly in the two different commercial code publishers, but only after the point when the code component of the statutory law is exhausted (which will be covered in the section below on session laws). The search for updated code sections is the same in both versions: after the pocket part you turn to a separate set of paperback updates, periodically issued and typically shelved at the end of the code set. The *U.S.C.S.* updating volumes, entitled "Cumulative Later Case and Statutory Service," include the "latest statutory additions, amendments, and repeals, classified to Code titles and sections." As with the pocket part, all you need to do here is to look up the code section of interest, and any changes or additions will be laid out in code format. The *U.S.C.A.* updating supplements, called "Pamphlets" although they can be hefty paperback volumes of well over a thousand pages, are similar, although non-cumulating as between themselves.

Since these Code updates are already laid out in Code format, i.e., since substantial (and therefore time-consuming) editorial work has been done, they cannot get you all that up to date. You can also consult these paperback updates for changes to the Code by looking in their subject indexes: unlike the pocket part supplements, these volumes do have their own indexing, which is more up to date than the annual General Indexes. Do not restrict the language you use to that which proved successful in searching the General Index, since new developments since then may have suggested new indexing terms. To improve your currency further, you need to go beyond the Code into the as-yet uncodified Public Laws, which will be discussed in the section below on researching session laws.

2.10   CHOOSING A FORMAT IN WHICH TO DO YOUR CODE RESEARCH

When deciding how to do your code research, check a variety of sources to make sure that the version of the code you are using is as up to date as possible. If you are researching in print codes you should definitely plan to check your work for currency by comparing it to what is available in the online code databases (and beyond). The other advantages of online code searching include easier accessibility (always available on your desktop or laptop, no problem with missing volumes, no multiple volumes to haul around), and the perennial electronic advantage when you are trying to locate specific language within a haystack of verbiage. Searching for a term in a full-text code database can, under some circumstances, speed the finding of a code section, and can also help with pinpointing a particular portion of a lengthy code section. The latter task is usually not onerous enough to constitute a serious advantage for the electronic code searcher, but that situation changes radically when the context changes to session laws, typically much longer and more convoluted than code sections.

In the code context, however, you should give serious consideration to the advantages of paper research for the initial stages, at least, of your research. We already saw the greater functionality of the print code indexes, the most direct way in to the code when you seek statutory law on a given subject. But the print code publications offer other advantages as well. Seeing the code in paper makes it much easier to understand the context of any given section. Instead of seeing only the section retrieved by your query, you are made unavoidably aware of the sections surrounding your own. The electronic versions do offer various means to get to those surrounding sections, but, since it takes an active choice to do so, many researchers will be tempted to skip that added step, or to give it short shrift.

The print researcher is automatically exposed not only to surrounding sections, but also, within longer stretches of statutory language, to the context of the language within the section itself, without the need to scroll through multiple sections to see the whole thing. On a larger scale, clearly and graphically seeing the end of one section or subsection and the beginning of another as one does in the print volumes makes it easier to grasp the organizational logic and structure of the code. Finally, having different subjects and different chronological iterations of the code available in different physical volumes makes comparison of the same handy and efficient—once, that is, you have assembled all the relevant volumes and cleared off enough desk space to arrange them all usefully!

2.11 CHOOSING A CODE SOURCE

In addition to choosing between print and electronic versions of the statutory code, you may need to choose a publisher. As mentioned at the outset of this discussion of codes, the text of the United States Code is available in print and electronically from three different publishers. Each of the three versions has different things to offer, speaking strictly from the perspective of the code text itself. Obviously the USC offers authoritativeness, as the very output of the U.S. Government. Both the USCA and the USCS offer greater currency within a single iteration of the code. The USCA and USCS have historically varied in terms of the source of their code text, and this may actually lead to differences in the language they publish. The USCA, published by West, uses as its source the text of the USC, which from the beginning has been produced for the government largely by employees of West. This close connection between West and the official Code may also explain why the indexes of the USC and the USCA are much more similar to each other than either is to the index of the USCS. The source of the code language in USCS, by comparison, is drawn from the language of the Statutes at Large, in case of conflict between those Statutes and the USC language. Typically this comes up where the codifiers have altered subdivision labels or devised them from scratch in non-statutory language to make them more "code-like". For one example, see 2 USC 30a versus 2 USCA 30a versus 2 USCS 30a versus P.L.101–520, Title III, section 310, 104 Stat. 2278, where only the USCS section heading is based on the language used in the underlying statute.

Usually, legal researchers will start off their print-based code research with a commercial version of the code (more current, more convenient), switching over to the official version only to verify that the text found in the commercial publication is accurate. Recent informal surveys have suggested that while large law libraries will have all three print versions of the Code, smaller ones will most often have only the USC and the USCA, or even just the USCA. The annotation material in the commercially published codes is much more likely to vary than is the code text, and this will be discussed in the chapter on case law.

So why would you use the official *United States Code* itself? The quick answer would be "because the *Bluebook* requires it," rule 12.3 instructing the writer to cite the official code (from any jurisdiction) whenever possible. In any serious legal research, you will eventually need to obtain access to a print copy of the *United States Code*. No matter what combination of other Code versions you consult (the online USCA or USCS for currency, the print *U.S.C.A.* or *U.S.C.S.* for clarity of organization, or the online U.S.C. for a combination of authoritativeness and moderate currency) you will always need to check the print U.S.C. as a final check of accuracy and authenticity. In the language of the Law Revision Counsel's own website: "While every effort has been made to ensure that the Code database on the website is accurate, those using it for legal research should verify their results against the printed version

THOMSON

WEST ™

PACKING SLIP
Not a Remittable Document

Shipped From:
THOMSON-WEST
545 WESCOTT RD
EAGAN MN 55123-1310

Shipped To:
NANCY ARMSTRONG
OHIO NORTHERN UNIV PETTIT COLLEGE O
TAGGART LAW LIBRARY
4611 STATE ROUTE 235
ADA OH 45810-9517

Ship To Account #	Purchase Order #	Order Date	Order #	Delivery #
1003328072		10/03/2006	3037347	655027981

ISBN	Material #	Product Description	Order Qty	Ship Qty
031416296B	40396696	ARMSTRONG WHERE THE LAW IS: AN INTRODUCTION TO ADVANCED LEGAL RESEARCH 2D	1	1
		Product(s) provided at no charge.		

Group # 476236

of the *United States Code* available through the Government Printing Office." Note that Rule 12.2.1(a) specifies the *Bluebook*'s order of preference for statutory sources where the official version is not yet available: commercially published print codes are preferred over other quickly-updated sources.

In the state law context, researchers may also have the choice of more than one version of the state's statutory code. Sometimes the state publishes an official code, or designates one of the commercially published versions as "official." In some states there is no official code at all, but only commercially published ones. Typically, Westlaw and Lexis each include the version of the code published by their affiliated print publisher; Lois and the states' own websites tend to carry the official versions. In print, the different publishers are associated with different updating methods, with some specializing in pocket part or looseleaf updating and others reprinting the code in full each year. The availability and status of these different code versions can be reviewed in the annually updated book by Kendall F. Svengalis, *Legal Information Buyer's Guide and Reference Manual*.

2.12 CODES OF THE PAST

When you need to figure out what the statutory law was at some specific earlier time, previous editions of the relevant code can often provide the easiest way to pin down the statutory environment as of the time in question. Lexis and Westlaw both provide "archival" files of their previous editions of the United States Code, no longer being updated with new developments, but closed as of a certain date. These files are only available for the years since 1992 for the USCS (Lexis) and 1990 for the USCA (Westlaw) (and for similarly limited ranges of dates for some states). Westlaw also offers, for an even more limited range of years, a beautifully designed "Versions" service that retrieves code material that was in effect on a specific date in the past. This service is available for the USCA starting with January 1, 1996 (and for the New York and California codes starting with January 1, 1999 and the New Jersey and Texas codes starting with December 31, 1999).

The United States Code itself is only available online from the 1994 edition on. Each print edition of the United States Code is designed for permanent retention, along with all supplementary volumes. All editions are also available in microfiche. In the state law context (outside the very limited confines of the Westlaw "Versions" service), consult a bibliography of that state's statutory law to see which code edition or which collection of revised statutes would most likely contain the law that was applicable during the period in which you are interested **(see Appendix)**.

The commercial Code publications, designed for completely dynamic and ongoing revision, are trickier to capture in amber. When individual volumes are replaced and retired from the *U.S.C.A.*, they are preserved in a microfiche set by Wm. Hein Publishing. Those pocket parts which were in the main volumes at the time of their replacement are included in the set, and Hein also produces a separate set which includes as many of the intervening pocket parts as can be located. By far the trickiest maneuver in this area of research is to locate code text that came into and went out of existence between publications of revised main volumes. Such fugitive text can most easily be tracked down in the *U.S.C.A.* by consulting superseded volumes of its General Index, which comprises part of the Hein microfiche set. Some law libraries also retain superseded print volumes of the *U.S.C.S.*, as it is not republished in microfiche. In the state law context, note that Hein also publishes a microfiche set of superseded state codes.

2.13 RENUMBERED CODES

Researchers into the law as of a particular date in the past may encounter old citations to code sections that have since been re-numbered. Re-numbering is not done often, but when it does occur, it usually affects a whole title (or large subdivisions thereof) at once. The subject arrangement of the code may require shifting of some code sections to open up space for newly developing areas of law. Renumbering sometimes accompanies a title's revision and re-enactment as positive law (see section 2.23 below).

All the print versions of the Code contain a table at the head of each renumbered title, showing the disposition of all the previous sections of the old title. In the electronic versions of the Code, these disposition tables are separate documents that show up at the head of the relevant title in the code's Table of Contents file. In print, the *USC* and *USCS* also have consolidated lists of all renumbered code sections in the Tables volumes. This kind of shifting of the numbered ground under the researcher's feet doesn't happen often, but it does happen often enough that if the reference you are pursuing seems weirdly inappropriate, one of the first things you should do is to poke around in the prefatory material to that title to see if a renumbering has occurred.

2.14 SESSION LAWS

Most legislatures publish their output in two ways: originally as session laws, then reworked as a code. While a code is arranged by subject, involving complex and time-consuming editorial work to fit it all together and make it work, the session laws are simply the raw output of the legislature's session, published in chronological order with only minimal editorial work. There is no subject arrangement or any other arrangement imposed on them. As they fall off the governmental assembly line, they go into the session laws. The convenient subject arrangement of the U.S. Code, the increasing percentage of it that has been reenacted as positive law, and the increasing speed of access to updated code sections are forcing the session laws of the United States, the Statutes at Large, increasingly into the background. Many a third year law student has never cracked open a volume of same. Yet knowledge of how to work with session laws **(see Table 2.B)** is indispensable.

One of the simplest ways that researchers encounter the session laws is when they seek to update known code sections beyond the most recent version of the code: you will need to use the session laws for statutes which have not yet made it into the code. But you will also need to use the session laws for statutes that will never go into the code, and for statutes that are unwieldy and dispersed in the code. Finally, you will need to use the session laws for verifying the accuracy of non-positively reenacted Titles of the Code (see section 2.23 below).

2.15   USING SESSION LAWS TO UPDATE THE CODE

Because of the minimal editorial work required to publish session laws, they can sometimes be ready for consultation much faster than the code sections to which they will contribute, especially during times of heavy legislating, such as at the end of a session of Congress. Since as a collection they may, therefore, be more current than the code, the legal researcher must supplement any code work with a search of the relevant session laws. The simplest part of the task is that of seeing whether any session law has been enacted which explicitly alters the text of the code section on which you are relying. We have seen how in the electronic databases the code sections are flagged in various ways when a subsequent session law not yet incorporated into the code has altered it. The process is a bit more laborious in paper, and this is one reason why the finishing touches to your statutory research are probably best done online, when that is feasible. If you do have to use print for this, you must use a commercial product that specializes in rapid publication of current session laws, since you need to obtain specifically those session laws that postdate the most updated version available of the code. In most jurisdictions this print product is a separate publication from the code, frequently a freestanding supplement to the session law set which it updates.

In the states, these publications are frequently titled "Session Law News" or "Advance Legislative Service," and the latter is the generic term for them. Newly-minted state session laws are frequently presented in these publications as "redlined" versions of the pre-existing code. The new session law specifies how an existing section of the state's statutory code is to be changed, typically by underlining the new additions to the text (or, online, by highlighting them in a different color or rendering them all caps) and by crossing out the parts of the previous statutory language that it repeals or changes (or sometimes, online, by putting the excised language in parentheses, not a happy graphic device).

In the Federal jurisdiction, changes to the existing code are described in the words of the amending session law, rather than graphically shown by redlining. There are several Federal advance legislative services available **(see Table 2.C)**. One is provided by the softcover supplements published to accompany the *U.S.C.S.*, entitled *USCS Advance*. This publication, which comes out monthly, includes a feature entitled "Table of Code Sections Added, Amended, Repealed, or Otherwise Affected," the "TCSA." The TCSA shows, for each affected section of the U.S. Code, which Public Law is responsible. The analogous tool in the West system is the table within the monthly advance sheets to *U.S.C.C.A.N.* entitled "U.S. Code and U.S. Code Annotated Sections Amended, Repealed, New, Etc." The *U.S.C.C.A.N.* table is a bit faster to appear than is *U.S.C.S.*'s TCSA, and includes page references to the Statutes at Large pages where these Public Laws will eventually appear. Another tool which can be used to ascertain whether a given print code section has been changed by subsequent session laws is the Shepard's citator for the code. *Shepard's Federal Statute Citations*, for instance, notes for each section of the U.S. Code when it has been amended by a session law that will appear in the *Statutes at Large*.

2.16 USING SESSION LAWS TO FIND NEW LAWS WITHOUT REFERENCE TO EARLIER CODE SECTIONS

Useful though these finding tools may be, you cannot rely upon them entirely to find all new statutes that affect your situation. Remember, you originally found your code section either by consulting a subject index, by reference from a secondary source or other citing source, or by full-text searching. There is nothing to say that some new statute, which on its terms does not affect the code section you identified by any of these means, could not be equally germane to your research. You will need to delve more deeply into the session laws than merely looking for statutes that specifically and explicitly affect your code section.

As in your code research, consultation of the subject index to the session laws can be an efficient way in. The critical difference is that there is no overarching subject index to the session law set, no "General

Table 2.B: Sources for United States Session Laws

1. United States, *United States Statutes at Large*. Washington, United States Government Printing Office.

    Coverage begins in 1789 (1st Congress)

2. Hein Online, U.S. Statutes at Large Collection. This subscription web database offers .pdf files of all but the most recent volume of the GPO series.

3. Westlaw:
    Database = **USCCAN-PL** (for most recent coverage; coverage begins 1973)
    US-PL (current session, text only)
    US-PLOLD (1973–2004, 93rd-Congress prior to present one, text only)
    US-STATLRG (1789–1972, 1st–92nd Congress, .pdf only)

4. Library of Congress, American Memory: Statutes at Large

    http://memory.loc.gov/ammem/amlaw/lwsl.html

    Coverage is from 1789–1875, image files only

5. *United States Code Congressional and Administrative News*. St. Paul, Minn.Thomson/West

    Coverage begins in 1951 (82d Congress). Its predecessor publication, *United States Code Congressional Service*, offered coverage beginning in 1941 (77th Congress).

6. Library of Congress, Thomas: Legislative Information on the Internet: Public Laws

    http://thomas.loc.gov/bss/d109/d109laws.html

    Coverage begins in 1973 (93rd Congress), with laws prior to the 104th presented as text only, taken from the bill that passed. Laws from the 104th and later link to the GPO site, below.

7. Lexis:
    Legal > Legislation & Politics–U.S. & U.K. > U.S. Congress > USCS Public Laws

    Coverage begins 1988, 100th Congress, 2d Session, text only. Additionally, individual earlier Public Laws can be retrieved as .pdf images of pages from the Statutes at Large. These earlier .pdfs can also be clicked to via the source notes at the end of a USCS section. (Library and File = **GENFED;PUBLAW**)

8. United States, GPO Access, Public and Private Laws. http://www.gpoaccess.gov/plaws/index.html

Coverage begins in 1995 (104th Congress). Offers text and .pdf files.

9. Lois: Jurisdiction = Federal, File = **Public Laws of the United States**

   Coverage begins 1997, 105th Congress, text only.

10. LLMC Digital: subscription web database. Includes image files of most volumes of the U.S. Statutes at Large.

11. *United States Code Service: Advance.* Charlottesville, Va.: LexisNexis

Table 2.C: Sources For New Federal Session Laws

1. United States, GPO Access, Public and Private Laws.
    http://www.gpoaccess.gov/plaws/index.html

2. Library of Congress, Thomas: Legislative Information on
    the Internet: Public Laws

    http://thomas.loc.gov/bss/d109/d109laws.html

3. *United States Code Congressional and Administrative News.*
    St. Paul, Minn.: Thomson/West

4. Westlaw:
    Databases = **USCCAN-PL** or **US-PL**

5. *United States Code Service: Advance.* Charlottesville, Va.:
    LexisNexis

6. Lexis:
    Library and File = **GENFED;PUBLAW**

7. Lois: Jurisdiction = Federal, File = **Public Laws of the
    United States**

Index" that covers all the volumes. Rather, each publication unit comes with its own index. Thus, each volume of the *United States Statutes at Large* (which in reality means the physical book containing the last "Part" of each volume) contains a Subject Index. That index covers only the statutes published in that volume. The same is true for *U.S.C.C.A.N.*, the commercial publication which issues the Statutes at Large in permanent form. How, then, can we say that the subject index to session laws can be efficient, if each volume has a separate index that must be searched separately?

The non-cumulative nature of the session law indexes is not a problem for most legal researchers because usually they will only need the indexes to the most very recent publication units of the session laws, namely the indexes in the paperback issues of the commercial services which undertake to provide print coverage of current statutes. In the West system, that would be the "advance" paperback volumes of *U.S.C.C.A.N.* These are published monthly, and the indexes in the back cumulate until the publication of the final hardback edition. Pagination of the statutes published currently in *U.S.C.C.A.N.* is the same as the pagination that will be used in the *Statutes at Large* when they are eventually published. *U.S.C.S.* also offers publication of new Public Laws, and indicates their ultimate Stat. paging as well, in their *USCS Advance* pamphlets, mentioned above. The indexing in the *USCS Advance* issues, as in the *U.S.C.C.A.N.* advance issues, cumulates from issue to issue.

We did not refer to any indexing of session laws in the electronic databases of the same, because it does not exist. On Westlaw, neither the Public Laws database for the current session of Congress, nor the backfiles of older Public Laws have indexes as separate documents. On Lexis, the Public Laws are included in the United States Code Service file, and also have no separate index document. Nor does the Federal Government's electronic database of public and private laws (accessible via GPO Access and numerous other online venues) include a separate index. So again, as with the codes, if you want to use a subject index, rather than to search the full text of the session laws directly, you will do it in print.

One of the main reasons one would wish to use a subject index rather than simply to search the full text of the session laws, would be if one wanted to have access to alternative search terms. If one has not correctly anticipated the actual language that was used by the legislators, one may miss the statute by putting in the wrong search terms. One looks to the indexer for assistance in suggesting other search terms. The indexers of session laws do not disappoint. The indexing in the advance sheet pamphlets does not necessarily use the same terms as does the indexing in the statutory code (which is not terribly surprising), nor even as does the indexing in the permanent edition of the session laws (a bit more surprising). This is especially true in the advance sheet pamphlets of state session laws, commonly referred to as "Advance Legislative Services" (ALS). Sometimes an ALS indexer will even add outrageously lay language to the index, to try and ease the use of the index for the uninitiated. Thus, in one extreme example, where the code indexer had demurely put licensing laws under "taverns," the ALS indexer had added an additional heading for a brand new licensing provision, filing it under the considerably more informal "booze shops".

2.17 CITATIONS TO SESSION LAWS

Either the index, or a full-text search, or a secondary source citation will eventually lead you to a page number or to a law number within the session laws. The numbering systems used with respect to session laws tend to be bipartite, with the first element referring to the date or to the numbered session of the legislature and the second element being the number assigned in sequential order to this particular statute. Thus, since 1957 the Public Laws of the United States have been numbered in the form [number of Congress]—[order of this public law in the numerical list of public laws from this Congress]. The laws are "through-numbered" within a two year Congress: if the first session of the 109th Congress ends with P.L. 109–312, the first law passed by the second session of the 109th Congress will be P.L. 109–313. The Office of the Federal Register, which is part of the National Archives and Records Administration, assigns law numbers to the bills once the latter have received Presidential approval (or have been passed over a Presidential veto), and posts the newly-assigned law numbers on their website.

Citations to session laws, though, don't stop with just the law number. The *Bluebook* requires all session law citations to include identification of the volume in which the law appears, as well as the law's name and number. You can think of this as being like the name and address of the session law. For example, in citing the Museum and Library Services Act of 2003, Pub.L. No. 108–81, 117 Stat. 991, all three elements of the citation are mandatory. The "108" is like the family name, in that it indicates the law's provenance is the 108th Congress. The "81" serves as the law's first name, particular to that law within the "108" family. "117 Stat. 991" is like the law's home address, with the volume number, "117 Stat." serving as the street name, and the page number serving as the law's particular address on that street. Note that the home address alone cannot adequately identify the session law because more than one law may commence on that same page, so it is not a unique identifier.

Session laws differ from codes in this respect, since codes are identified only by code titles and section numbers, and their tangible enshrinement on a physical page is indicated only by a mention of the publication year of a code version, if that. Code sections need to remain untethered to a page number so that as their surroundings swell, shrink and shift they can still be found in their right place in relationship to those surroundings. Session laws, by contrast, are immutable. They may lose all or part of their clout, thanks to subsequent actions by the legislature or courts, but their passage is what the session laws memorialize, and that cannot be affected by anyone after it has occurred. A page number in a physical volume, widely distributed among the population through the Government Printing Office's Federal Depository Library program, ensures that this historical fact of the session law's passage remains verifiable by all.

2.18 CHOOSING A SOURCE FOR SESSION LAWS

As ever, the problem with the GPO's official version is the slowness of its publication. Prior to the appearance in print of the *United States Statutes at Large*, the researching public has already long had access to what it will contain, both on government and commercial online databases, and in the print *U.S.C.C.A.N.* and the *USCS Advance*. Since 1975, *U.S.C.C.A.N.* has provided a mockup of the actual page setups of the eventual Statutes at Large, and therefore of the expected pagination of the official source. Prior to 1975, the page numbers of session laws published in *U.S.C.C.A.N.* were completely independent of Statutes at Large pagination. Even with the current close physical resemblance between the *U.S.C.C.A.N.* pages and the eventual official publication, the Bluebook rule we mentioned in our first chapter remains: you cannot read the statute in *U.S.C.C.A.N.* and cite as though you had read it in the Statutes at Large.

Although many print and online sources offer faster access to the Public Laws than does the *Statutes at Large*, these other sources also vary greatly between themselves in the speed of access they provide. You always need to check the data source that you are using to see how up to date it is that very day. In the legal databases, there is generally an "information" link for each file which tells either specifically or as a matter of policy how up to date the information in that file is. You are always more interested in specific information about currency than in an updating policy which might be merely aspirational! Sometimes individual documents within the files have a note at the top about the specific currency of the database from which the document is drawn. However, even specific information about currency may be inaccurate: adding new laws to the database appears to be a higher priority than does adding the notice to a coverage information page that this has been done.

As of this writing, there is no faster way to get information about newly enacted public laws than to search the public laws database on Westlaw. It incorporates language from enrolled bills passed by Congress, signed by the President, and entered as Public Law before even the government's fastest public law website does, although the government does offer the same text still in its bill format. The language for Westlaw's version is taken from the Thomas data base of the Library of Congress, and so despite its labelling in Westlaw as Public Law (and indeed its simultaneous incorporation into the USCA database) it is actually, at least at first, the final language of the bill as signed. The Lexis session law database of Public Laws is just as up to date as Westlaw's, but the corresponding USCS database lags a bit behind the USCA database in incorporating these new laws, perhaps waiting for them at least to be released officially as Public Laws before incorporating them into the code. The real problem with the USCS database is the lack of a clear path to follow to update a very recently amended section. In all the databases, in order to be sure of having the latest material, you have to independently continue your research into the realm of pending legislation. This is discussed below in the section on researching bills.

For updating statutory law beyond the code, therefore, you will almost always be using unofficial sources like electronic databases, *U.S.C.C.A.N.*, or *USCS Advance*. Where do the official volumes of the *Statutes at Large* come into play? We mentioned at the end of section 2.14 that there were four principal reasons why you need to use session law sets. The first, to find laws that have not yet made it into the code, will never involve use of the actual *Statutes at Large*, simply because of the time lag in publication of the latter. But the other three uses of the session laws can all oblige the researcher to refer to the official set.

In the state law context, note that some states offer only an official set of session laws, published by the state. Others offer competing versions produced by different publishers (New York, for example, offers an official publication and two competing commercial publications!). As usual, Westlaw and Lexis offer the versions published by their affiliated print publishers; Lois and the states' own websites tend to offer the official texts. The Svengalis *Legal Information Buyer's Guide* offers a frequently updated overview of state session law publication.

2.19 FINDING LAWS THAT WILL NEVER MAKE IT INTO THE CODE

Codes aim to include statutes of a general and permanent nature. "General" means applicable to everyone that comes under a statute's substantive terms: this is what is meant by the "Public" law nomenclature in the *Statutes at Large*. The alternative is a Private Law, and while these are not as common as they once were, they are still enacted and still published in the *Statutes at Large*. These Private Laws provide for the specific relief of named parties in their dealings with the government. Historically, many of them provided pension coverage to widows of Civil War veterans; today the typical Private Law involves immigration relief for a worthy individual.

Private Laws are published in slip (uncollected) form and in the official *Statutes at Large*, which contains the only index to them. This single point of entry to the printed record illustrates the precariousness of access to non-commercially significant information. In the 107th Congress, one Private Law was passed, Act for the Relief of Rita Mirembe Revell, Private Law 107–1, 115 Stat. 2471. In theory the only way to find your way to this law in the *Statutes at Large* would be to look in the index for each year. In the subject index to vol. 115, there is an index entry under "Revell, Rita Mirembe" . . . the only problem is that the page number to which it refers is 200 pages off. Nor can you find the correct page number by searching the Catalog of Public and Private Laws which GPO Access makes available online. This access tool covering both Public and Private Laws since the 104th Congress is searchable by the "find in page" function of web browsers, but while the Catalog provides access to text and .pdf files of the Laws, it does not provide page references to the *Statutes at Large*. In actual practice, the only way to find this Private Law would be to look through the Private Laws section in each volume that might have it. Private Laws being as few and far between as they are these days, that practice is actually even quicker than looking at an accurate index would be.

While few will ever be concerned with finding Private Laws, the non-"general" statutes that don't go into the Code, many may at some point wish to find one of the non-"permanent" laws that also are not Code candidates. Prominent among laws that are not destined for the Code are such one-off statutes as appropriations acts, appointments, and laws which by their terms apply only for a very short time. For seeking out the likes of these, the researcher may need access to the whole chronological stretch of uncodified statutes. The problem that could basically be laughed off in the context of pre-codified session laws looms a bit larger in the world of never-codified statutes. How does one search for them in the absence of a unified index? Clearly one would want to search full text across a database comprising all the session laws.

The only way to do such a search is via Hein Online's U.S. Statutes at Large collection, which offers the whole set as .pdf files. The entire collection can be searched for files in which the search term is present. Yet valuable though this database is, using it can be extremely uncomfortable. Although the result files can be very lengthy and sometimes contain more than one law, there is no mechanism for locating a search term within an individual result file. In some instances you may find it most efficient to use Hein Online to identify the session laws in which your search term appears, but then to actually look over those known statutes in print, if it's available to you. This way you can avoid waiting for each successive page to load so you can eyeball it for your search term and figure out if the statute is useful to you.

Actual searchable text of the Statutes at Large is only shallowly available online. The uncodified Public Laws are available in text on Westlaw only back to 1973, on Lexis only back to 1988, and on GPO Access only back to 1995. The Library of Congress's American Memory website offers access to image files of the first eighteen volumes of the Statutes at Large (covering the first forty-three Congresses, 1789–1875), along with searchable indexing of each. The first eight volumes included in the American Memory project share an online index. With that one small exception, however, for Statutes prior to 1973 one would have to either use Hein Online, search the separate subject indexes for each Congress, or obtain citations through research in secondary sources.

2.20 UPDATING UNCODIFIED SESSION LAWS

Whereas subsequent amendments to or repealing of codified laws are indicated in the ever-changing code itself, amendments to or repealing of never-codified session laws must be researched differently. Notice that even though an uncodified session law may be reproduced in a "note" to the Code, it is still updatable only via the Public Law number. For this task there is only one tool specifically made for the job: *Shepard's Federal Statute Citations* in print. Neither Shepard's on Lexis nor KeyCite on Westlaw offer updating of the uncodified sections of the *Statutes at Large*, even for those portions that are represented in the statutory databases of the respective services. By using this Shepard's print product you can check to see if an uncodified Public Law has been amended or repealed, in whole or in part. Since Shepard's publication involves editorial work which requires time, you should also do a keyword search in the full text session law databases to verify that nothing new has come up that could affect your statute since Shepard's did their work.

In the state law environment, as you would expect, the technique for updating non-codified statutes will be different in each jurisdiction, but can get quite complicated. In New York, for example, session laws not part of the Compiled Laws of New York (the New York equivalent of the United States Code) are updated via *Shepard's New York Statute Citations* in print, but cannot be updated on Shepard's on Lexis nor (except for a limited subset) on Westlaw.

The commercial publishers who produce the collected Compiled Laws of New York have each cobbled together a set of Unconsolidated Laws that they have selected from those session laws that are not assigned by the Legislature to an existing part of the Compiled Laws. The complication is that the two publishers have selected different laws to treat in this way, so their numbering systems are completely different from each other. In *McKinney's Consolidated Laws of New York*, a session law selected for this treatment will be assigned a McKinney's Unconsolidated Laws number which will then function within McKinney's as a code section number, i.e., subsequent session laws that amend the original session law will be used to refashion the existing McKinney's Unconsolidated Laws section, and will be added to the list of underlying statutory authorities for that section in the parenthetical information following the text of the refashioned section. Subsequent citation to this subset of the session laws outside the Compiled Laws can be researched via KeyCite, but no others can.

A similar approach is used in the *New York Consolidated Laws Service* volume of Unconsolidated Laws, each of which gets its own CLS Unconsol.L. number and gets similarly updated. The *CLS* set provides a helpful table correlating its own Unconsolidated Laws with those of McKinney's (no equivalent table exists in McKinney's), and with the underlying session laws. For details on this process in each of the several states, consult a research guide for the particular state **(see Appendix)**.

2.21 STATUTES MORE CONVENIENTLY DISCUSSED IN THEIR ORIGINAL SESSION LAW FORM

The third use of the session laws is for those laws which are more usefully cited to the session law than to the code. A session law citation would usually be more useful than a code citation when the original statute was broken up and the pieces scattered into farflung corners of the code, such that lining them up to talk about them collectively would be awkward. The *Bluebook* discusses this in Rule 12.2.2 (a), giving in its examples some idea of how scattered the sections have to be in order to be considered unwieldy. The other chief circumstance in which session law citation would be more useful than code citation would be when you wish to discuss the history of the actual passage of the statute. The session law citation, tied as it is to a particular date, gives a historical precision that is indispensable in the historical context. Both of these uses of the session laws may well involve use of any part of the whole chronological range of the set, and thus necessitate access to the paper set.

2.22 SESSION LAW NOMENCLATURE VS. CODE NOMENCLATURE

Once one is cognizant of both the session law version and the codified version of the same law, one is struck by the very different numerical labels that get affixed to the same language in its different contexts. It is crucial that the researcher keep these different labels straight and distinct; confusion between a session law and a code section is one of the easiest and most common mistakes made by beginning legal researchers. We have already seen that a code section is labeled by the title of the code in which it appears, the name of the code, and finally its own section number. We saw, too, that the code sections can be grouped together in subgroupings called chapters and subchapters, but that these subject groupings do not function as part of the citation to any section. By contrast, a session law is labeled by its own name and law number, and then with a citation to where it is physically printed, i.e., a volume and page number of a particular statutory set.

The complications arise when we look within the individual statutes: session laws can be very long indeed, and require multiple subdivisions. And here's the rub: the principal subdivisions within the Public Laws are (like the subdivisions of the U.S. Code) known as Titles. This kind of title can indeed be properly incorporated into a citation of that particular portion of a session law. Sometimes these subdivisions are the most useful way to refer to a particular set of provisions, and so they enter the common legal parlance. Think of Title VII civil rights actions. To be precise you would need to say Title VII of what specific statute you were talking about, but within the civil rights area, say Title VII and everybody knows what you mean. In order to avoid confusion in any particular instance about whether you are looking at something that pertains to a big portion of the U.S. Code or, rather, to a subdivision of an individual session law, note that the former always involves a regular number (e.g., Title 17) and the latter a capital Roman numeral.

The other form of confusion that arises from statutory labels involves chapters. The kind of chapter that denotes a grouping together for arrangement purposes in a statutory code gets a capital "C", as though you were talking about a chapter in a book. However, some session law series use a numbering scheme where each statute is assigned a chapter number as its individual identification number. The *Statutes at Large* used this system until 1957. Many state legislatures still assign chapter numbers to each enacted law. What you need to remember here is that the sort of chapter number that refers only to an individual statute gets a lower-case "c", and is frequently abbreviated "ch.", or even "c". Since your research may well need to go back and forth between the session laws and the code, you will need to keep all these labels straight so that it remains clear to you and to your readers which you are talking about at any particular time.

2.23 SESSION LAWS AS AUTHENTICATION OF CODE LANGUAGE

The fourth reason you will need to use the session laws is to verify the accuracy of language in the code. As of this writing, twenty-four of the fifty titles of the U.S. Code have been reenacted by Congress as positive law, meaning that they serve as legal evidence of the law they contain, without reference back to their source in the *Statutes at Large*. A list of which titles have been reenacted is provided by the Office of the

Law Revision Counsel at http://uscode.house.gov/about/info.shtml. Subsequent enactments on subjects pertaining to the reenacted titles must be framed by Congress as amendments to the appropriate reenacted Code title, rather than leaving this task to the Law Revision Counsel to do *ex post facto*. The other Code titles, as yet not reenacted, are only *prima facie* evidence of the law they contain. This means that code sections from titles that have not been reenacted can be rebutted as evidence of the law if their language conflicts with that of the *Statutes at Large*. This, in turn, means that if you are relying on language from such a code section, you are supposed to verify its language against that of the *Statutes at Large*. If the language of the two conflicts, the language of the *Statutes at Large* governs.

Once a statute is passed by Congress, its text receives first official publication as a freestanding "slip law," identified by its law number. That text is then sent both to the National Archives and Records Administration for incorporation in session law format into the *United States Statutes at Large*, and to the Law Revision Counsel of the House of Representatives for codification, i.e., to be added, as the Counsel sees fit, to the edifice of current general and permanent federal statutory law: the United States Code. Sometimes the new law needs to have a little something added, or subtracted, or changed in order to make it fit coherently into the existing body of the Code. Sometimes (or always, with respect to those titles of the Code that have already been reenacted as positive law by Congress) all the codifiers have to do is to give effect to language specifically stating how a particular portion of the code is to be amended by the session law in question. Other times the codifiers have to choose, based on the subject matter of earlier code sections, where to put the new content and what might need to be excised from the existing code. Making these changes frequently obliges the codifiers to alter the language of the code to accommodate the additions, changes, and deletions while maintaining a logical and readable whole. It is the job of the Law Revision Counsel to make all these changes as unsubstantive as possible. Nonetheless, it is here that the possibility of error arises.

In the words of Charles J. Zinn, long a member of the Law Revision Counsel, "classification is a matter of opinion and judgment." Occasionally (only very occasionally, in light of the amount of codification they do), the Counsel goes astray, and makes what turns out to be a substantive change to the statute in the course of revising it for the code.

This is why the statutes in their original formats are the governing authority. The original legislation is the expression of both houses of Congress, but the unreenacted Titles of the Code are in part merely a creation of the codification scribes. The statutes in their original format (session laws) are "positive law." The code, as it emerges from the hands of the codification body, is just a useful system of evidence as to what the positive law is, which must be verified in the last analysis, against the positive law of the *Statutes at Large*.

2.24 GETTING FROM A CODE SECTION TO ITS SOURCE IN THE SESSION LAWS

In case you do need to verify the accuracy of a code section, you will have to find out where exactly in the *Statutes at Large* your code language came from. At the end of each code section, in all versions, there is parenthetical information that is sometimes all you need to get to the original language of the session law. It contains one or a series of citations to Public Laws: these are the session laws that furnish the basis for the code section in question. The first citation given was the original source for the code section; any subsequent session laws cited furnished the basis for amendment of or addition to the original language of the section. In the USCS on Lexis and the USCA on Westlaw you can click through from the parenthetical information following each code section to those text-based session law sources that are part of the respective service's session law databases. In the USCS on Lexis you can also click through to many of the earlier session law source documents in .pdf format. The USC online gives the parenthetical source information, but without offering any clickthrough functionality.

In all but the simplest cases, however, you may need to go further to identify what was added when. After the parenthetical information comes a section (which in the print editions, helpfully, is in a different font to differentiate it from the code itself) called "Historical and Statutory Notes" (USCA), "History; Ancillary Laws and Directives" (USCS), or "Historical and Revision Notes" and "Amendments" (USC): these sections give brief indications of which statutes did what to the code section in question. This section of the annotations is also where a lot of statutory material not incorporated into the code is presented, in the form of a "note" to the code. These notes (references to which frequently refer to "nts") often include language of purpose from the statute. They are cited by courts, but are not covered by any citators, so tracing the judicial impact of a "note" requires either working with its source in the Statutes at Large or, when it is not taken from there, by a full text search of the appropriate case law database.

In Westlaw, as with the parenthetical source attributions, one can click through directly from these notes to an unofficial version of the Public Law, limited to the years for which Westlaw offers text-based Public Laws, i.e., 1973 to date. The procedure in Lexis is less direct, since it involves clicking through to notes in USCS that in turn quote from the Public Laws. The Law Revision Counsel's online version of the Code does not offer clicking through to anything, but does give citations to the amending Public Laws.

For laws enacted or amended before the period covered by the electronic databases, you need to resort to the *Statutes at Large* in print to retrieve the original language. The problem here is that many of the statutes are so long that finding the desired language within them either in print or in image-based files is arduous and frustrating if all you have is the citation to the statute as a whole, or to a subsection of a statute without a *Statutes at Large* page number particular to that subsection, which is all you can get either from the parenthetical information or from the historical notes. Happily, there is a separate tool which will enable you to find the language relatively easily: the Tables volume of the Code.

Each of the three publications of the Code has a section entitled "Tables." The Tables lay out where everything in the *Statutes at Large* has been placed in the U.S. Code, including in the notes to the U.S. Code. The breakdown of the Public Laws for this purpose is down to the individual section number, which is given with the actual page of the *Statutes at Large* on which it appears. Since the principal purpose of the Tables is to show the disposition of the *Statutes at Large* in the Code, the Tables are arranged in Public Law number order. But the savvy researcher will also resort to the Tables when trying to pin down a particular location within the *Statutes at Large* for a known code section. In the print Tables, once you know which Public Law is involved, you can then sweep your eyes over the Code sections listed for that Public Law in the right hand column. When your eye alights upon the desired code section number, you can look back to the left to see which exact page in the *Statutes at Large* was the source for your code section. Though this method be slightly unsystematic, it still beats skimming through the statute itself! This technique works both in print and online, and covers the full range of dates of the *Statutes at Large* in both. For long and very long statutes, this locating function is essential. Remember that for much of the *Statutes at Large* there is no full text available for searching.

Not only is the arrangement of the information different in the USCS, USCA, and USC Tables, but their content varies slightly as well. This means that if there is an error in one, it can be worthwhile to try one of the others. As ever, the USCS Tables vary more in content from the other two than the other two do from each other. The USCS Tables on Lexis include an additional column which usefully characterizes what the given Public Law did to each code section indicated, not just those which are repealed or unclassified. The USCS Tables also go into much more granular detail than the others, both as to which subsection of the Code was the destination of a given section of the session law, and indicating such subdivisions as Titles on the session law side of the Table. On the other hand, the *U.S.C.A.* Tables in print are conveniently reprinted in toto frequently, and navigating to a desired section of the *Statutes at Large* is much more direct in the Westlaw version of the Tables than in the Lexis version. The online Tables produced by the Law Revision Counsel only cover Public Laws back to 2001, but they are unique in offering a choice between arrangement in Public Law order or in U.S. Code order.

2.25 MONSTER SESSION LAWS:
OMNIBUS STATUTES

Our concern over the difficulty of locating statutory language precisely within a long law may seem overwrought, until, that is, your first encounter with an omnibus statute. *Black's Law Dictionary* defines omnibus as "relating to or dealing with numerous objects or items at once; including many things or having various purposes," and an omnibus bill as either "1. A single bill containing various distinct matters, usu. drafted in this way to force the executive either to accept all the unrelated minor provisions or to veto the major provision," or "2. A bill that deals with all proposals relating to a particular subject, such as an 'omnibus judgeship bill' covering all proposals for new judgeships or an 'omnibus crime bill' dealing with different subjects such as new crimes and grants to states for crime control." Some states have long had constitutional provisions prohibiting such legislation, precisely to counter their obfuscatory potential.

The most difficult problems when working with such statutes involve legislative history, but looking for uncodified topics or even looking for codified language within them to check the accuracy of code sections can be brutal. Whether by design or by necessity (of cramming things in before the end of the legislative session so all that work need not have been in vain), these omnibus statutes can be incredibly long. Remember how we said that the law number is a necessary part of the session law citation so you can know which law is meant when more than one law starts on the same page? No such problem with these omnibus monstrosities: some of them (e.g., the Omnibus Consolidated Appropriations Act of 1997) tip the scales at over 700 pages of pure law, couched in unremitting statutory English.

The titles of the omnibus acts can seem bizarre when one peruses the components that get shoehorned into them. The outlines or tables of contents included at the beginning of such statutes are usually skeletal and not much help. Also, there is no provision of running heads of the subdivisions throughout the text, and there are so many different levels of subdivisions (including the subdivisions of the Code or of earlier session laws that are being designated for amendment) that flipping through the pages of these statutes looking for the subdivision indicated in the table of contents is confusing and frustrating. Finally, the type faces used to differentiate subdivisions are inconsistent, which further complicates finding something. This is a situation where full-text searching is truly indispensible, and yet not always available.

2.26 READING THE SESSION LAW AS AN
AID TO UNDERSTANDING THE CODE

Another kind of verification of accuracy involves reviewing the whole original session law for its internal cross-references. For situations where you want to read an original statute as a unit, the best solution is to use the Popular Name Table in any of the versions of the Code (or the Popular Name Index, as it is called in Westlaw). This gem of a publication includes citations for named "acts" subsumed into larger Public Laws, showing not only their dispersal into the Code, but also both which subdivision of which Public Law contains it and what its initial page is (i.e., within that public law) in the *Statutes at Large*. The desire to read the whole statute together as originally passed probably most often arises when the codification process has created some ambiguity about the coverage or applicability of a particular provision. References to "herein" or "hereinafter," for instance, may be clearer or indeed different in the session law than in the Code.

2.27 FINDING STATUTES BY "NAME"

The Popular Name Table, a feature in all editions of the U.S. Code (each offering a slightly different array of names), introduces us to the last major access point in indexes generally: name of item. We have seen in sections 2.3 through 2.8 how to find statutes by subject either through use of a subject index or through a subject hierarchy structure. We saw in section 2.14 that the chronological arrangement of the *Statutes at Large* enables you to find statutes by date or by law number. Finally, we come to a resource that permits us to look for a statute whose name we know, through an alphabetical index of statute names. The Popular Name Tables in the commercially published codes take you from the statute name to session law and code citations for the original act and all subsequent amendments; the one in the official U.S. Code takes you to the original session law cite only.

What are these "popular names" that are indexed in the Popular Name Table? Often they are names given by Congress to statutes in the language of their own opening section: "This Act may be cited as the 'Consolidated Omnibus Budget Reconciliation Act of 1985' " (Pub. L. No. 99–272, sec. 1, 100 Stat. 82 (1986)). Within the statute, such statements usually bear the caption "Short Title." But on the street the statute is called "COBRA," and this even more "popular" name is also indexed, referring the reader to the entry under the official short title.

Occasionally the Office of the Federal Register of the National Archives and Records Administration, which edits the *Statutes at Large*, creates a title for a statute where the legislature was silent on the matter, and puts that title into the margin of the session law. This goes into the popular name table as well, as does the occasional "popular name" that is neither acronym nor official short title but a real nickname, like the Switchblade Knife Act (actually the Ballistic Knife Prohibition Act of 1986) or the Taft–Hartley Act (actually the Labor Management Relations Act, 1947). It also distinguishes between, e.g., the two completely different Volstead Acts. Contemplation of the Popular Name Table gives rise to an appreciation of the wide ranging activities of Congress: think of the Popcorn Promotion, Research, and Consumer Information Act (Pub. L. 104–127, Title V, Subtitle E, Apr. 4, 1996, 110

Stat. 1074.) It also cuts through all the byzantine layers of the legislative act, so that you can easily find the "Use of Assisted Housing by Aliens Act of 1996" nested within the "Illegal Immigration Reform and Immigrant Responsibility Act of 1996," which in turn resides within the mammoth "Omnibus Consolidated Appropriations Act, 1997" (Sept. 30, 1996). But do not mistake the Popular Name Table for an index to all of the *Statutes at Large*: many Acts within the latter are denominated simply "Act of [date]," and consequently make no appearance in the Table.

2.28　GETTING FROM A SESSION LAW TO THE CORRESPONDING CODE SECTIONS

We have seen that the arrangement of the Tables to the Codes is in Public Law number order; now we will get to the uses for which that order is actually appropriate. We started out with the code for reasons of efficiency, and then needed to get from the code to the session law for a variety of reasons. What about when you are starting off with a session law?

There are three main reasons why you would be interested in proceeding from the session law to working with the code, and they comprise the reasons why the Code was devised in the first place. The first reason would be to see the current state of the law on the subject matter that was covered by your session law: since the code collates the various general and permanent laws on the same subject, it should fill you in on later enactments that have affected your original statute. Secondly, locating your statute within the code enables you to see it within its larger subject context, i.e., in the context of other laws on related matters. Finally, because of the subject collocation provided by the code, it enables you to go on to find other related legal authorities and annotating materials.

How, then, do you go about finding where your session law was put into the code? The easiest case is when the code destination is indicated within the language of the session law itself, sometimes even in its title, as in Public Law 108–92, titled "An Act To amend chapter 84 of title 5, United States Code. . . . " We saw above how the language of the session law is frequently framed in terms of how a particular section or subsection of the code is to be amended thereby. However, where the destination of the code is a section that has not been reenacted as positive law, the code section (or sections) where the new statute will reside is not necessarily spelled out in its own language. In some versions of the session laws, marginal notes created by the codifiers and indicating code destination may be included alongside the text. But the most thorough and comprehensive source of code destinations is the aforementioned Tables feature of every version of the Code. It offers a high level of precision of location, and since it is updated periodically, it is kept up to date with changes to the Code. Superseded paper editions, moreover, can provide navigational aid to those working with archival back editions of the Code.

2.29 FINDING BILLS

Sometimes your situation dictates that you must be concerned with laws that are on the horizon as well as with laws that are already in effect. In such circumstances, the final step in researching statutory authority on a subject is finding any nascent statutes, i.e., current bills, that deal with your subject. Moreover, the search for bills can also reap a bonus: you may come up with an actual law that has only just been enacted, and has not yet been incorporated into either the latest session laws or—*a fortiori*— the code.

When looking for possible imminent changes to the legislative landscape, you are concerned only with those bills pending in the current legislative session, and will want to look for them by subject. You will of course want to look for bills that on their terms propose to affect an already existing statute. But if you only look for bills that on their terms would affect a particular section of the Code or an existing Public Law, you might miss something relevant to your subject. We mentioned in section 2.18 above on choosing a source for session laws that in the USCS database you would be obliged to look into the Public Laws database to get the latest statutes, since there is a lag between their appearance there and in the USCS online code. In fact, you would be just as well or better served to do your updating search in the bills database, since then you would find in one search everything too recent to go into the code: bills, very newly enacted Public Laws, everything. To narrow your results down to just those bills that have already become law, you can add the search term "P.L."

2.30 FINDING A BILL BY SUBJECT

The electronic legal databases offer a variety of ways to look for bills on a subject. The text for all of these services originates in the U.S. Government Printing Office. The Library of Congress's Thomas website offers keyword searching of the full text of current bills. Again, as with the U.S. Code site provided by the Law Revision Counsel and the Public Laws database provided by the Government Printing Office, the Library of Congress specifies that the online text is unofficial and is subordinate to the official, physically printed text (in slip form) of the bills. Thomas also offers an "index" of searchable words, which is just that: an alphabetical list of the searchable words in all of the bills, with links to the bills containing those words. Lexis and Westlaw also offer full text searching of bills, and the bill texts get picked up by a variety of other sites **(see Table 2.D)**.

Table 2.D: Sources of Congressional Bills

1. Library of Congress, Thomas: Legislative Information on the Internet.

    http://thomas.loc.gov/

    Includes bill texts starting with the 101st Congress (1989)

2. United States, GPOAccess. Congressional Bills. http://www.gpoaccess.gov/bills/index.html

    Coverage begins with the 103rd Congress (1993–94). Offers both text and .pdf files.

3. Westlaw:
    Directory Location = All Databases > U.S. Federal Materials > Bill Tracking

4. Lexis:
    Sources = Legal > Legislation and Politics—U.S. & U.K. > U.S. Congress >

5. *Congressional Bills, Resolutions, and Laws* [Microform]. Bethesda, Md.: Congressional Information Service

6. *Congressional Bills, Resolutions, and Amendments* [Microform]. Washington: U.S.G.P.O.

    Note that this set is no longer produced by the G.P.O., but has been taken over by Court Record Services, Inc., working from the G.P.O.'s online data.

Of course the full text searches make you completely dependent on the actual language employed by the bills, and even the "index" on Thomas adds no further indexing terms. In order to search bills by subject headings that may not track the bill language exactly, you need to consult the only subject index to bills: the *CCH Congressional Index*. The *Congressional Index*, a two volume looseleaf publication available in print only, is updated weekly with a wide variety of information about current legislation in the U.S. Congress.

For our current purposes, you are concerned with the *Congressional Index's* subject indexes to bills. Each volume contains, among other things, a subject index to bills introduced in one of the houses of the current Congress. The subject headings used in the index include broad terms that group bills under general topics, such as agriculture or education, with subheadings for more specific topics within them.

One peculiarity of this index is its division into a number of layers of currency (a typical CCH technique, used to avoid excessive weekly republication of the same material): you will need to look through as many as three layers of alphabetical subject indexing in each chamber of Congress to do a thorough subject search. As with the electronic sources, note the date of currency of these indexes. You will want to do a full text search in the online bill databases for material that was too late to be caught in the most recent issue of the *Congressional Index*. Also, since the *Congressional Index* contains only summaries describing the content of each bill very briefly, you will need to retrieve the full text of the bill from one of the sources listed in Table 2.D, above.

2.31 FINDING A BILL BY BILL NUMBER, BY DATE, OR BY SPONSOR

You may already have information about a bill that would make it more efficient to locate the bill text or other information by bill number, by date, or by sponsor. You can use any of these access points in the electronic bill databases and in the *Congressional Index*. Bill numbers are typically composed of first an abbreviation denoting the legislative chamber into which the bill was originally introduced, and second a sequential number in order of the bill's introduction into that chamber. To make the citation complete, you need to add information specifying the legislature during which the bill was introduced, and the year of publication. Since the bill numbers are assigned in chronological sequence, a numerical list of bills will also enable you to pick out a bill by its date, if that is what you have to go on (frequently the case if you are working from, e.g., a newspaper story). If you want to find a bill by a known sponsor, you can consult the "Author Index" in the Senate volume of the *Congressional Index* (this covers House authors as well), or use the form-based query on Thomas reached by clicking on "Bill Summary and Status."

In the state law context, the states vary in how they make public the text of proposed legislation, but in no state is the documentation as highly developed as it is in the federal jurisdiction. For information about the different ways that you can access pending state bills, consult a bibliography like William H. Manz's *Guide to State Legislative and Administrative Materials* (2002 ed., AALL Publications Series No. 61. Buffalo, N.Y.: William S. Hein & Co., 2002) or a state legal research guide **(see Appendix)**. Common bill retrieval methods in the state context include use of the state legislature's website, employment of a specialized document delivery service, or telephone contact with the state legislature.

For possible future statutes that are even further out toward the horizon, perhaps just a glimmer (but a persistent glimmer) in a legislator's eye, you would need to look further than the bill resources. Don't overlook the value of full text searching in newspapers of record, principally (for this purpose) the *New York Times* and the *Washington Post*. In the state law context, check out the websites of interest groups focussed on the subject of concern to you, and the sites of associations of state legislatures, which frequently comment on matters that are expected to be the subject of upcoming legislation in more than one state.

2.32   CASES INTERPRETING STATUTES

As advanced students of legal research, you know that mere awareness of the current statute relevant to your situation is not enough. In our common law system, you need to know what precedents, if any, exist in the application of that statute by the courts. So important a role does this court interpretation play in determining the significance of your statute, that finding all relevant cases construing it is as indispensible to legal research as is finding an absolutely current statutory text. While there are many different ways to find case law (see Chapter Five, below), there are a number of specialized ways to sift the caselaw for those cases that apply (or construe, perhaps declining to apply) your statute.

When all you want is the famous, leading cases interpreting an important statute, you should think in terms of looking in law review articles for exactly those cases, the cream of the crop, that can furnish the basis for much of your further research. Another important type of secondary resource would be the many treatises on statutorily-based subjects which are arranged in code section number order, and which offer selective annotations either in a separate section or in footnotes (e.g., works on federal or state practice, evidence, copyright, the U.C.C., etc.). See Chapter Four below on law reviews and Chapter Six below on treatises for more on this type of research.

2.33   FINDING CASES IN AN ANNOTATED CODE

Let us assume, however, that you are looking for more and that you are ready to do some detailed research. The *sine qua non* of this type of research is the annotated code, already encountered in the form of the *U.S.C.A.* and the *U.S.C.S.* Annotated codes follow each section of code text with references to sources that will aid in the interpretation of that section. Chief among these interpretive sources are citations to relevant cases with brief summaries of how the statute was applied in each. Typically, these case descriptions come after all the information about the code section itself (the text, the derivation information, the legislative history information, the references to commentary on the statute).

In the *U.S.C.A.* the case descriptions are called Notes of Decision, and are preceded by a little alphabetical table of contents grouping the decisions under hierarchically numbered subject headings called "catchlines." In the *U.S.C.S.* they are called Interpretive Notes and Decisions, and the little table of contents is just numbered hierarchically, with no alphabetical arrangement. The significance of this distinction is usually *de minimis*, but when you come to a section with hundreds and hundreds of case descriptions, and a correspondingly high number of subject headings classifying them, the difference may loom a bit larger.

Note that these numbered subject headings are used only in this one context, and have no connection to any other numbered subject heading scheme (like the Key Number system, or the subject headings in the competing publisher's annotated code). The subject headings used are different, for instance, in the two electronic annotated codes, so you may want to check both in case the concept or point you are interested in is not addressed in the one you try first. In Westlaw's USCA, you can click on the number of the subject heading to jump to the part of the Notes of Decision that falls under that subject heading, a feature that makes scanning these case summaries a bit more like the print process, which is easiest of all. Where both online sources shine, of course, is in the ability to click through from the case descriptions to the cases themselves. Hard to argue with the convenience of that!

Each case description in the USCA (and in other West annotated codes) is identical to a headnote in the cited case, and thus to a digest entry for that case, with only one significant difference. The headnote in the case reporter and the entry in the digest both list all the statutory sections cited by the court for the point of law discussed therein. The case description in the code annotation, on the other hand, omits this list. Consequently, you may wish to click through to see the original headnote (or pull the case, if working with print sources) so that you get the full list of statute sections and don't focus your attention prematurely on only the section under which you found the case.

Whenever (as here) you have a lot of cases to look up from a source that is on Lexis or Westlaw, you should consider working at the computer with the analogous print source in your hand. That way you can, for instance, scan the Notes of Decision in print (faster than scrolling and reading online), and when you see something you want to look at, do a "find in page" search for a distinctive word from the case name. After jumping to the note about that case, you would click through to take a look at the whole case online. If it still looks good, add it to a list to print, in whole or in part (the latter if you prefer to read from the print volumes). This technique, marrying the most convenient parts of print and online formats, minimizes the chance that you will allow gaps in your research either through error or frustration.

Where a case cites to a whole act (whether the choice to do so is technically correct or incorrect), and the act has been codified into numerous sections, the case will usually be noted under the first of the code sections, frequently the introductory one. Therefore, you should make a practice of looking not only at the notes of decision listed for your particular code section, but also under those listed for the adjacent sections and for the introductory sections to the chapter (finally a use for those chapter subdivisions!). If you don't have a code section but only a Public Law number to work with, first determine the relevant code section (see section 2.28, above, for instructions on how to do this), and then look up case annotations in the annotated code. Remember also that citation rules dictate using the code citation, except in limited exceptional circumstances. If you confirm that there actually is no code citation for your statute, then you will need to resort to other techniques to find cases tied to it (see sections 2.38 and 2.39 below).

2.34 CURRENCY OF THE CASE ANNOTATIONS

Searching the USCA or USCS online for case annotations, you will need to be concerned (as you were when looking for the current statute) with the currency of the database. In both the USCA and USCS online the information provided for the file as a whole does not give a "current through" date. Once you get to an individual code section, the heading at the top of the document tells you up through which public law number this section has been updated. However, neither database offers information about the currency of the case annotations. By contrast, in both the print *U.S.C.A.* and *U.S.C.S.*, each volume or issue contains at the front not only information about the currency of the statutory text, given in terms of last public law number incorporated (or excluded from incorporation), but also information about the cutoff point for case annotation, given in terms of the last page of each case reporter reviewed for relevant cases. While the database is as current in its case annotations as the latest print supplement to the *U.S.C.A.* or *U.S.C.S.*, without access to the print books you would have no way of knowing how current that actually was. This is another instance where you can usefully supplement the convenience of the online format with the fuller documentation associated with the print format.

Of course, no matter how up to date the annotations are, you can get cases that are more recent by mining the most recent cases in the case law databases via a full-text search for references to your statute. This is analogous to searching the most recent public laws for subject terms, in order to get more current than the most updated version of the code. You are essentially eliminating the editorial middleman, and going straight to the data as yet unsifted by that middleman. While you do sacrifice the orderliness of the subject arrangement of the catchlines, you gain not only in currency but in the ability to customize your search by the inclusion of particular terms.

2.35 REVISION OF THE ANNOTATIONS

The annotated codes, as we saw above in the section on using codes, are not republished on a fixed schedule as the official code is. Rather, each volume is republished as the need arises, usually when the annual pocket part that is cumulating all changes to that volume since its last republication gets too fat for the book's spine, or when a wholesale revision of a title makes it indispensible to republish right away (as with Title 17, Copyright, following enactment of the Copyright Act of 1976). When the pocket part gets too fat, the first step is often to publish a softcover supplement that takes the place of the pocket part; this gets shelved adjacent to the supplemented volume. Usually the existence of such a supplement indicates that republication of the main volume in question is on the way.

When republication of an annotated code volume occurs, what changes does it include? Obviously all the material that is still valid from the most recent pocket part is incorporated into the appropriate section of the new main volume. But other changes can occur at this point as well. Errors that crept in to the original volume can now be corrected, significant subsequent history of annotating cases can be appended to their case descriptions, and, curiously, the catchlines for annotations within the sections can be renamed, reorganized, and reassigned. This latter revision occurs with surprising frequency, and the text of the annotations themselves are sometimes rewritten, but the actual selection of cases from earlier editions is usually carried forward into all successive editions. Occasionally there is an exception, so if you want to find absolutely all cases that have ever been selected to annotate a given code section, you can consult superseded volumes of the *U.S.C.A.*, available in the Hein microfiche set. As we saw above, the *U.S.C.S.* is not preserved in microfiche, so you would need to seek out a library that has retained archival copies of superseded *U.S.C.S.* volumes in order to do an exhaustive historical search.

2.36   CASES INCLUDED IN
THE ANNOTATIONS

The selection of cases for annotations varies from publisher to publisher. The two annotated versions of the U.S. Code have historically differed in their approach to case annotations. Of old, the *U.S.C.A.* aspired to "completeness," while the *U.S.C.S.* aimed to be more selective. Currently, the *U.S.C.S.* is also being marketed as having "comprehensive" annotations. In fact, however, neither set is comprehensive, whether through active editorial discretion or just the exigencies of dealing with the tidal wave of decisions that must be sorted through: while the *U.S.C.A.* will frequently have more annotations after a given code section, the *U.S.C.S.* often has cases that the *U.S.C.A.* does not. The obvious moral: check both codes for the most complete picture possible, and don't assume that even the combination of the two is comprehensive.

2.37   CASE ANNOTATIONS IN
SPECIALIZED SOURCES

You may also wish to look for case annotations in more specialized sources, many of which offer such annotations in code section order. For example, the *CCH Standard Federal Tax Reporter* offers case annotations arranged under thematic catchlines after each section of the Internal Revenue Code (Title 26). The catchlines are devised from a more specialized viewpoint and, since it does not limit itself to officially published cases, the coverage of the annotations is broader. Similar services exist for annotations to such statute–like authorities as rules of procedure and evidence. For more information on this kind of research, see Chapter Nine below on looseleafs.

In the state law context, the annotated code (and some states, as with the federal code, have codes published by more than one publisher) is again your primary source for judicial interpretations of statutes. However, there are also some additional resources for the state law researcher. If your statute was based on a uniform statute (see Chapter Eleven for more on this concept), the *Uniform Laws Annotated* set will provide annotations to cases from a range of jurisdictions which have statutes based on the uniform source. Similarly, the various UCC services will provide citations to cases from a variety of jurisdictions. But even using specialized annotation services **(see Table 2.E)** cannot assure you of complete coverage, because of the editorial time required to put the annotations together, if for no other reason. To be sure that you have found absolutely every relevant decision, you will need to supplement your annotation search with either or both of the other two principal methods of finding cases pertaining to your statute.

Table 2.E: Examples of Specialized Sources of Statute Annotations and How They Work

1. *Copyright Law Reporter.* Chicago: Commerce Clearing House

This looseleaf service is a good example of the multi-step process used to get from statutory section to interpreting case in such publications. The copyright statutes appear in one volume, and each section of the statute is assigned a paragraph number. Cases are found by consulting a list of cases organized by the paragraph number(s) (and therefore the statutory sections) to which they are relevant. The payoff for going through this comparatively cumbersome process is subject access to many cases not published in print elsewhere and thus not picked up by the general indexing systems.

2. *Federal Rules Service.* St. Paul, Minn.: Thomson/West

Here, too, a multi-step finding process leads to ''unpublished'' cases. In this set, the text of each Federal Rule is followed by a detailed breakdown of subject headings pertaining to that section (analogous to the catchnotes following the statutory sections in the annotated codes), and then cases are listed in a ''Findex'' under those numbered subject headings.

3. *Uniform Laws Annotated.* St. Paul, Minn.: Thomson/West

This set covers only those laws that have been adopted by states on the basis, to at least some extent, of a Uniform Law (these are discussed at some length in Chapter Eleven), but in the familiar format of a West annotated code. The text of each section is followed by official commentary and then by notes of decisions.

Case annotations of statutes can be found in many treatises, as well as in looseleaf services, specialized reporters, and specialized statutory compilations like those listed here.

2.38   USING A CITATOR TO FIND CASES INTERPRETING A STATUTE

The first of these alternative methods should be the use of a citator. The citator process will catch the newer judicial applications of your statute faster than the code annotators will, so you can gain valuable currency of coverage without sacrificing the organizational efficacy of an edited resource. Shepards and KeyCite will both provide you with citations to cases (including cases not yet published) that construe your statute. The reason they should be regarded as secondary to use of the annotations is that unlike the annotations they provide only finding information, no description of content. Even when working electronically with a citator, where you can simply click through from each citation to the underlying case, you would waste a lot of time compared with the quick sweep you can make of an annotation to determine whether it is possibly relevant.

When working with a citator, make sure to check under all the possible ways that your statute could have been cited, i.e., as the section as a whole, as the specific subsection invoked in the case, or as the section in context of a sequence of sections identified by a section number followed by "*et seq.*". Again, it is definitely worthwhile to check more than one online citator, since they do not necessarily pick up the same cases, and they certainly do not necessarily pick them up at the same time. The online citators do have several immense advantages over the print alternative: they furnish you with the case name of the citing reference and with its initial page as well as the page on which your statute was cited, and they allow you to see all the citing references in one pass, instead of obligating you to look through multiple volumes and supplements (any of which could be off the shelf just at the moment you need it!). However, Shepards in print (in this instance, *Shepard's Federal Statute Citations*) remains the only resource available for the researcher needing to find cases construing an uncodified session law. Also, for those who like to get a sense of what sort of context you are dealing with, it can be easier to pick up on the magnitude of judicial commentary on a particular statute by taking note of how many pages of citations there are to it as opposed to scrolling through a long, long list of them. After a certain amount of scrolling, all such lists tend to seem equally endless!

2.39   USING FULL–TEXT SEARCHING TO FIND CASES INTERPRETING A STATUTE

The final way to find cases applying a given statute, and by far the most problematic, is to do a full–text search in a case law database. This is something you will definitely need to do at some point, so it is important to consider the challenges it poses. Fully aware of the potential difficulties, you will be better prepared to avoid the pitfalls that lie in wait. The twofold lure of the full-text search consists of the more current database you will be using, and the opportunity to override the possible errors of the editor (or the algorithm) that prepared the annotations or the citator. On the first count, the case law databases of Westlaw and Lexis are updated in something much closer to real time than are their code or even their public law databases, so you have additional, fresh material to look at. On the second count, since you get to choose how to look for the statutory references in the cases, you may think of some way to do so that catches something that others missed.

But herein lies the problem: the authors of decisions, the *Bluebook* notwithstanding, refer to statutes in many, many different ways, and you must cover them all to be successful in a full–text search. You can, of course, reasonably expect that every case dealing with your statute will cite to it in some manner. If you search for the code section number in some reasonably close proximity to the title number, you should get most of the relevant cases. But be assured that you will probably not get all of them, since you will miss the ones where for some reason only the underlying session law was cited, or where some fanciful version of the citing information is used, or where the statutory authority cited was a much broader grouping of code sections than you anticipated. Moreover, you may also retrieve many false drops, documents that also include those two numbers in the requested degree of proximity to each other but which do not concern your statute. You need to acknowledge to yourself that whenever you get a lot of false drops, your potential disposition to err shoots up, since the parade of irrelevant material up your screen can make your head swim just long enough to miss the one relevant item that is caught up in that crowd.

One way to try to achieve greater precision in a full-text search for cases construing a statute is to base the search on the precise statutory language that is of interest, rather than on the statute's citation, or to combine both these elements into a single search or series of searches. The downside of this is that here too you will probably miss some relevant cases, since the court cannot be assumed in every case to have actually quoted the statute. You have to be creative in doing this kind of full–text searching, and you also have to reconcile yourself to the idea that you cannot rely on this kind of searching alone. Once you have run whatever course of research you have set for yourself along these lines (e.g., annotations plus citator plus full-text search), one final step remains to check that your work is complete: you can do case law research on the subject matter of the statute, without mentioning the particular statute. Full advice on this kind of case law research is included in Chapter Five, below.

2.40 SPECIAL ISSUES IN STATE STATUTORY RESEARCH

Throughout this chapter on statutes we have raised points pertaining to state statutory research when they have varied from the federal model, or to confirm their similarity. Now we will address the single biggest issue in working with state statutes: the difficulty of comparative research. The legal researcher has many different reasons to want to do comparative state statutory research. She may wish to locate the ideal jurisdiction for a certain kind of activity, or a certain kind of lawsuit. She may wish to draw upon the statutes of different states as part of the work of drafting a new statute. She may wish to explain why the statutes of some states result in the different case law jurisprudence of those jurisdictions.

Doing this kind of research—locating the statutes from different jurisdictions that address the same legal issue though possibly couched in different terms (e.g., "criminal" rather than "penal")—is more difficult than case law comparative research for a number of reasons. First, there is no national index to statutes that assigns subjects to them as do the case indexing systems. Second, language is used differently in statutes than it is in cases: the statutory language of a jurisdiction is liable to be more standardized than the judicial language within that jurisdiction; as a result, the full-text researcher is less likely to get a hit based on the smaller universe of possible terms that will be used with respect to a given topic. The reasons we gravitate away from full-text searching in the U.S. Code databases as a whole are still in play here, but the need to cover a lot of ground at once pretty much compels you to do full-text searches in entire state statutory databases at once. Thirdly, the variations of language amongst jurisdictions are more likely to remain hermetically sealed off from each other. Whereas judges in one jurisdiction may cite (and quote from) cases from elsewhere as persuasive authority, it is far rarer for a judge to even mention a statute from another jurisdiction.

How, then, to accomplish this difficult legal research task? The first step, as ever, is to ascertain whether someone else has already done it for you. Comparative state statutes on a particular topic are a relatively common subject of law review articles (see Chapter Four, below). Many of these comparative analyses of state statutes are indexed in a series of bibliographies entitled *Subject Compilations of State Laws* (see **Table 2.F**). These bibliographies also index other sources of comparisons of state laws on particular topics, including charts and tables in subject treatises. Another good source is the websites of interest groups with a brief on that particular topic. Groups of legislators, such as the National Conference of State Legislatures, are another source of information on comparative state statutes.

Table 2.F: Some Sources of Comparative State Statutes

1.   Cheryl Rae Nyberg, *Subject Compilations of State Laws, 2003–2004*. Twin Falls, Idaho: Carol Boast and Cheryl Rae Nyberg, 2005

This is the latest in a series of annotated bibliographies of different sorts of subject compilations of statutes that cover multiple states. Compilations indexed include law review articles, appendices to treatises, and websites. There is some cross-referencing and some cumulation of the indexing within the set.

2.   *National Survey of State Laws*. 5th ed. Richard A. Leiter, editor. Farmington Hills, Michigan: Thomson/Gale, 2005

Citations and summaries of state laws arranged in tables for 45 subjects.

3.   Inter-state political, advocacy, and governmental organizations are often useful sources of information on recent and proposed legislation on a particular subject. One particularly useful site is that of the National Conference of State Legislatures:

http://www.ncsl.org/

4.   Westlaw:
All Databases > U.S. State Materials > Statutes > 50 State Surveys

Database = **SURVEYS**

Includes surveys on selected topics of state law drawn from a variety of sources including the Leiter book, above. Also reachable via Statutes Plus cross-reference from the statutes included in a survey.

5.   Lexis:
Legal > States Legal–U.S. > Combined States > Statutes & Legislative Materials

Library; File = **STATES;NCSLBR**

Publications of the National Conference of State Legislatures, including a backfile of their LegisBriefs from 1993–2003.

Chapter 3

LEGISLATIVE HISTORY

3.1 LEGISLATIVE HISTORY: WHEN AND WHY?

Legislative history takes a back seat to case law as an interpretive tool for statutes. Unless there is arguably an ambiguity on the face of the statute, the first place to look beyond the statute's own text for legal authority is to judicial interpretation, not legislative history. That said, in the proper circumstances an argument from legislative history can be decisive. The idea behind it is that the judiciary must give effect to the will of the sovereign legislature and so must ascertain that will correctly, even if it involves looking beyond the language of the statute for the legislature's intent.

This idea has had far longer play in the United States than in closely related jurisprudential systems such as the United Kingdom. Up until the 1993 turning point of the English House of Lords case Pepper v. Hart [1993] 1 All E.R. 42 (H.L.), the use of legislative history as an aid to statutory interpretation was traditionally viewed as barred from English courts. See, e.g., Michael P. Healy, *Legislative Intent and Statutory Interpretation in England and the United States: An Assessment of the Impact of Pepper v. Hart*, 35 Stan. J. Int'l L. 231 (1999).

Even here in the United States, there has long been lively debate about the proper role of legislative history in statutory interpretation. But the demand by researchers, both legal and historical, for the stuff of legislative history has been strong enough over a long period of time to support the creation of a robust and thorough publication system for this type of material, at least in the context of the U.S. government. The situation in the states, we shall see, is rather different.

3.2 COMPILED LEGISLATIVE HISTORIES

Before discussing how to conduct legislative history research yourself, we urge you to by all means ascertain whether someone has already done this work for you. Many important federal statutes have been subjected to this kind of research, and this research has often found its way into print. Compiled legislative histories may consist of reprints of documents, or simply of a list of citations to the documents identified. Both kinds of legislative history are indexed in specialized subject bibliographies, and in general bibliographies of federal legislative histories **(see Table 3.A)**. In the latter category, the standard sources are Nancy P. Johnson's looseleaf *Sources of Compiled Legislative Histories* and Bernard D. Reams Jr.'s *Federal Legislative Histories* (1994). Since the citation types of legislative history are often published in law reviews, you can check law review indexes for works not yet listed in the legislative history indexes (see Chapter Four on law reviews, below); book-length compilations that have not yet been included in indexes can be sought in library and publisher catalogs.

The next step, if you are not fortunate enough to find that someone else has already done all your work for you, is to see if the general lists of legislative documents will suit your purposes. From the *CIS Index* to lists included in certain years of the *Statutes at Large* and *U.S.C.C.A.N.*, a variety of lists of documents associated with particular enacted statutes are readily available. Some of these lists describe the content of the documents in considerable detail, others essentially just put you on notice as to the documents' existence. We mentioned in section 2.25 above the problems posed by researching the sources of text for omnibus statutes, and alluded to the even greater difficulties created by such statutes for legislative historians. If we take as an example the Omnibus Appropriations Act of 1997 (P.L. 104–208, 110 Stat. 3009) we can see how differently the various legislative history document lists would handle such an unwieldy task. The list in the *CIS Index*, for instance, includes 33 committee reports from the 104th Congress alone; the list in *U.S.C.C.A.N.*, by contrast, lists three. Your choice of which to work with will depend on the depth of your need and the sources you conveniently have at hand. In any event, working with these lists will require you to know the relative value of different sorts of legislative history documents.

3.3   TYPES OF LEGISLATIVE HISTORY DOCUMENTS

The underlying quest of the legal researcher is for material that indicates what the legislature had in its collective mind when it voted to enact a certain statute. Of course, the cold hard truth is that different legislators may well have had different things in mind. The exploration of that type of political reality, however, is really more the province of the legislative historian, who will concern herself more with the machinations of individual legislators and of the large supporting cast of figures peripheral to the legislative process.

Table 3.A: Selected Sources of Compiled
Federal Legislative Histories

1. Nancy P. Johnson, *Sources of Compiled Legislative Histo-ries*. Buffalo, New York: William S. Hein.

    This looseleaf publication, sponsored by the American Asso-ciation of Law Libraries, lists in Public Law number order the legislative histories included in government documents, law review articles, books, and microfiche sets. For each compiled legislative history listed, the nature of its contents is noted: i.e., whether it contains cites or full texts, and of which legislative history components. Also available in the subscription web database HeinOnline, in the Legislative History Library.

2. Bernard D. Reams, Jr., *Federal Legislative Histories*. West-port, Connecticut: Greenwood Press, 1994.

    This bibliography covers narrower ground, since it only includes legislative histories published by the government, but it includes much more descriptive detail about each one.

3. Congressional Information Service, *CIS Index*. Bethesda, Maryland: LexisNexis.

    Since its beginning in 1970, this annual publication has pulled together the components of a basic legislative history for each Public Law enacted; since 1984, the annual Legis-lative Histories volumes have compiled comprehensive lists of legislative history components, including background his-tory from earlier Congresses. This material is also available in LexisNexis Congressional, a subscription database on the web.

4. Lexis: Legal > Legislation and Politics—U.S. & U.K. > U.S. Congress > Legislative Histories

    Includes CIS Index material (Library and File = **GEN-FED;CISLH**).

5. *United States Code Congressional and Administrative News*. St. Paul, Minnesota: Thomson/West.

    This annual contains not only a list of the basic legislative history for each Public Law enacted, but also excerpts from what the editors deem to be the most significant committee report.

6. Westlaw: All Databases > U.S. Federal Materials > Legisla-tive History

7. HeinOnline: U.S. Federal Legislative History Library

    In addition to the Johnson bibliography described in number 1, above, this subscription database includes the U.S. Federal Legislative History Title Collection, a selection of compiled full-text legislative histories.

In the strictly legal researcher's pursuit of the theoretical contents of the fictitious collective legislative mind, the evidence that legislative history offers is that of the material that was available to the legislators generally when they were casting their votes. The U.S. Congress can generate a lot of documentation in the course of its work. The legal researcher must be able to identify which kinds of documentation may arguably be probative of legislative intent, and it is under this lens that evaluation of the relative value of the different kinds of documentation can be made.

The principal kinds of legislative history documents for the U.S. Congress are (in rough order by their order of production)

— (Investigative Hearings)

— Bills

— Committee hearings

— Committee prints

— House or Senate Documents

— Committee reports

— Floor debate

3.4   COMMITTEE REPORTS

Of these, the Committee Reports are universally regarded as by far the most important: this is what the legislators were aware of as they decided how to vote on a bill, and it therefore furnishes evidence of their intent. So significant are the committee reports that the text of the reports or of excerpts from them are made widely available in conjunction with the statutes in whose construction they aid (**see Table 3.B**, below). Note that although Committee Reports are widely cited in court decisions these Reports cannot be systematically traced through to the body of case law to see how the courts have made use of them.

No citator, in other words, undertakes to provide citing references for Committee Reports. Finding court citations to these reports will require full–text searching. There are myriad ways you could approach such a full-text search. You could run the statute through the citator of your choice, and then limit the results to those cases that include the word "Report" (or its various abbreviations, such as Rept. or Rep.) and other key words (or numbers) from the report citation. You could also do a full–text search in the appropriate case law database looking for cases that use the word report (or its abbreviations) in proximity to the report number.

It may seem odd to you that we are basically starting off this section about legislative history by talking about how to work around the lack of a citator for Committee Reports, even before, for example, having said anything about how to find the text of such Reports. This matter of finding case law is so important that we are putting it up front because of another doctrine of legislative history: once a court has judicially weighed in on how the legislative history demonstrates legislative intent, it is relatively rare for a subsequent court to reconsider the issue of intent *de novo*. Rather, subsequent courts often cite the earlier court's inquiry into the historical evidence of legislative intent as dispositive of the issue. Consequently, finding what earlier courts have said about the legislative history of your statute is a task you will want to prioritize.

Doing the searches described above can be done without reference to a report number, because the citing court will of necessity also cite the underlying statute. But a report number will make the search easier by enabling you to use the close proximity between the word "report" and the report number to minimize false drops. And of course you will need the report number if you are going to seek out the text of the report first yourself, if, for example, it transpires that no court has ever cited any committee report on your statute. Happily, there are a number of excellently organized resources that will enable you to find Congressional Committee Reports on any federal statute for which they were produced.

3.5 IDENTIFYING COMMITTEE REPORTS ABOUT A KNOWN STATUTE OR BILL

For those researchers starting off with a code section, there may be information available to you without even switching files or turning a page. The *U.S.C.A.* includes annotations pointing you to selected legislative history relevant to the code section whose text has just been laid out. These annotations lead you to excerpts of reports printed in *U.S.C.C.A.N.*; their great convenience is that they do not require you to pin down by yourself the particular source for the code section, in terms of public law number or bill number, prior to starting your legislative history research.

Table 3.B: Sources for Committee Reports

1. *United States Code Congressional and Administrative News.* St. Paul, Minnesota: Thomson/West

   Often, this is all you will need. Reprints the highlights of the principal committee report where the editors deem it potentially significant for the discernment of legislative intent. 1948–Present. Updated with monthly softcover supplements.

2. Library of Congress, Thomas: Legislative Information on the Internet.

   http://thomas.loc.gov/

   Coverage begins in 1995.

3. United States, GPOAccess, Congressional Reports

   http://www.gpoaccess.gov/serialset/creports/index.html

   Coverage begins in 1995.

4. Westlaw: All Databases > U.S. Federal Materials > Legislative History > Legislative History—U.S. Code (Database = **LH**)

   Reports from 1948 to 1989 are from USCCAN; thereafter from the GPO.

5. Lexis: Legal > Legislation and Politics—U.S. & U.K. > U.S. Congress > Committee Reports (Library and File = **GEN-FED;CMTRPT**)

   Coverage begins in 1990.

   The same data is available in the subscription database LexisNexis Congressional.

6. United States, *United States Congressional Serial Set.* Washington: U.S. G.P.O., 1817–

   The Committee Reports and Congressional Documents bound in permanent volumes. Note that there is no indexing, and no through pagination in this set.

   Subsets of this series are being republished in two privately-produced text and image databases. The U.S. Congressional Serial Set, 1817–1980, distributed by Readex as part of their "Archive of Americana," currently covers 1817–1883. The U.S. Serial Set Digital Collection, distributed by LexisNexis Congressional, contains documents produced between 1817 and 1969 (the 15th through 91st Congresses). Finally, the Library of Congress has also put selected reports from the period 1855–1917 on the web in image files as part of its American Memory project at

   http://memory.loc.gov/ammem/amlaw/lwss.html.

By contrast, in all original legislative history research, the crucial piece of information that you will need in order to use any of the finding tools is the bill number. For legislative history of those bills that did eventually succeed in becoming law, the other crucial piece of information will be the Public Law number. How you get these numbers most efficiently will vary with your circumstances. If you are starting off with a code citation (and the legislative history annotations in the code do not suffice for your purposes), all you may need to do to get the public law number is to look in the parenthetical source information after the code section. If there is more than one session law source listed there, you should be able to establish which one (or ones) you are interested in by referring to the historical notes described above in section 2.24. To get the bill number of a public law, find the text of the law itself **(see sources in Table 2.B, above)**. The bill number will be prominently displayed near the beginning of the statute. Alternatively, for the period covered by the Thomas database, the List of Public Laws there gives the bill number for each session law enacted.

When looking for reports pertaining to a particular statute, the easiest tools to use are those which combine the finding mechanism with text from the reports themselves. The Library of Congress's Thomas website is hard to beat, if your statute falls within its very limited coverage dates. Having obtained the bill number (as described in the previous paragraph), you can either simply click on that bill number in the List of Public Laws, or enter it in the search forms on the Bill Summaries and Status part of the website. From the menu that results, you can select the choice indicated for committee reports. You can also go directly to the menu for Committee Reports and plug in a bill number. Note that Thomas offers the complete text of reports, and that it offers them for all bills, not only those bills that actually do become law.

Another source which offers both a finding tool and some text of reports in one fell swoop is the *United States Code Congressional and Administrative News (U.S.C.C.A.N.)*. We already saw that the USCA, both on Westlaw and in print, offers references within the individual code section annotations to reports reprinted in *U.S.C.C.A.N.*. You can also find these reports directly in *U.S.C.C.A.N.*. On Westlaw (database = **USCCAN–REP)** complete committee report coverage (i.e., full text, and coverage for both enacted and unenacted bills) goes back to 1990; for the period 1948–1990, reports are presented for enacted laws only, and as they appeared in the print *U.S.C.C.A.N.*. There are also reports going back to 1933 for statutes bearing on securities.

In the print *U.S.C.C.A.N.*, which (with its predecessor publication, *United States Code Congressional Service*) goes back to 1941, the committee reports are arranged in public law number order and appear in Part II of each session and in the paperback advance supplements. The editors of *U.S.C.C.A.N.* reprint, for each bill that became a public law, those portions of the relevant committee reports that (in their own words) they deem "necessary to the interpretation of the laws". In practice this means that most frequently only one report is reprinted (although all will be cited), and that the one is frequently reprinted only in excerpts.

Note that even though reports on Westlaw since 1990 include a cite to USCCAN, the text differs between the online and print versions, since the print *U.S.C.C.A.N.* continues to offer an edited text. You will find that the edited text is sometimes all you need and therefore can be a big timesaver if you are actually reading through the text, rather than searching for a particular term therein. This divergence of the print and online versions of USCCAN is promising, in one sense, since it demonstrates how the strengths of different presentational formats can be maximized by tailoring the underlying content differently for each. Yet it is ominous, in another sense, because of the possibility for confusion over two different versions being labelled with the same name (or citation).

The researcher using the traditional version of U.S.C.C.A.N., either online (prior to 1990) or in print (1944–present) will be using an edited version of a single committee report. While in many instances this will prove sufficient, the researcher needs to bear several questions in mind about the edited version of the report excerpts. How are the reports selected? Are important ones ever omitted? How are they excerpted? What is cut out? Is the excerpt always a good indicator of what else there might be in the full report?

It may well happen that you wish to read the portions of a committee report that were omitted from *U.S.C.C.A.N.*, or a report that was omitted in its entirety. You will then need to refer (prior to the 1990 start date for G.P.O. electronic coverage) to the print version officially published by the Government Printing Office. Unlike the sources we have discussed so far, the official committee reports have no finding mechanism internal to their structure. Rather, you will need to use an extrinsic finding aid to locate your committee report within the official set. The best such finding aid is the *CIS Index*, the gold standard for legislative history research since 1970 **(see Table 3.A)**. The information in the *CIS Index* is also contained in the subscription web database LexisNexis Congressional ("LNC"). While the *CIS Index* excels particularly as a subject index, it also facilitates considerably finding reports associated with a particular Public Law or bill. In print, the organizational structure of the presentation can be very helpful to the researcher, but, on the other hand, the electronic presentation of the data (available on Lexis and LNC) eliminates the need to look through multiple volumes to reach the desired material.

The *CIS Index* is currently published in print in four parts. The primary part to consult if you are looking for reports pertaining to a particular public law is the part called "Legislative History." Up until 1984 this part was included in the Abstracts volumes. Since 1984, however, Legislative History gets an annual volume of its own, and quite a feast it provides. Under each of that year's Public Laws (arranged sequentially) CIS lists citations and summaries for all the legislative history documents relevant to that law, including reports. Since the expansion of the section in 1984, citations are provided not only for those documents within the current Congress that bear directly on the bill or bills that were eventually passed into this law, but also to material from earlier Congresses, pertaining to related bills that didn't make it.

Another part of the *CIS Index*, called the Subject Index (or simply, in the annual volume, the Index), contains in addition to the subject listings a host of other invaluable finding aids. These include an index that takes you from bill number to CIS accession numbers for reports and other legislative history documents pertaining to that bill. CIS accession numbers are in three parts: typically they start with "H" or "S" for House or Senate. Within the House and Senate sections of the Abstracts, the documents are categorized according to the Congressional committee (arranged in alphabetical order) that produced them. The Committee involved and also the type of material are indicated by the number immediately following the "H" or "S". Thus, the House Judiciary Committee includes numbers H520 through H523. House Judiciary Committee materials are further categorized into type: H520 being Documents, H521 being Hearings, H522 being Prints, and H523 being Reports. Finally, the third component of the accession number is the sequential number assigned to each individual document within its category, the first House Judiciary Report (by date) within the period covered being number–1, the second being number–2, and so forth.

When these components are all combined, they give a unique identifying number to each document within that year's *CIS Index*. For example, the report by the House Judiciary Committee dated October 15, 2002 which recommends passage of the Border Commuter Student Act of 2002 is given the number H523–54 within the 2002 volumes of the CIS

Index. In cumulative subject indexes that cover more than one year of *CIS Index*, this number will get an additional prefix: it will become **02** H523–54. The **02** refers not to the year of the report's publication, nor to the title of the proposed legislation, but to the volume of the *CIS Index* in which the document is described. Once you have a CIS accession number, you can go to the part of the set called Abstracts and look up a brief summary of the contents of the report (or other document) and see if it warrants further pursuit.

For locating a pre–1970 committee report that discusses a particular statute, or an unenacted bill, you will have to take the more roundabout route of either doing a subject search that would encompass the subject matter of the statute or bill (discussed further below), or you would need to consult one of the several tables or indexes that go back further than the CIS, but are not endowed with summaries as is the latter. *U.S.C.C.A.N.* contains tables of Legislative History (printed in the last volume for the session (1964–present), also available as an image file on Westlaw **(database = USCCAN–TABLE)** (2000–present)) which take you from Public Law numbers within that session to report numbers; the same information is in two other places in the same set: in small print at the end of each Public Law in Part I (print only, 1975–present), and at the head of the coverage for each Public Law in the Legislative History section, Part II (also in Westlaw, **database = USCCAN–REP)** (1948–present). The same information appears either in tables or at the end of each public law in the official *Statutes at Large* volumes (1963–present).

For bills prior to 1970 that were not enacted into law, you can get citations to pertinent reports by referring to the Status of Bills sections in the *CCH Congressional Index*. These listings enumerate in chronological order all actions taken on each bill in the House and Senate, and when that action is the filing of a committee report, the listing gives the report number.

3.6 ACCESSING CONGRESSIONAL COMMITTEE REPORTS

If you like what you see in CIS, you can obtain the full text of the official report in a number of sources **(see Table 3.B)**. Since we already saw that Westlaw only has the full text of the full range of committee reports going back to 1990, and both Thomas and GPO Access back to 1995, it should not be much of a surprise to learn that Lexis also has them back only to 1990. The text for all of these electronic versions is provided by the U.S. Government Printing Office.

There are many reports, therefore, prior to 1990 that can only be read *in toto* in the officially printed version from the GPO, or from a database or microfiche set made from that version. The reports were printed originally by the GPO in slip form, and then collected into the *United States Congressional Serial Set*, a set of bound volumes which contains not only House and Senate Committee Reports, but also House and Senate Documents. Materials from the first fifteen Congresses, i.e., prior to the Serial Set, were collected by subject into a series called American State Papers.

Some libraries, over the years, have bound their slip reports into permanent bound volumes rather than obtain the *United States Congressional Serial Set* itself. This has given rise to a variety of different volume numbering schemes in different collections. Some libraries have simply bound the reports in numerical order, and indicated which reports are in which volume by listing them on the spine. It's not, however, always so simple. In order to tell in which volume of the officially bound Serial Set your report appears, you can check it by looking in the Numerical List at the front of a GPO publication called *United States Congressional Serial Set Catalog*. Prior to the 97th Congress, this list appeared in an earlier GPO publication called *Numerical List and Schedule of Volumes*; in the 97th Congress an experiment was undertaken of dropping this publication in favor of the *Monthly Catalog*, and the following year the current arrangement began. The same information is available commercially in the Finding Lists volumes of the *CIS US Serial Set Index*, with coverage through the 91st Congress, 1st Session (1969). The Schedule of Volumes is a list of the report and document numbers for the contents of each officially bound volume of the serial set. This is available online for Congresses since the 91st (1970) at a web page created by the Law Librarians' Society of Washington, D.C., available at http://www.llsdc.org/sourcebook/sch-v.htm.

3.7 FINDING COMMITTEE REPORTS BY SUBJECT

Some (but not all) of the print sources used in locating reports by bill number or statute number can also be used for subject searching. As you will see, there are many different ways to access the same information on federal legislative history. The tools available to you under different circumstances will vary, and people can devise very ingenious ways to get by with whatever they have on hand. That said, if all possible tools are in fact at your disposal, you would be wrong to use a shoe rather than a hammer to drive in a nail. It's not good for the shoe, the nail, or the wall, and you waste a lot of time. It's true that you can use the subject index to bills that is in the *CCH Congressional Index* or the subject indexes to session laws that are in the *Statutes at Large* or *U.S.C.C.A.N.* to wend your way around to finding committee reports on a given subject. However, that would be wrong: you should, instead, use the tool that is made for the very purpose of looking up committee reports by subject. The *CIS Index* is primarily a very detailed subject index to, among other materials, committee reports. When searching for reports on a given subject after 1969, the *CIS Index*, or its online spinoff, LexisNexis Congressional, should definitely be your first stop. When searching for a report by subject, think not only of what type of action is being legislated about, but also of geographical locations, and of people associated with the legislation or the report you expect to find.

For identifying reports on a subject before the *CIS Index* start date of 1970, you should use the *CIS Serial Set Index*, a source that offers subject searching and searching by bill number. The *CIS Serial Set Index* goes back to the earliest committee reports in 1817 (and further back still to *American State Papers* dating back as far as 1789). However, the *CIS Serial Set Index*, unlike the later *CIS Index*, does not provide any summary of the contents of these items beyond what you can glean from their titles.

Another source of both early committee reports and a means of identifying them is provided by historical Serial Set databases from two different publishers. Both Readex and Lexis have prepared massive databases which they distribute to subscribers over the web. Here, too, you can search by title, but also by full text. The databases offer both searchable text files and linked image files that reproduce individual pages of the Serial Set.

Remember that the full text coverage of committee reports via Westlaw, Lexis, and the U.S. Government is shallow, going back only to 1990 at the earliest. However, Lexis has *CIS Index*-type locating information (but not summaries of content) going back to the earliest Congressional materials in its CIS/Historical Index database (Library;File = **Legislation;CISHST**). And for the recent reports that are available online, full text searching takes the place of subject indexing.

At the other end of the temporal spectrum from the old reports that furnish the *raison d'etre* of these historical databases, you may have occasion to try to find a very recently filed committee report that has not yet been published and distributed to the public. This is less of a problem today than it used to be, since reports are now published online soon after they are filed. However, the tools developed for handling this situation in days of yore still exist, and can come in handy on occasion. The aforementioned *CCH Congressional Index*, in its aforementioned Bill Status sections, will list the filing of a report, with its report number, within a week of that event. Similar notifications appear on Lexis, Westlaw, and Thomas. An earlier event in the history of a report, i.e., the referral of a bill to committee for consideration, will also be duly noted in all these lists. Since the report may be ready for filing, or even filed already, before notice of that fact appears, you can use your knowledge of which committee received the bill to try and track down the report at its source. All of the committees are set up to handle public inquiries, and the appropriate contacts for this are listed in the various Congressional directories **(see Table 14.A, below)**. The Committees themselves have websites where this same information may be available, and these can all be accessed through Thomas.

3.8   IDENTIFYING CONGRESSIONAL COMMITTEE HEARINGS

After committee reports, the type of legislative history material that is logically the next most likely to furnish evidence of legislative intent is the committee hearing. Some sorts of hearings are more likely to be important than others. Congress holds periodic supervisory hearings that are mandated by law, and it holds hearings in contemplation of confirming executive appointments of officials. Neither of these would be useful for establishing legislative intent. The kind of hearings you are looking for are the hearings on proposed bills and investigative hearings held in contemplation of the drafting of bills, whether those bills become law or not.

Again, the name to remember here is the *CIS Index* (or the online LexisNexis Congressional). The finding lists mentioned above in section 3.5 will take you from bill number or Public Law number to hearings, as well as to reports. The subject index discussed above in section 3.7 is, if anything, even more useful for identifying hearings than it is for reports. The subject index includes not only the subjects covered at the hearing, but also indexes each and every person who testified, either in person or in writing. The summaries of the hearings give the name and position of each witness, and brief accounts of the testimony which was given; these summaries are often substantial enough to give a clear indication about whether it is worth tracking down that hearing or not.

Other tools which can be used to identify hearings include the charts of legislative history which appear in *U.S.C.C.A.N.* and the *Statutes at Large* (and the small print information after the text of the public law in *U.S.C.C.A.N.*). Since these only indicate the date and committee, they are inferior to the information in *CIS Index* for the period covered by the latter. Indeed, the only other direct subject access to hearings in print is through the cumbersome *Monthly Catalog of Government Publications*, now online (with coverage from 1994 through April 2005) at GPO Access. The Senate's own website notes, however, that "it is often difficult to locate [hearings]in GPO's Catalog ..."

Since there is such a multiplicity of ways to find hearings by subject, it is instructive to compare the different kinds of subject access. For example, the Senate Special Committee on Aging held a hearing on March 21, 1995. This hearing was published as "Gaming the Health Care System: Trends in Health Care Fraud." As so often with bipartite titles, the first part of the title may be catchy, but the real gist of the content is conveyed by the second part. In the *Monthly Catalog* print issue for December 1995, accordingly, the subject headings assigned to this item for library cataloging of the same include "Medicare fraud" and "Insurance crimes". In the subject index, you can find this hearing by looking under "Health care reform—United States". However, there are no subject entries for either "fraud" or "insurance crime". The *Monthly Catalog* print edition also includes a separate title keyword index, and in that index you can find the hearing under "gaming", but not under "fraud".

In the print *CIS Index*, by contrast, you can find the hearing under any of the following headings in the subject index: "Fraud—health care fraud and abuse problems and control initiatives", "Insurance—health care fraud and abuse problems and control initiatives", "Health Facilities and Services—health care fraud and abuse problems and control initiatives", and "Health Insurance—health care fraud and abuse problems and control initiatives". You can also find it under "Health Insurance Association [the president of which was a witness]—health care fraud and abuse problems and control initiatives", and "Medicare—health care fraud and abuse problems and control initiatives". Unlike the GPO index, however, you cannot find the hearing by searching under the word "Gaming". One lesson reinforced here is that by using multiple indexes you can pick up additional entries, since the subject headings used will be different.

If we go on to compare the same indexes in their online versions, another lesson emerges. GPO Access, the GPO website, offers searchable hearings back only to 1997. Prior to that you can search the entries in the online Catalog of U. S. Government Publications (CGP), the data in which goes back to 1994. All of the data is combined; there is no need to search through multiple sources as you had to search through multiple books with the paper *Monthly Catalog*. The CGP retrieves the citation for the hearing when searched for Health AND Fraud (showing that unlike the print title keyword index ALL the title words are indexed online) and also when searched for "health care reform" (a subject heading assigned to the item). Had the hearing been from 1997 or later, you would have been able to click through to its full text, if it had been selected by its originating committee for distribution via GPO Access.

On Lexis, the content of the CIS Index is contained in the file called US–CIS Legislative Histories (abbreviated CISLH), and again, you can search the whole record at once (both the summary content and the subject headings) and all the available years of data (back to 1970) at once. Given the greater convenience of both these online indexes, why would one want to schlep out all the necessary volumes of the print format if the same data is available so much more handily online?

The answer to this conundrum is one that comes up again and again in legal research: serendipity. The convenience of the one-shot search is achieved at a cost: no longer do you have the opportunity to let your gaze wander above and below your target on the index page, taking in the fact that the indexer created many other subject headings closely related to the one you selected, and that the items under those other subject headings look pretty good as well, maybe even better than what you chose to look for the first time through. The second lesson reiterated here, then, is that you may want to supplement your online search with use of the print materials, and vice versa. In this particular instance, you can in some ways attain the best of both worlds by using the subscription web database LexisNexis Congressional, which allows not only targeted searching but also browsing of a list of index terms à la the *CIS Index*—in fact, it is the CIS Index!

3.9   ACCESSING CONGRESSIONAL COMMITTEE HEARINGS

Finding the text of a hearing can be more tricky than was getting your hands on the text of the committee reports. **(See Table 3.C)** Online availability is even more limited than was that for reports: as mentioned above, GPO Access offers the full text of hearings back only to 1997 (1995 for the House). Moreover, it only contains those hearings that the committees have given it to distribute. However, the GPO site is especially valuable because it makes the hearings available not only as text but as image files. The image format allows for more reliable citation to the archived original, while the text file allows for full text searching. Lexis and Westlaw, for once, have even less available in the way of hearings. Lexis and Westlaw both have some hearing transcripts back to 1993 (text only), but these are not the officially published hearings. The committee's own websites also provide piecemeal access to some recent hearings, but frequently only to the testimony that was submitted to them electronically by witnesses, not to the colloquy that took place with Senators on the day of the hearing, so these, too, are not official. As with reports, you may wish to try contacting staff at the committee to see if they can provide you with a hearing that is not available any other way.

Hearings are published officially by the Government Printing Office. The print editions of the hearings are distributed individually, not as part of a compilation like the Serial Set. This means that the titles of the hearings are important tools in locating them, since they are frequently cataloged separately, like books, in library collections. There is a CIS microfiche collection of hearings which reproduces over 31,000 published hearings found in the U.S. Senate Library or in other libraries. If you want to find an individual hearing in print, you can try to locate it by searching merged library holdings databases like RLIN (or Eureka) or OCLC (WorldCat) for the hearing's title. Materials from the 1970's and earlier, that may not have been included in some libraries' electronic catalog records, might be found in old printed union lists of library holdings, again by title. You can also search in all of these holdings catalogs by the hearing's author: United States. Congress. House of Representatives. (or Senate.) Committee on Blah. Sub-committee on Blip. Then you would look through the entries for the title that looks good. This is much easier to do in print than online, because the length of the author line usually means that it gets truncated way before it gets specific enough to be of any use. There is no point even waiting for all the publications authored by "United States. Congress. House of Representatives. Committee on … [involuntarily truncate here]" to load, much less to look through them for good titles, or a specific title. If the catalog offers keyword in author, however, you may be able to cobble together a useable search.

Another way that hearings may be arranged in collections is by the numbering scheme used by the GPO for all its documents (the SuDoc number). The SuDoc number is the number you will see in bibliographic records for hearings and other government documents that is a long combination of letters and numbers with slashes and colons. Those documents emanating from Congress get a SuDoc number that starts with "Y". The SuDoc number for the hearing we used as an example above, for instance, is Y 4.AG 4:S.HRG.104–110. The SuDoc number can be helpful in the course of your research, but it is not part of the *Bluebook* citation and is not used in legal literature.

3.10　UNPUBLISHED HEARINGS

All the hearings discussed above were open hearings, published by the committees through the Government Printing Office. But the committees of Congress also often conduct closed hearings, usually involving material sensitive because of concerns over national security or personal privacy, or during the working markup sessions in the final stages of legislative drafting. You may have been alerted to the existence of a closed hearing on your topic by the work schedules in the Congressional Record or on the committees' websites. The records of this kind of hearing, captured and maintained with varying degrees of attention over the years, have generally been treated by the committee involved as internal documents for the committee's use only, and retained only as archival records of the committee's operations. Many of them (with a time lag dictated by the nature of the material) have been obtained by CIS, and published in microfiche with a print index. The indexing of these documents is also included in LexisNexis Congressional.

Table 3.C: Sources of Committee Hearings

1. United States, GPOAccess, Congressional Hearings

   http://www.gpoaccess.gov/chearings/index.html

   Coverage begins in 1997 (1995 for the House).

2. Congressional Information Service, *CIS US Congressional Committee Hearings on Microfiche.* Bethesda, Maryland: CIS

   Covers 1833 through 1969.

3. Individual libraries' holdings of individual hearings as published by the G.P.O.

4. Congressional Information Service, *CIS Unpublished US Senate Committee Hearings on Microfiche.* Bethesda, Maryland: CIS

   Covers 1823 through 1980.

5. Congressional Information Service, *CIS Unpublished US House of Representatives Committee Hearings on Microfiche.* Bethesda, Maryland: CIS

   Covers 1833 through 1972.

How useful are these unpublished hearings? We can logically compare them to other sorts of legal research materials. While the publication of statutes is not specifically mandated by our Constitution, a statute intended to be unpublished is completely antithetical to our system of government. Statutes are the state speaking in a normative vein to those subject to its authority, and publication of those statutes is the broadcast that allows the distant public to hear the promulgating speech. While the statute may exist, in some sense, even without publication, its effect would be curtailed by (among other things) the Due Process Clause of the Fifth Amendment. For a historical overview of the needfulness of publication of statutes, see *U.S. v. Burgess*, 1987 WL 39092, 1987 U.S. Dist. LEXIS 11227, No. 133066 (N.D. Ill., Dec. 1, 1987). For a case to be unpublished, by contrast, is extremely common. Only the tip of the iceberg of judicial opinions gets published as case reports. An unpublished case may or may not be citeable, depending on the jurisdiction. But even if you are not permitted to cite a case, it still retains some importance to the researcher as an indicator of how that judge (or others of similar inclination) is likely to lean in particular circumstances. An unpublished hearing, however, loses almost nothing of its probative value by virtue of being unpublished. Whatever effect the closed hearing had on legislators when they were forming legislative intent is at least as likely to be significant as with open hearings.

3.11 IDENTIFYING AND LOCATING COMMITTEE PRINTS AND HOUSE AND SENATE DOCUMENTS

Next most significant, logically, are other materials relied upon by the committee during its deliberations and in preparing its report. These run the gamut from investigative reports to statistical tables, from draft bills to annual reports of executive agencies submitted to Congress as mandated by law. These sorts of materials may be selected for publication either as committee prints, only some of which are numbered (Senate only), or as House or Senate Documents (especially the communications from the executive branch to Congress), which are deemed to contain information which will be in wider demand. Note that "Documents" here is a term of art, and not a reference to legislative history documents generally. Those materials picked or otherwise designated for publication as Documents are included by the GPO in the physical Serial Set (see section 3.6 above), and thus get wider distribution than the Committee Prints, which are primarily for internal use. Occasionally a Committee Print proves to contain information for which there is wider demand, and it will be reprinted as a House or Senate Document.

House and Senate Documents, as part of the Serial Set, are widely available. Prints, however, are more fugitive, and the efforts of CIS to assemble many of them has been central to providing access for researchers. Both of these types of material are indexed and summarized back to 1970 in the *CIS Index*. The earlier Documents, as part of the

Serial Set, are indexed without summaries in the earlier Serial Set Index; the earlier Committee Prints are indexed and reproduced in a separate *CIS U.S. Congressional Committee Prints Index* and companion microfiche set. Online access to these materials is shallow: GPO Access has Committee Prints beginning with the 105th Congress (1997–1998) in text, with some in .pdf as well, and selected House and Senate Documents beginning with the 104th Congress (1995–1996), in both text and .pdf files. Lexis has select Committee Prints gathered by CIS beginning with the 104th Congress (starting from January 1995) in text only, and the same House and Senate Documents beginning in 1995 that GPO Access provides (but in text only).

3.12 IDENTIFYING AND LOCATING BILLS AS A SOURCE OF LEGISLATIVE HISTORY

All of the legislative history sources explored above contain commentary or background, of one sort or another, about Congressional thinking concerning proposed legislation. Another sort of source to consider is the actual texts of the proposed legislation as it developed into the form that was eventually enacted into law. Many of the techniques used when searching recent bills for relevant pending legislation (see section 2.30 above) can be projected back into the past to find variant bills on a subject, the differences between which can shed light on Congress's intent in making the changes that were eventually made. You may find useful information by comparing different states of the same bill at different stages in its evolution, or by comparing related but unsuccessful bills in earlier Congresses. Particularly useful, of course, would be finding that Congress had specifically rejected a text that supports an interpretation proposed by your opponent.

The best way to start off in this activity, when researching the legislative history of a post–1983 statute, is with the Legislative History volumes of the *CIS Index*. In 1984, the *CIS Index* switched from the undeniably useful but still relatively modest legislative history format that they used from 1970 through 1983 to the all stops out approach they have used since then. Prior to 1984 the CIS Legislative Histories would lead you from the public law enacted that year to the bill that was enacted, along with related bills considered as part of the same process during the same Congress. Since 1984, the Legislative Histories volumes lead you from the public law enacted that year to all related bills from the same Congress and to bills on the same subject from preceding Congresses. For earlier years than 1984, you would have to look for these yourself. Remember (section 2.30 above) that the *CCH Congressional Index* is the only subject index to bills. It first appeared in 1937, and since there is no overarching index to the set, a historical search on a subject would require looking through the indexes of each individual volume during the period of interest. If you do have to do that, remember to be open to alternate terms, as the terminology used for what you now perceive to be the same concept may have changed over time. Since each chamber begins numbering its bills anew in order of introduction at the commencement of each new Congress, there will generally be no correspondence between bill numbers on related topics from Congress to Congress.

Where to go for the bills themselves will depend on their vintage. In electronic full text, the government itself offers the best coverage: GPO Access has all published versions of all bills from the 103rd Congress forward, each Congress in a separate file, in both text and .pdf files. Thomas, the Library of Congress site, has all versions of all bills from the 101st through the current congress, each Congress in a separate file, text only. The American Memory project of the Library of Congress has text, .pdf, and high quality image files for bills from selected sessions of Congress between 1799 and 1873.

The commercial sites have even shallower coverage, but do enjoy some search advantages due to combined files. Westlaw and Lexis both have all versions of all bills (from Thomas) starting with the 104th Congress, with each Congress in a separate file. Lexis, additionally, has full text of bills from the 101st through 103rd Congress (with no source other than Lexis given). Note that each electronic provider of bills in full text has different conventions for indicating changes in the text ("redlining") between versions. Check their user guides for up to date information on this.

Another electronic option for bill research is the databases of bill summaries available on Thomas (back to 1973 with each Congress in a separate file) and on Westlaw (two different single file databases going back to 1990 and 1985).

There are gaps in the above electronic coverage, and especially large gaps if you are looking for official and citeable text. Locating a bill in hard copy will probably mean using a microfiche set, since very few libraries maintain their old collections of the official GPO-published slip bills in paper any more. There are at least two microfiche publishers of sets of the bills, CIS and the GPO. Some bills are also reproduced in the Congressional Record. The most likely location for them is the day on which they were introduced, so the first date to look for is the earliest date on which the bill is mentioned in the index.

3.13   THE CONGRESSIONAL RECORD

Finally, we consider the chronicle of Congressional activity enshrined in the Congressional Record. When the *Congressional Record* commenced in March of 1873, it was the first publication to present the full text of Congressional floor debate and comment. It was preceded by four earlier publications, the *Annals of Congress* (1789–1824), the *Abridgement of the Debates of Congress* (1789–1850), the *Register of the*

Debates in Congress (1824–1837), and the *Congressional Globe* (1833–1873) which were primarily paraphrased reporting of what had transpired on the floor.

Novice legal researchers frequently make the mistake of thinking that what they are going to do when looking for legislative intent is to look in the Congressional Record. They expect to find clarification through floor debate of what was in the legislative mind at the time of passage. But we have saved the Congressional Record for last in this consideration of legislative history sources precisely because it offers a lot of very questionable evidence of legislative intent. The reproduced bill texts, to be sure, offer both high evidentiary value and convenience. Occasionally some last minute colloquy between members of Congress about the intended meaning of some wording in the legislation about to be voted on can indeed provide a solid gold nugget of evidence as to intent. But the bulk of material contained in the Congressional Record can be completely discounted as a source of such evidence, for the simple reason that it only occurred *ex post facto*. Much of the content of the Congressional Record consists of the "extensions of remarks" which Members of Congress are entitled to insert into the Record even though they never delivered the same on the floor of Congress nor, therefore, into the ears of their colleagues as they prepared to vote. Even material not designated as an extension of remarks may not actually have been uttered on the floor, thanks to the extremely liberal editorial license granted the Members of Congress. While their subsequent remarks may be rich fodder indeed for the political historian, their timing makes them pretty slim pickings for the legal researcher. This is not to say that nothing of any value can be gleaned from the extensions of remarks. Since they frequently deal with politically significant aspects of the topic under discussion, even *ex post facto* remarks can act as signposts to important issues that should be researched carefully in the more probative documents such as Committee Reports.

How, then, to find things in the Congressional Record **(see Table 3.D)**? The handiest method by far, in terms of assembling your materials, is searching full text in the Congressional Record databases. In Westlaw, Lexis, and Thomas, fielded searching includes searching by a Congressional Record date, but you yourself have to construct a search that would mention your bill number and a keyword. GPO Access offers coverage back only to 1994, but, as so often, offers both text and .pdf images. Since it offers page images, it also offers a special search method for retrieving known pages. Its explanatory material includes detailed suggestions for how to construct a search that will retrieve entries pertaining to a particular bill. GPO Access also contains a separate resource called History of Bills (text only), which on a biweekly basis provides page numbers in the Congressional Record for actions on bills.

Since the date coverage of the electronic versions of the Record is limited, recourse to other finding methods may well prove necessary.

The legal researcher is likely only to approach the Congressional Record with respect to a particular bill or law, not with merely an interest in a subject generally. Happily, many of the legislative history sources that we have already explored provide helpful pointers from Public Law numbers or bill numbers to relevant entries in the Congressional Record. The *CCH Congressional Index*, which commenced in 1937, gives the dates of Congressional actions in its Senate and House bill status sections, and these dates can be used as a guide to where to look in the Congressional Record.

Other sources cover a more limited range of dates, but are more specifically tied to the Congressional Record publication dates. In the *CIS Index*, the legislative history sections going back to 1970 contain lists of dates in the Congressional Record for when each Public Law was considered and passed. *U.S.C.C.A.N.* goes back further, with a table showing Congressional Record dates of consideration and passage for each Public Law from 1964 to 1991, and, since 1991, dates of passage only. The *Statutes at Large* has a similar table going back one year further, starting in 1963. In 1975 the *Statutes at Large* switched from tabular presentation of this information to a statement following the text of each public law, and *U.S.C.C.A.N.* added these statements to its Laws volumes, thereby duplicating the information it includes in its legislative history tables. Of course, the Congressional Record itself has indexing features, which differ from these external finding aids in one critical way: they actually give page numbers, a complicated matter to which we now turn.

3.14 CONGRESSIONAL RECORD PAGINATION

Prior to 1985, you will need to hunt down your Congressional Record references either in paper or on microfiche. You will probably have noticed that most sources pointing you to the Congressional Record references for a particular bill or law do so by date only, not by page. This is because the Record goes through two different iterations, and each is paginated differently. The print Congressional Record appears first in a Daily Edition, which is paginated in separate sections for the House and Senate. Once material is carried over to the Permanent Edition (the bound compilation volumes that have been amended and added to by members of Congress and are repaginated in one continuous sequence), the *Bluebook* requires citation to that, rather than to the Daily Edition (Rule 13.5). This can pose a problem from the mid-eighties on, when production and distribution of the permanent edition became intermittent and spotty. Currently, the usual way to get access to the permanent edition is via either the GPO or CIS microfiche sets. So far, GPO Access offers one volume only of the bound edition: vol. 145 (1999), in both text and image files.

Table 3.D: Sources of the Congressional Record

1. Library of Congress, Thomas: Legislative Information on the Internet.

   http://thomas.loc.gov/

   Coverage begins in 1989.

2. United States, GPOAccess, Congressional Record

   http://www.gpoaccess.gov/crecord/index.html

   Coverage begins in 1994.

3. United States Congress, *Congressional Record.* Daily edition. Washington: G.P.O

4. United States Congress, *Congressional Record.* [microform] Permanent edition. Washington: G.P.O

5. Westlaw: All Databases > U.S. Federal Materials > Congressional Information > Congressional Record (Database = **CR**)

   Coverage begins in 1985.

6. Lexis: Legal > Legislation and Politics—U.S. & U.K. > U.S. Congress

   From that point you can choose various subsets of data, e.g., by Congress or by section of the Congressional Record (for the combined data, Library and File = **GEN-FED;RECORD**). Coverage begins in 1985.

Citing to the Congressional Record date only, as do all of the indexing sources listed above, puts the burden on the researcher to obtain the page number for herself. Working with only the date can be onerous, since a single dated issue can be quite lengthy. To get a particular page number, the researcher must usually turn to the internal indexing of the Record, which is, of course, provided separately for the two different print editions.

3.15   CONGRESSIONAL RECORD INDEXING

The print Permanent Edition includes, in the final book of each volume, an index entitled "History of Bills and Resolutions". This gives, for each bill introduced in that session, the page numbers in the permanent edition where action was taken on that bill. There is also a subject index, in the unlikely case that you are not looking for references to a particular bill. In the Daily Edition, very brief descriptions of the proceedings for that day are grouped in the Daily Digest section under broad rubrics like "Measures Passed", giving the appropriate daily edition page numbers within that issue. While there is no numerical list of bills in the Daily Digest, the descriptions are brief enough that scanning the material for mentions of a particular bill number is quite easily doable, and certainly more efficient than reading through the whole issue looking for your bill. Note that the online History of Bills at GPO Access, described above, gives page numbers to the daily edition since 1983.

These Daily Digest sections are eventually revised and collected in bound volumes for each session of Congress; in this format they refer the researcher to pages in the permanent edition. These bound volumes can usefully be employed as a way to get from a known date to a particular page of the permanent edition on microfiche without having to pore over an index on microfiche. While they still do not contain a list of bills by bill number, these volumes of collected Daily Digests do include tables of legislative history by public law number for those bills that did pass, including page numbers in the permanent edition of the Congressional Record.

3.16   STATE LEGISLATIVE HISTORY

While the same principles apply in state legislative history as in federal, the state legislative historian does face some special problems. The principal problem is that of paucity of raw material. Many states do not publish all or indeed any of the deliberative materials that would provide evidence of legislative intent. The Manz guide, which we already encountered in section 2.31 as a good source for information about state bills, is also full of information about other state legislative history documentation. One source that comes up frequently in the state context is the work product of various law reform commissions. Again, individual state legal research manuals will provide more detail **(see Appendix)**.

As state legislatures put more legislative material online, the situation is changing to one more similar to the federal context. Using what you know about the federal legislature's documentation of its work, you can search the state website or speak with a state librarian looking for analogous documentation in the state context.

If your state statute's source was a Uniform or Model Act, you can tap into the larger body of legislative history and commentary that pertains to the Act in its proposed generic form, and also in other jurisdictions (see Chapter Eleven for more on this). One component of this legislative history is the law itself: the variations between versions from jurisdiction to jurisdiction and between any one jurisdiction and the original uniform version can all be telling. Given the aims of Uniform Acts, to unify statutory law where inter-jurisdictional need dictates, and to replace common law in a rational manner, they are popular subjects for analysis in law reviews, and the commentary they contain (see Chapter Four, below) will provide much grist for the state legislative historian.

Chapter 4

INTRODUCING SECONDARY SOURCES: LAW REVIEW ARTICLES

4.1 LAW REVIEWS AS A TOOL FOR THE LEGAL RESEARCHER

It would be difficult to overstate the utility of secondary sources to the legal researcher. Law review articles in particular can save much time and heartache by offering a jumping off place into an unfamiliar area of the law. Moreover, since law review articles serve both explicative and normative functions with regard to the law, the researcher is doubly bound to take notice of their content and the trends in jurisprudence they indicate.

Law journals are academically–based periodicals, the editorial work for which is provided by law students. Whereas the prestige–conferring journals in other disciplines are typically peer-reviewed, the law reviews which serve this purpose in academic law are edited by the publishing institution's own top students. The typical journal publishes a number of different types of articles, and they vary in their usefulness to the legal researcher. "Lead articles" are the first article or two in an issue, usually written by a prominent judge or a prominent law professor. These articles are typically contentious pieces which put forward ideas about how the author feels the law should develop in a particular area. Lead articles are the most likely type of article to be cited either to or by courts. Other articles follow, written by less prominent judges, by academics, and by practitioners. Since these authors have less clout, their articles may branch off into the merely analytical and explicative, although some articles in this category maintain the prescriptive model of the lead articles. Articles of this type written by law student staffers are usually shorter and are frequently called "comments". The uniquely student-written contribution to law reviews is the type of piece called a "note": a shorter piece going deeply into the background and the likely impact of some recent statutory or case law development. While these student notes (traditionally unsigned, although that tradition is now all but dead) are unlikely to be cited, the mass of footnotes they contain can still be a legal researcher's best friend.

The conventional structure of most of these articles facilitates their use as a road map for someone starting off in the area. You can count on the first few paragraphs, in which the author is setting out the context for his presentation, to be a very rich source of background material on the topic at hand. Typically the footnotes to these initial paragraphs contain citations to all the big primary sources that are central to understanding the article's subject (statutes, cases, regulations, administrative rulings), and also citations to seminal commentary (especially other law review articles). The middle of the article usually includes lots of case citations, along with analysis which helps to determine the significance of the cases cited. By sorting out the important cases in an area and discussing how they interact with relevant statutes, this part of an article helps the researcher identify what is critically important. Finally, these pieces wind up with policy recommendations, which may be interesting, but, except in the case of lead articles by big players in the area, are clearly of limited utility for legal research. The same might be said of the book reviews which usually round out the law review bill of fare.

4.2 FINDING LAW REVIEW ARTICLES

As with so many tasks in legal research, you have two basic choices when it comes to looking for law review articles. You can use an index, or you can search full-text databases of articles. For most purposes, you will be better served by starting off with a legal periodical index, since that way your search results will focus on articles that are devoted to your subject of interest, rather than be diluted with articles where your subject is merely mentioned. Also, while the gap in number of journals covered is smaller than it used to be, a greater number of law reviews is still indexed in the periodical indexes than is presented in the full-text databases.

The two principal general indexes for this purpose are the *Index to Legal Periodicals*, published since 1908 by H.W. Wilson, and the *Current Law Index* which started in 1980. Both indexes are currently available both in print and in a variety of formats electronically. Earlier indexes go back even further (see Table 4.A). For journals and years that are covered, you will want to use the electronic version whenever it is available to you. The electronic versions of these indexes offer the ability to combine multiple search criteria, and eliminate the need to search

Table 4.A : Selected Legal Periodical Indexes

1. WilsonWeb: Index to Legal Periodicals Retrospective and Index to Legal Periodicals and Books

   These subscription web databases offer coverage for 1918–1981 and1981–present, respectively.

2. Westlaw:

   All Databases > Legal Periodicals & Current Awareness > Periodical Indexes > Index to Legal Periodicals (Database = **ILP**)

   Coverage begins in August 1981.

   All Databases > Legal Periodicals & Current Awareness > Periodical Indexes > Legal Resource Index (Database = **LRI**)

   Coverage begins in 1980.

3. Lexis:

   Legal > Secondary Legal > Annotations & Indexes > Index to Legal Periodicals (Library and File = **LAWREV;ILP**)

   Coverage begins in 1978.

   Legal > Secondary Legal > Annotations & Indexes > Legal Resource Index (Library and File = **LAWREV;LGLIND**)

   Coverage begins in January 1977.

4. Leonard A. Jones (vols. 1–2) and Frank E. Chipman (vols. 3–6), *An Index to Legal Periodical Literature*. Various publishers. This series, known as the "Jones–Chipman index," was published between 1888 and 1939, and covers articles published between 1770 and 1937.

5. University of Washington, Marion Gould Gallagher Law Library, *Current Index to Legal Periodicals*. This publication is available by subscription in paper and by e-mail; the most recent eight weeks are also available on Westlaw.

through multiple volumes and non-cumulative supplements to cover a range of dates. The electronic versions are for the most part taken from the print indexes, so the contents and currency of the different formats of a given index should be the same. The principal exception is the LegalTrac/Legal Resource Index electronic products, which add coverage of legal newspapers and law-related articles from the general press to the law reviews and journals indexed by the paper *Current Law Index*.

If it is important to you to get absolutely every article, as when, for example, you are doing a preemption check to ascertain whether another article has already been written on a topic on which you propose to write, it is worth it to check each index via all vendors. An identical search of the *Index to Legal Periodicals* on Westlaw and on Lexis, for instance, can easily bring up non-identical results lists. There are also differences in display between the Westlaw and Lexis versions of ILP. In the short citation displays, book reviews on Westlaw's ILP are listed with the reviewer shown as the author, while on Lexis's ILP the same piece shows the author of the reviewed book as the author. Lexis retains the print ILP's identification of student authors as such, while Westlaw omits that information from its ILP records. Westlaw indicates in the short citations which pieces are book reviews, even if that was not part of your search. Note that searching ILP and CLI in Westlaw or Lexis permits you to use refined searching techniques like requiring one term to appear within a certain proximity to another, which can cut down on false drops. However, the absence of this search flexibility in the stand-alone web versions of the indexes is not too serious, since the documents you are searching, bibliographic records of articles, are already so short.

Another index, the *Current Index to Legal Periodicals*, offers less elaborate indexing of a narrower range of journals with a faster turn-around time than the two primary indexes. Other law review indexes focus on the journal output of particular jurisdictions (e.g., English and Canadian). Indexing of law review articles is also provided in various subject–specific treatises and looseleaf services (such as the CCH services); their advantage is the inclusion of articles from more specialized sources than those covered in the general indexes, and the use of more precise and specialized subject headings.

The other principal method for finding law review articles is by full–text search. The law review databases on Westlaw and Lexis offer coverage of a large number of law reviews (although not as many as are indexed in ILP and CLI); however they generally only go back in their coverage to about 1994. For earlier articles, the principal online source is Hein Online, a subscription database on the web that offers full–text searchable .pdf images of many law reviews from the beginning of their runs. The searching in Hein Online is not as flexible as that offered by Lexis and Westlaw, but the coverage is an extremely valuable addition to the universe of online legal resources.

4.3   LOOKING FOR ARTICLES BY SUBJECT

When you are just starting out, a general subject may be all you have to go on. In order to avoid casual mentions of the terms you are using to describe your subject, you should start off with an index, rather than full–text searching. The subject indexing varies considerably among the three general legal periodical indexes, so searching in all of them might well be fruitful. The *Current Law Index* and its electronic progeny Legal Trac and the Legal Resources Index use subject headings from the Library of Congress system. The *Index to Legal Periodicals* tends to have much more general subject headings, which can be either a blessing or a curse. Some of the subject headings (e.g., constitutional law) are so general as to be almost useless when conducting legal research; fortunately, when searching these indexes electronically you can combine a subject heading with a word from the title or with a second subject heading for much more precise targeting.

The longevity of the *Index to Legal Periodicals* has meant that some subject headings have become obsolete or anachronistic; Wilson has undertaken to change the subject headings for more consistency with modern usage. Therefore, the electronic version of the Wilson indexing for pre–1981 articles may use different subject headings than the print volumes do. If one or the other is not working out for you, it may be worth trying the other even though the articles indexed are the same.

In general, if your attempts to guess at good subject headings are not panning out, there are two techniques you should use. First, you can usually find an appropriate subject heading by starting off with a reference to just one good article, found by a keyword in the title or subject. While it's a bit backwards, you could also resort to fishing around in the full-text database for that one good article, which you would then look up in an index, for our current purpose. Once you have found the record for that one good article in the index, go down to the very bottom of the record for a list of what subject headings were assigned to that article. Usually one or a combination of those subject headings will get you to other good articles, and possibly even more good subject headings. A second method to find good subject headings is to scan a list of all the subject headings used by an index.

4.4   LOOKING FOR ARTICLES BY CASE NAME OR CITATION

If your purpose in looking for law review articles is to investigate the legal penumbra of a particular case, there are numerous ways to zero in on the appropriate articles. When an article is devoted to consideration of a particular case (as is true of many student-written articles in particular), the index record for that article may include the name of the case and its citation, even if that information is not included in the article's title. The decision to add the case name and citation to the article's record is made by the indexer, and while the index entry for an article may get a case name slapped on it in one index, the same may not be true in another index. This is another reason to do your searches for articles in both of the major indexes.

The electronic indexes can all be searched for articles by case name and citation. ILP in its stand-alone incarnation permits fielded searching by case party name or case citation. On Westlaw's and Lexis's ILP and LRI the records that you are searching include case name and citation. The stand-alone CLI-related products have added case name and citation to the area searched by a keyword search. While CILP does not offer fielded searching, you can use your web browser's search function to look for the beginning of a citation. Since the format of the citation may not be what you are expecting, it's probably most efficient to type in only "volume number<space>first letter of the reporter title". The print indexes also offer article lookup by case name.

Since the association of an article with a particular case in the journal indexes is a matter of editorial discretion, you may wish to dispense with the judgment of the editorial middleman and construct a search in a full-text journal database (JLR on Westlaw or Lawrev;Allrev on Lexis) that will retrieve articles about your case. The trick here is to find the articles that are devoted to the case, without getting mired down in every article that ever merely mentioned it. On both Lexis and Westlaw you can use the "atleast" command to require a certain number of appearances of your search term within the document, and this could be pressed into service to find just those articles that mention the name of your case (or a distinctive word from that name) over and over again.

If you are unable to find an article devoted to your case, and are ready to settle for any old article that at least cites to your case, you can use a citator. KeyCite on Westlaw includes references to law review articles in the Secondary Sources category of Citing References to cases. Shepards on Lexis puts references to law review articles in a category of citing references called Law Reviews and Periodicals. Shepards in print puts citations to law review articles about the case in a group at the end of the citations for that case. This is another instance of how you can enhance your results by using both competing citators. KeyCite indicates, via use of a headnote signal, which legal point in the case is the subject of discussion in the law review article. KeyCite also includes references in law reviews not covered by Shepards, but Shepards (both on Lexis and in print) includes citing articles going farther back, before the period of online journal availability. For the most complete coverage, you should check your case in both citators.

4.5   LOOKING FOR ARTICLES
ABOUT A STATUTE

As when looking for articles about a case, you will need to distinguish between articles that are about your statute, and articles that merely mention your statute in passing. All the techniques and sources described above in the section on articles about cases should be pressed into service here as well, but only after checking one very valuable additional source: the annotated code containing your statute. In the *U.S.C.A.*, after a code section which has been the subject of a law review article, there appears in the Library References annotations a listing of "Law Review and Journal Commentaries" pertaining to that section. Similarly, in the *U.S.C.S.*, the Research Guide after such a section will have a list of relevant law review articles. When using the print versions of the codes, more recent article citations will appear in the pocket parts and in the paperback supplements.

4.6   LOOKING FOR AN ARTICLE
BY A PARTICULAR AUTHOR

Occasionally the legal researcher may have call to look for articles by a particular author. A judge or colleague may have remembered a relevant article but only by its author, or the work of a certain writer may be acknowledged as significant in a particular area. In case you do need to find an article by a particular author, you should use electronic means if possible. Full-text searching in a law review database becomes more reliable for this purpose than for the purposes described above, since Westlaw, Lexis, and HeinOnline all provide the ability to limit your search amongst their data by author. All of the electronic periodical indexes also offer fielded searching by author. The only complicating wrinkle in an author search arises when using the paper ILP prior to September 1983, which of course will sometimes be necessary because of date limitations on the other sources or because of lack of access to the WilsonWeb Retrospective database.

The complication involved in author searching in the old paper ILP arose from the publisher's desire to avoid unnecessary duplicative printing of information. We encountered this motivation in section 2.30 above, in the indexing to the paper *Congressional Index*, in which multiple indexes are issued in the course of a Congress to avoid having to reprint earlier entries later in the term. In the pre–9/83 *Index to Legal Periodicals*, the aim was to avoid having to print an article's record multiple times, under each of the possible entry points. Instead, the article's full record was printed only once, under the first subject heading assigned to the article. Under the heading of the author's name, the article was identified only by listing its first subject heading, with the initial letter of the article's title in parentheses thereafter. The researcher then turned to that subject, and scanned through the alphabetical list of article titles underneath it. At least one of those articles starting with the specified letter would be by the desired author. Multiple subject headings were dealt with by cross-references to the primary subject heading. This roundabout system was abandoned shortly after the introduction of the rival *Current Law Index*, which announces itself as offering "multiple access to legal periodicals"!

Occasionally problems arise in working from authors' names because of an old citation rule that mandated use of only the author's last name in citing to article authors (and only last name plus first initial in citing to book authors). This rule was abrogated by the 15th Edition of the *Bluebook* in 1991, when Rules 15.1 and 16.1 were amended to require use of the author's full name. Should you ever encounter difficulties in connection with overly-brief versions of authors' names, you can use periodical indexes (or library catalogs), which always required use of the author's full name, to fill in the blanks. When you encounter what appear to be different variants of an author's name and wish to confirm that you are in fact dealing with one and the same person, one handy method is to look up law review articles listed under the different forms of the name. The author's name at the head of the article is usually followed by an asterisk which leads to a footnote giving identifying information (such as institutional affiliation) about the person.

4.7 EVALUATING THE USEFULNESS OF LAW REVIEW ARTICLES

Once you have identified a list of law review articles that look helpful, and even read them, you will still need to evaluate the usefulness of any particular article that you find. Obviously, the content of the article itself will either prove useful or not, in terms of leading you to citeable authority for your legal proposition or in terms of educating and orienting you with respect to a previously unfamiliar area of the law. But the article's content is not the only aspect you need to consider when working with law review articles. Especially if you are considering citing to an article as evidence of the direction in which the law should be moving, you will want to consider the prestige or standing of that article.

The most straightforward indication of the prestige of the article is the status of the person who is named as the author. A roughly descending order of punch is probably packed by the following types of authors: United States Supreme Court justice, other judge, famous law professor, other law professor, famous practitioner, other practitioner, and student. Of course the identity of the author can be important to you for reasons other than prestige. The different experiences and backgrounds of these different types of author can offer valuably different perspectives on the issue at hand. Useful information on what that perspective might be can be gleaned from the information in the first (usually non-numbered) footnote of the article, which includes the author's place of employ, and acknowledgments of intellectual and other gratitude. Since these footnotes are part of the full text of the articles, they can be searched and analyzed to follow the influence of a particular individual or coterie. Another subject for reflection with respect to article authorship is whether the article is the author's first, or whether this is the latest of many articles. If the latter, is the repeat author focussed on one subject, or wide-ranging?

Another component in the prestige of an article is the prestige of the law review which published it. Among the different types of student-edited law journals, the school's top journal usually confers more cachet than the other journals. The top journal at a school is the one that gets the top students to work for it, the one that probably is more generously supported financially (either by the school or by alumni, as well as by subscriptions), the one which has more clerical and/or business management support, and (sometimes) the one which offers more academic credit to student staffers. At most schools this publication is a generalist publication, with only the name of the school and either "Law Review," "Law Journal," or "Law Quarterly" in its title. This is the publication that tends to attract higher caliber articles, in terms of the authors that publish in it, and in terms of the citedness of those articles by other law reviews and by judicial opinions. In some cases the footnotes are better edited, either because of higher standards imposed by editorial policies, or because of preferential treatment and training by the law librarians working with the student staffers.

By comparison, most law journals devoted to a particular subject are the secondary journals at their school. Some of these publications, particularly at the top schools or if the journal was groundbreaking in introducing scholarship in a new topic, are moderately prestigious, with all that the modifier implies about editing quality and content quality. These journals may be the only place where certain topics are covered, but arguably the best articles about most subjects go to the generalist law reviews at the top schools anyway. If you have lots of articles from which to choose and limited time to review them, you will need to balance these factors in deciding how to allocate your reading time, particularly when it comes to scanning articles which are not available electronically.

Another factor to consider in evaluating the potential value to you of a law review article is its length. Length by itself is clearly not always an indicator of worth: consider that the average law review article is now somewhere over 40 pages long. However, in choosing which to read from an otherwise undifferentiated list of articles, realize that at least a longer one will go into more detail about the topic, and probably have either lots of background, or lots of statistical information, or lots of policy discussion, as well as analysis of the legal issue and its treatment in courts. In accordance with Bluebook Rule 3.3(a), most of the time when you encounter a citation to an article only the number of its first page will be indicated. Again, as with incomplete name information, you can use a periodical index to fill in the final page number, and thus learn for evaluation purposes how long the article is. The *Index to Legal Periodicals* started supplying terminal page numbers for articles in 1973, and *Current Law Index* had them right from its beginning in 1980.

You will probably also be interested in the date of the articles you find. Very recent articles are preferable for the purpose of mining the footnotes for still-current references. Note that articles retrieved via searching the Westlaw JLR database of articles will display in reverse chronological order, so you will see the more recent ones first. The same display order applies in the Index to Legal Periodicals on Westlaw and on Lexis, and can be chosen in ILP's freestanding incarnation on Wilson-Web. Reverse chronological display is also employed by LRI on Westlaw and Lexis, and by the freestanding LegalTrac on the Web. If, on the other hand, you would prefer to see your results grouped initially by publication in which they appeared, your wish can be fulfilled by searching in the LAWREV;ALLREV file on Lexis.

Since 1948, the University of Washington's Marion Gould Gallagher Law Library has published the weekly *Current Index to Legal Periodicals*, providing indexing of law review articles up to 6 weeks earlier than the commercial indexing publications. CILP is available in a variety of formats **(see Table 4.A)** including as an e-mail alert by subscription (SmartCILP). The database versions of CILP consist of a series of separate documents, each of which must be searched separately. Sometimes the newest issue of CILP will appear in one venue earlier than in others, and sometimes particular articles may turn up earlier in the commercial indexes. For articles even newer than those listed in CILP, you can seek out articles as yet unindexed by full-text searching with a date restriction in the law review databases of Westlaw and Lexis. Some law reviews put their current issues up on their websites, or at least abstracts of the current issue's contents.

For even more recent material, articles that are not only as yet unindexed but as yet unpublished, you can turn to working papers, a comparatively recent import from the world of economics to the world of academic law. **(See Table 4.B)** Originally actual papers, distributed in print by the institution where the authors worked, working papers today are more likely to be electronic, distributed in abstract by subject-oriented extra-institutional organizations such as the Social Science Research Network. When you encounter unpublished material like a working paper you should always check to see if it was subsequently published. Be careful here! Just because something has not yet been published doesn't mean it is fresh and new: the Internet is, among other things, a boneyard of stale research.

At the other end of the spectrum, older articles that are still being cited long after their publication are particularly likely to have good analysis in the text, so determining citedness is another reasonable way

Table 4.B: Examples of Sources for Working Papers in Law

1. Legal Scholarship Network. A component part of the Social Science Research Network (SSRN), which also embraces research in accounting, economics, and finance.

   http://www.ssrn.com/lsn/index.html

2. NELLCO Legal Scholarship Repository. Maintained by the New England Law Library Consortium.

   http://lsr.nellco.org/

3. American Bar Foundation. An example of a different sort of source of working papers, the ABF is a research institute which develops a research program, and funds and publishes research.

   http://www.abf-sociolegal.org/

to evaluate articles, especially older ones. This can be done to a limited extent (limited in that only articles present in full text can be researched) on Westlaw's KeyCite. Citations to older articles are available via *Shepard's Law Review Citations*, available both in print and on Lexis. This citator refers you to citations since 1957, both in subsequent law review articles and in the published decisions of federal and state courts, of law review articles published after 1946. Within these date limits, the electronic service on Lexis does include coverage of articles that are too old to be on Lexis. Since for these there is no document from which you can click through to Shepardize, you will have to bring up Shepard's and then enter the citation for the article. The query box for Shepards in the web version of Lexis will provide you with the appropriate citation form for any law review covered, and the software version of Lexis will give you the opportunity to type in the full name of the publication you wish to Shepardize and then return to you the citation format to use. Happily, these (but not the abbreviations in the print Shepard's) are the same as the *Bluebook* abbreviations for law reviews.

4.8   USING THE FOOTNOTES IN
LAW REVIEW ARTICLES

Most legal researchers working with law review articles find their reward in the mass of footnotes they contain. Especially with regard to student writing, the real meat of the articles is the collation of relevant legal authorities and other sources, rather than in the students' opining. While the plenitude of law review footnotes is the butt of many jokes, that same plenitude can be impressive and useful. The footnotes to the best articles are plentiful, detailed, logical, and accurate.

Getting to the footnotes is more of a pain than it should be. In print law reviews, the footnotes are traditionally at the bottom of the page of text which cites to them, the assumption being that the reader is at least as interested in the footnotes as in the text. In the electronic text versions, what was the graphical simplicity of geographically segregating print footnotes and text on a single page becomes a complicated matter of jumping back and forth from a text document to a footnote document. This issue of footnote display is handled differently in the different databases and it does change (usually for the better) with some frequency; suffice it here to note that it is still less graceful than reading the footnotes in print (or in image files). Yet the electronic reading of law review articles in text files offers an enormous advantage to the legal researcher over the reading of print: the citations in the footnotes are frequently links to the full text of the documents cited. Again, hard to beat that convenience!

Not all the footnotes will be links, however, and those references you will need to hunt down yourself. The information gathered in footnotes is recorded in the highly standardized forms prescribed by the *Bluebook*. Thus, you may encounter abbreviations that you cannot understand without reference to that indispensable volume. The abbreviations table in the back of the *Bluebook* contains not only the specific abbreviated titles for many publications, but also the accepted "Bluebookese" for many words that commonly come up in the titles of legal publications not specifically listed. Remember, for instance, that "L." means "Law," but that "Law." means "Lawyer"! You are likely to encounter abbreviations in the footnotes of law reviews for which the *Bluebook* offers no guidance. Rule 20.1.3 specifies that for foreign legal materials with no *Bluebook* abbreviation, you should follow the usage of the source. Numerous legal abbreviation dictionaries can rescue you here. **See Table 4.C** for the most important ones.

Footnotes can be used not only as a source of citations, but as a source of information about citations. If you find an ambiguous cite in a reference, or if you are having trouble with an incomplete or erroneous cite from any source, you should check the citations to that material in more than one article. Frequently, looking at the work of the student staffs of several different law reviews will reveal the origin of the problem. One of the thorniest problems that arises is that of ghost references: an author didn't look at the underlying cited document, but just appropriated someone else's (invalid) cite. Passing along a ghost reference like this is a blot on the law review's escutcheon, and a reminder to the entire research community of the need to maintain the integrity of our common enterprise.

Table 4.C: Selected Dictionaries of Legal Abbreviations

1. Mary Miles Prince, *Bieber's Dictionary of Legal Abbreviations*. 5th ed. Buffalo, N.Y.: W.S. Hein, 2001.

   The first two editions of this indispensable companion to law reviews were written by Doris M. Bieber.

2. Lexis: Legal > Secondary Legal > Annotations & Indexes > Bieber's Dictionary of Legal Abbreviations (Library and File = **LEXREF;BIEBLA**). Note that this is the 4th edition (1993).

3. *World dictionary of legal abbreviations*. Igor I. Kavass and Mary Miles Prince, general editors. Buffalo, N.Y.: W.S. Hein, 1991–

   Multi-volume looseleaf set.

Chapter 5

CASES

5.1 THE CORE OF OUR ENTERPRISE

Despite the primacy of statutes in our research scheme of things, case law research is the *sine qua non* of the lawyer's art. "Finding out the law" in a statute book is something a diligent lay person with a real interest can manage. Ascertaining the law from the vast array of possibly relevant cases, however, requires a legal education. Knowledge of substantive law, experience in issue spotting, and familiarity with legal analysis and synthesis all contribute to successful case law research. Thus, the finer points of working with cases are better appreciated in an advanced legal research course than in the initial whirlwind exposure to the subject. Hence we begin this discussion of case law research with a general overview of how to do it. As an advanced student, you need to become comfortable with finding all of the cases that have to be found, and with determining their significance by analysis and by investigation of their background and of both their progeny and commentary.

5.2 FINDING ALL THE RIGHT CASES

The first year of law school frequently offers research experiences that bear little resemblance to research in the larger worlds of scholarship and practice. Scavenger–hunt type library exercises are devised to see whether the student can find a known item. Moot court problems, often the first–year student's principal research experience, are usually purposely composed of live legal issues in areas rife with recent judicial developments. Again, there is definitely something out there, by design, for the student to find.

By contrast, when a student begins to work outside the academic walls, she may well find the whole enterprise transformed: all of a sudden there don't seem to be any answers out there anymore. Research assignments seem more often than not to lead to a dead end, or a huge question mark. This is only natural, given the structure of the legal workplace: the research assignment is given by a more experienced lawyer who has a real problem; that lawyer's questions about the law will tend to cluster around unconventional or unlikely points of interpretation. The saving grace, for the novice researcher, is that their law school spent a lot of time teaching them to think like a lawyer. In order, however, for that lawyerly thinking to have the proper grist on which to work, the researcher must have found all the necessary cases to form a correct and defensible view of the law.

We have already explored, in Chapter Two, how to find the cases that interpret a particular statute. Given the structure of our legal system, that has to be the starting place for most legal research. However, pure case law research still has a role to play: there may be no controlling statute, the matter may be in an area governed by common law, you may want to compare the case law of many jurisdictions subject to different statutes without initial reference to those statutes, or you may be checking your statute–based work by reference to case law generally to make sure you found the right statutes.

The researcher in search of cases without reference to a statute has three basic options. The first option, and often the best for the tyro, is to start off by finding a secondary source that has identified principal cases and work from those. Chapter Four explored how to do this by using journal articles, and Chapter Six will do the same for treatises. The second option is to employ the highly–developed tools of case indexing which categorize and organize the enormous body of decisional law by a number of different criteria. The third option is to dive directly into full–text searching of case law databases.

Beginning researchers engage most often (at their peril) in this third option, full–text searching. We say "at their peril" because of the twin dangers of the full–text researcher becoming either overwhelmed by the amount of decisional law, or overly charmed by the apparent suitability of a retrieved case for the purpose at hand (or both). While these pitfalls can certainly threaten the index–employing researcher as well, they sit more squarely in the path of the researcher who relies on the Way of Full–Text. That said, the allure and convenience of full–text searching is such that we open our discussion of how to find cases with a rundown of its dos and don'ts.

5.3 FULL TEXT SEARCHING OF CASE LAW DATABASES

Full–text searching is actually an index of almost every word in the case. While an index produced by a human indexer subjects you to the limitations of that writer's wisdom and abilities, with full–text you are avoiding possible errors in judgment by the editorial middleman because you can look up every actual word in the case (except common stop words). However, by the same token, with pure full–text you are constricted by ONLY being able to look up those words that actually appeared in the case (with certain structural variants). The full text researcher, therefore, must leave no plausible synonym unturned. The case law databases have supplemented their full text of the cases with added descriptive terms in order to make this easier, thereby reinserting the human editorial eye, either directly or via the application of an algorithm, into the process.

The legal landscape is dominated by two competing online information vendors, Westlaw and Lexis. Other players (including, currently, Bloomberg Law and Lois) provide specialty information or niche pricing of a subset of similar information, but the big two provide the most legal content and the most sophisticated mechanisms for using it. Their competition has prompted a stream of constant changes and improvements, and it would be futile to try to capture here the details of how to search optimally in either system. Instead, our discussion will focus on the broader principles of how to engage in full–text searching, in the hopes that those principles will usefully inform how you go about using both Westlaw and Lexis and any other full–text system you encounter.

Your first choice involves picking a search method. Choosing whether to use Boolean or relevance–based searching will depend on the degree of precision with which you wish to control the terms of the search, and on how you wish to have the results presented to you. In Boolean connector–based searching (called "Terms and Connectors" on both Westlaw and Lexis; analogous to the "advanced" searching in many web–based search engines) you have the ability to specify the exact criteria for documents to be returned to you, in accordance with a defined list of conditions that you can apply. This kind of control is essential when you are dealing with concepts that you understand very well, where the vocabulary and turns of phrase you can anticipate in the case language are both significant to you and familiar. This kind of searching enables you to specify, via the connectors, exactly what relationship the search terms must have to each other in the retrieved documents. Boolean searching is also indicated where you wish to require many different variables and then swap them in and out to control for different ones. The order of presentation of results with Boolean searching may be subject to your control, but as a matter of default it will usually, within any given jurisdiction, be by court (with higher courts presenting first) and then by date (reverse chronological order).

By contrast, relevance–based searching (called "natural language" in both Westlaw and Lexis) algorithmically infers a relationship between your search terms by their identity and the order in which you entered them, and returns results in order of their relevance ranking according to a concealed set of rules based on that relationship. This process takes you out of the driver's seat, to a large extent, and for that reason should never be used exclusively in any legal research project. Note especially that some of the criteria you enter in your search may not be present in the results, even toward the top of the list, depending on how the relevance ranking operated on your search terms. Think of how you can get some weird stuff toward the top of a list of Google results and you'll be thinking along the right lines.

Relevance–based searching can be great, however, when you are starting out in a broad area that is unfamiliar to you, since the algorithm's judgment about which of the 600 results returned are more important is likely to be superior to your judgment after having had to scan 600 cases returned in date order. Also, it can be your best bet if you are searching, for content reasons, in the service that you use less often, since it can let you at least get started without getting mired in command errors. Once you get at least one good case, relevance–based tools such as "more like this" and "more like selected text" on Lexis can enable the system to retrieve other cases that it deems to be of similar interest.

Choosing search terms to use calls upon all your legal training, and then some. When you receive a research assignment in an unfamiliar area, assume that the language used in describing the problem to you contains terms of art. Enclose in quotation marks any phrases that were used, or employ appropriate proximity connectors to ensure that you retrieve cases where the phrase is used in the precise form that you heard it. Later, when your initial results have given you some idea of what kind of concepts are in play, you can start thinking up lists of synonyms to expand your search.

Search components that are common to all Boolean searching are important tools in Westlaw and Lexis. You will want to be fully versed in the connectors available to specify maximum and minimum proximity of search terms to each other, to truncate search terms or substitute unspecified characters at any point in the term, and to specify the order or placement of terms within the document. Arm yourself with an actual list of connectors, printed out and sitting on the desk next to your keyboard, since otherwise you will be tempted to stick with only those connectors that you happen to remember from frequent use.

More specific to case law research is the ability to locate your search terms within fields of data particular to case law documents. The case is divided into portions ("fields") which can be searched separately, and the significance of a search term's appearance in one field versus another taken into account. Thus, one field in a case document is restricted to the name of the judge who wrote the opinion. Another consists of the editorially–produced summary (headnote) of a specific point of law touched upon in the case. Another is the court–produced summary of the entire case (e.g., the syllabus in U. S. Supreme Court cases). The ability to search these fields separately contributes enormously to the efficiency of full–text searching. Searching the headnotes or summary of a case for a combination of search terms is much more likely to avoid cases that only mention those terms peripherally. Note that each type of file on Westlaw and Lexis offers different fields that can be searched, and a list of such fields is available from the search screen.

5.4 USING SUBJECT INDEXES TO CASE LAW: DIGESTS AND THE KEY NUMBER SYSTEM ON WESTLAW

As with statutes, subject access to cases is paramount to the legal researcher. The chronological order in which cases appear is of minimal importance: even the reporters, so seemingly sequential in their long marches down the shelves, are not arranged in strict chronological order (a case published in one volume may actually have been decided prior to cases published in an earlier volume). Subject access is all, and although full text searching is one important way to find cases by subject, there are other ways that are powerful and more organized. The paradigm of these methods is that embodied in the Key Number System created by West in its American Digest System, and carried over and further developed in Westlaw.

Long the foundation of American legal research, West's American Digest System continues today as the principal print subject index to published American case law (as well as the "unpublished" cases printed in the *Federal Appendix*). Once the starting point for virtually all legal research, the West digests have been pushed increasingly into the shadows by both the advent of case law databases and the ascendancy of statutes. But researchers raised in the era of full text searching are frequently thrilled when they become aware of the structure, clarity, helpfulness, and ergonomic pleasure provided by these print tools. As you explore the West Digest System, note the different kinds of access to case law that its different features provide: access by subject, by name, and by reference to a hierarchically arranged set of subject rubrics (the Key Numbers). These same types of access are offered by many case indexing tools, and when you encounter any such tool for the first time, you should remember to look for each of these features (see, e.g., Chapter Nine, below, on looseleaf services).

The West American Digest System consists of indexes for federal law, for state law by region, for state law by state, for the whole country by historical period, and for different specialized subjects **(see Table 5.A)**. The heart of these indexes is a system of subject headings (called Topics) and sub–headings (called Key Numbers) which are used across virtually all jurisdictions covered by the system. Even though you will hear people refer to "Key Numbers," they almost always actually mean a "Topic and Key Number," since a Key Number needs to be identified in relation to the Topic under which it exists. For example, "Key Number 118" is meaningless; Trusts 118, however, signifies "Extrinsic circumstances" and Waters & Water Courses 118 signifies "Obstruction or repulsion of flow." These Topics and Key Numbers can be used on Westlaw as well: every current digest volume contains a list of the numerical equivalents for the Topics. These can, with their associated key numbers, be used to search for cases on Westlaw.

Table 5A: Principal Components of the American Digest System

1. Federal digests:

    West's Federal Practice Digest 4th, and its predecessors

    United States Supreme Court Digest, a subset of the *Federal Practice Digest*

    West's Bankruptcy Digest

2. Regional digests:

    West's Atlantic Digest, 2d, and its predecessor

    North Eastern Digest, discontinued in 1969

    West's North Western Digest, 2d, and its predecessor

    West's Pacific digest, beginning 585 P.2d, and its predecessors

    West's South Eastern Digest, 2d, and its predecessors

    Southern Digest, discontinued in 1991

3. State digests:

    Many states have West digests devoted to those cases from their state and federal courts published in West reporters.

4. Comprehensive digests:

    West's General Digest, 10th Series

    Eleventh Decennial Digest, and its predecessors

    Century Edition of The American Digest: A Complete Digest of All Reported American Cases From the Earliest Times to 1896 (a pre–Key Number digest)

5.5   FINDING A TOPIC AND KEY NUMBER

The West system aims to encompass all American law within its approximately four hundred Topics and the 100,000 or so specific Key Numbers which they contain. In the print digests, the Topics are arranged alphabetically (Abandoned and Lost Property in the first volume to Zoning and Planning in the last) in a series of volumes that make up the bulk of each set. Within each Topic, however, the indexing scheme changes from alphabetical to hierarchical.

The researcher unfamiliar with either the system or the legal topic being investigated will probably want to start with an overall subject index that can direct you to the appropriate Topic and Key Number. On Westlaw this can be done via the KeySearch feature, which presents you with a separate alphabetical (but searchable) list of subjects (and subsets thereof) which in turn can be used to show you the Topics, if any, (or, in certain instances and with a second level of menu checkoffs, a Topic and pertinent range of Key Numbers) that KeySearch considers related, or even to go ahead and run the search. KeySearch does not seek to direct you to Topics and Key Numbers from fact settings, but to do so only from legal concepts. Since the Topics themselves need to be fairly unchangeable, given that continuity of classification over time is one of the assets of West's system, this KeySearch feature offers a way to combine use of the system with searching for concepts that don't readily fit into it.

Another way to get to a good Topic and Key Number on Westlaw is simply to do a fulltext search that uses whatever terms you know to find some case, any case, that includes discussion of your topic. Perusal of the Topics and Key Numbers assigned to the headnotes of the case will identify at least some relevant ones, and you can proceed from there to branch out to other related parts of the hierarchical Key Number tree. You can focus your preliminary search for that "jumping–off point" case by limiting your search to the headnotes of the cases, so you have a greater chance of landing in the right subject area. Other good ways to head for the right ballpark include using a subject–defined subset of the case database in which to conduct your full text search ("Topical Practice Areas" on Westlaw and "Area of Law by Topic" on Lexis), and using a search guide to limit the subjects of the cases that your full text search will retrieve (KeySearch on Westlaw and Search Advisor on Lexis).

The classic tool for this task, the print–only Descriptive Word Index, is still, in some ways, the most extensive finding aid for Key Numbers. Each digest includes several volumes of Descriptive Word Index, a subject index that enables you to look up a legal term or a fact setting in a single alphabetical index and be referred to a topic and key number. Thus, entries under the legal concept "Color of Title" include key numbers under the topics Extortion, Easements, and Highways; entries under the fact component "Dogs" include key numbers under the topics Animals, Searches, and Theaters. The Descriptive Word Indexes are not related to actual cases indexed in that particular digest edition, but rather are virtually identical from digest to digest at any one time, and embody a set of rules about where cases with that characteristic would be (or, probably, have been, in at least one of the many digests) categorized within the Key Number System. If you look up "Treason", for instance, in the *Pacific Digest* (a digest that includes no federal cases), the descriptive word index includes the same detailed entries as does the *Federal Practice Digest*, even though almost all of the entries lead to key numbers under the topic "Treason," under which no cases appear in the current *Pacific Digest*, nor ever have.

At the beginning of each Topic is printed a valuable explanation of what subjects are included under that Topic and what subjects are excluded and covered by other topics. This explanation of the subjects included and excluded is also available in Westlaw (by right–clicking on the Topic and choosing "Scope"), but only in the software version, not on the Web. Also at the beginning of each Topic in the print digests is the complete outline of subtopics and key numbers under that Topic. Come here if you want to try a "top down" analytical approach akin to that of using the table of contents at the beginning of a statutory code chapter. Looking at the hierarchical arrangement of subtopics and Key Numbers under a Topic can clarify for you the importance of always checking overarching Key Numbers, such as "—in general," at the beginning of a Topic (or subtopic), in addition to focusing in on the Key Numbers more specifically related to your issue.

On Westlaw this subject outline can be viewed by expanding each level of Topics and subtopics in the Key Number menu. The online presentation is graphically less graceful than is the print outline, and of course it can tempt you to skip over possibly relevant subtopics by requiring you to click on them to see what Key Numbers they harbor. On the other hand, at this exploratory stage the convenience of not having to assemble a bunch of different volumes off the shelf to investigate the contents of a variety of plausible–looking Topics can be very appealing.

5.6   CHANGES TO THE TOPICS AND KEY NUMBERS

The infrequent changes to the classification and numbering scheme can also be traced only in the print digests. Such changes are, by design, infrequent: the topic "Duelling" was only dropped in the early 1990s. In order to maintain the alphabetical order of the Topics, new introductions generally get shoehorned into the existing lineup (when a place had to be made for Automobiles and Aviation they became topics 48A and 48B in between number 48 Audita Querela and number 49 Bail); the sole exception is the special Topic 450, Merit Systems Protection, put in at the end of the sequence, out of alphabetical order.

When renumbering of Key Numbers within a Topic does have to occur, the digest volume involved is reprinted (with a pair of tables going back and forth between the old and new numbers); on Westlaw, searches on the old number will retrieve results with the new number. The best place to see how the whole system works together is in a separate volume called *West's Analysis of American Law*, which sets out all the material from the head of each Topic in one series. This volume also lists all the Topics, including the ones that have been dropped from use, and contains a brief but highly detailed "Explanation of Key Number Analysis."

5.7 WORKING WITH KEY NUMBERS

Once you have found at least some Key Numbers which seem appropriate, the next step is to try them out and see what kind of cases they get you. In Westlaw, the numerical formulation for the Topic and Key Number can be used as a search term in the data file of your choice. Alternatively, you can drill down through the Key Number tree (reached by a drop down menu from any screen) until you get to your key number, and then either formulate a search or browse the cases under that Key Number.

In the print digests, once you have a Topic and Key Number, proceed to the alphabetical volume containing your Topic, and turn to your sequentially arranged Key Number within that Topic. Under the Key Number you will find short summaries of points of law, each of which is followed by citation to a case. The summaries are arranged in order of the court's level of authority, by jurisdiction, and by date. These summaries are actually the headnotes taken from cases as they appear in print reporters or online. Since most cases include more than one headnote, most cases will have multiple entries in the digest. What the digests and the Key Number system allow you to do quite efficiently is to compare the headnotes summarizing the legal content of individual points made within many cases. The beauty and strength of the West Key Number system lies in the continuity with which it has largely been maintained over almost a hundred years, permitting comparison of judicial discussion of a single legal concept across jurisdictions and throughout that period.

Looking for cases using this method on Westlaw offers the obvious advantage of convenience. Once you find references to cases that look promising, you need only click through to the case itself and read it, since only the very oldest cases are unavailable online. Yet there are still arguments to be made for preferring the print digests at this point in your research. For one thing, the procedure followed when working with the print digests compels you to make a plan that includes a range and variety of Key Numbers before you start retrieving cases, instead of just sequentially following one lead after another, as is encouraged by the online procedure. Having a list of Key Numbers in advance can keep you from straying down a blind alley, and remind you of all the places that you did want to go.

Secondly, the headnotes printed under a given Key Number may go on for pages and pages. When you see that in print, it puts what you are looking at in a different perspective than if you were just pulling up screen after screen, each displaying only a few headnotes. Your eye can scan the page, noting occasional details and getting the gist of most headnotes on it, much faster than you can glean the same information from a long series of screens of such information. Moreover, you are far less likely to throw in the towel inappropriately early when you can see, tangibly, just where you are in the sequence of cases.

You are also more likely, in the print digest, to note adjacent headnotes or even key numbers, and perhaps to be struck by their possible usefulness or even superiority to what you came there looking for. Again, serendipity! As with the print version of the statutory codes, the printed page can offer you more information at one glance and therefore greater likelihood that you will engage in productive browsing.

5.8   GETTING THE MOST RECENT KEY NUMBER INDEXING

No matter what method you used for your original Key Number research, for updating it you will want to use Westlaw, which retrieves all the most recent Key Number assignments. But where Westlaw use is not an option (for reasons of, e.g., money, access, or power blackout), you can get quite recent indexing materials (much more recent than digest pocket parts or even pamphlet supplements) through a system that nowadays functions primarily as a current awareness (rather than a research) tool.

Each West reporter volume contains pages which set out in digest format the Key Number indexing for the cases included within that particular volume. The first place that cases are published by West is in softcover updates to reporters, and these include the same kind of "digest" pages, again covering only those cases printed in that particular soft–cover update issue. These various updating pages can be used together efficiently by noting the exact coverage of the digest they supplement. On the back of each digest's title page is recorded at least one "stop cite," a case citation that shows which was the last sequentially published case whose indexing is contained in that edition of the digest (the digesting is done in order, working through the reporter). If the digest covers more than one reporter, there will be a stop cite for each reporter covered. Having used whatever is the latest edition available of the digest, be that main volume, pocket part, or supplementary pamphlet, you would note the stop cite on the reverse of the title page and then start looking in the appropriate reporter's "digest pages" starting with the first reporter volume or issue that goes beyond the stop cite. Repeat for each reporter covered. . . .

5.9 OTHER SUBJECT–BASED SEARCHING FOR CASES

As the old joke has it, if the West editors were not in the forest when the tree fell, would it have made a sound? Other indexing and subject–finding aids to case law research have indeed been produced by different editorial hands, and can be used as supplements to the West system. On Lexis, a feature called Search Advisor offers guided topical access to cases using its own list of subjects, called Core Concepts. On Westlaw itself, Key Search provides a means of topical access that can be used independently of the Key Number system. As noted above, you can also use it to narrow the searched universe of cases down to one where a full-text search is more likely to reveal appropriate Key Numbers. The *United States Supreme Court Digest*, a publication tied to a family of titles published by LexisNexis, combines the features of a typical digest (subject and name indexing of cases) with additional research references. Specialized finding aids abound for cases published in topically specific reporters or databases, either as part of those publications or as free-standing indexes **(see Table 5.B)**.

Citators also provide highly targeted subject–based searching for cases. The principle behind using a citator as a case finding tool is that a case which cites to an earlier case must logically discuss the same legal issue as that for which it cites the earlier case. By following the citations of a case for a particular point, therefore, you can find other cases on that point. Where possible, you will want to conduct this kind of research electronically, since once you find a case that does look useful, electronic citators enable you to click through to the full text of the citing case. Both KeyCite, on Westlaw, and Shepards on Lexis provide the case names of the citing cases, and KeyCite also provides signals about the substantiality of the citation. Shepards in print, by contrast, only provides the bare citation, without even a name. In order to retrieve the maximum number of cases, you should consider conducting your research in both KeyCite and Shepards (when both are available to you), since they return overlapping but not identical lists of cases.

Both Shepards (in print and on Lexis) and KeyCite (on Westlaw) provide information about which portion of the earlier case is the reason for the subsequent citation, based on headnote numbers of the original case. All three citators also provide some judgment as to the purpose of the citation for some citing cases, but you must not rely on these. The rules that the citators apply in order to arrive at these characterizations have led to individual choices with which few researchers would agree. Notoriously, *Shepard's United States Citations* indicated online at least as late as 1993 that the 1954 landmark case *Brown v. Board of Ed.* merely "questioned" the 1896 *Plessy v. Ferguson*, rather than overruled it. The print Shepards had changed the characterization of *Brown* only in 1987.

Table 5.B: Some Examples of Non–West Subject Indexes to Cases

Subject indexing of cases can be found not only in the standard digests, but also in many treatises, looseleaf services, and indexes to specialized reporters.

1. *Digest of United States Supreme Court Reports, Lawyers' Edition*, Charlottesville, Virginia: LexisNexis

   The companion digest to *United States Supreme Court Reports, Lawyers' Edition*, long a part of the Lawyers' Cooperative Publishing family of interconnected publications, uses a different system of subject headings.

2. *Housing Court Reporter Consolidated Index*, Vestal, New York: Treiman Publications

   Highly specialized subject indexing to a set of case reports concerned with a practice local to New York.

3. *PUR Digest, 4th Series*, Vienna, Virginia: Public Utilities Reports

   Subject indexing to the *Public Utilities Reports, Fourth Series* in a familiar digest format, but with a specialized subject classification system developed continually since 1915 to cover this particular area of the law.

4. James H. Pannabecker, *Banking Law Journal Digest*, Arlington, Virginia: A.S. Pratt & Sons

   Another specialized index to cases, covering decisions appearing in *The Banking Law Journal* and some important ones published elsewhere. Looseleaf format.

5.10   FINDING CASES BY NAME

In the course of your case law research, you may encounter a case name without a citation. Finding a case online by its name is just a matter of typing as much of the name as you know into the name field in an appropriate case law database. If you really know nothing about the case other than its name, this is one of the most appropriate uses for the expensive megafiles that cover all case law.

In print, you use a digest to find a case by name. Each West digest contains a Table of Cases (a name index of cases in alphabetical order by the principal named plaintiff or appellant) and a Defendant–Plaintiff Table (alphabetical index reversing the order of the names in the Table of Cases). If you don't know the jurisdiction you will have to use the Tables of Cases in the Decennial Digests and the unwieldy (because non–cumulating) *General Digest*. One exception to the general rule that you must use a digest to look up a citation by case name is presented by the *L.Ed. Quick Case Table*, a freestanding table of cases published annually as a name index to the headnoted cases in the *United States Supreme Court Reports (Lawyers' Edition)*.

If the only citation you have is a nickname for the case (e.g., "the Sick Chicken Case"), a proper citation for it should be easily obtainable by using the nickname as a search term in a full text law review or case law database. Non–electronically, *Shepard's Acts and Cases by Popular Names* includes some cases by "popular name."

5.11   FINDING CASES BY CITATION

Most case citations follow the straightforward and easy to use format of volume number followed by reporter abbreviation followed by initial page number. But beyond these most common citations, you are sure to encounter some others that require more interpretation. In order to follow your research trails where they ought to go, you will have to learn to work with these more unfamiliar citations. Do not write them off as unimportant! One of these might well turn out to be the most significant case on your point.

Most standard citations to American cases follow fairly predictable patterns. A reporter name given simply as an abbreviated or full name of a jurisdiction will be the official reporter for the cases of the jurisdiction's highest court (e.g., ___ U.S. ___, ___ Mich. ___, etc.). A citation to a state's name followed by the word "Reporter" usually indicates a commercially–published set of reports, which may include cases from lower courts as well as the state's highest court. Where the reporter name is the last name of a person, you are usually dealing with early reports published in what are called "nominative reporters" (or, in England, "nominate" reporters).

5.12 NOMINATIVE AND OTHER UNFAMILIAR REPORTERS

Nominative reporters bear the names of their court reporters or editors rather than the jurisdictional names that later became standard. Pre–1874 United States Supreme Court cases, for example, were published in series known as Dallas, Wheaton, etc. (abbreviated Dall., Wheat., and so forth). When a citation includes only this nominative reporter name, you may need to get the equivalent citation in the standard set (such as the *United States Reports*) into which these early volumes were later incorporated. Typing the nominative citation into the function that retrieves by citation in an electronic case law database will bring up all the equivalent citations in the standard reporters.

If you are working non–electronically with a nominative citation, you can ascertain the jurisdiction involved by looking up the abbreviation in a dictionary of legal abbreviations. Then, consult the *Bluebook* for that jurisdiction to see if a modern citation should also exist for that case, and if so, what the volume equivalents in the modern set will be. This same approach can be used wherever you do not recognize the abbreviation comprising the middle element in a case citation. Specialized case reporters exist to cover particular subject areas, and while some of these may be included in Westlaw and Lexis, and therefore be directly retrievable by citation without knowing the actual name of the reporter, some may not. For these, resort to a legal abbreviation dictionary **(see Table 4.C)** is your best bet.

5.13 DOCKET NUMBERS

Sometimes the problem is not an odd reporter name, but no reporter name. Probably most common among non–reporter citations are docket numbers. When a case has not been published, it may be cited by the identifying information that the court has assigned it within its own record keeping system. Typically, one of these docket numbers can be recognized because it includes a date component and then a sequential number assigned to the case as it was received into the court's workload. This number usually remains the same from the start of the court's involvement with the case.

The most familiar docket numbers are probably those for the United States Supreme Court, since the high level of interest in Supreme Court cases from their outset means that people want to find information about their progress through the Court long before they are eventually published. However, while a docket number in a Supreme Court citation means only that at the time of citation the case had not yet been published (and quite possibly not even decided yet), a docket number citation for a lower court case (especially a citation long after the date of the case) may mean that the case was never published.

The first step in tracking down a case cited by docket number is to ascertain whether the case was in fact eventually published. The easiest way to do this is to run a name search in Westlaw or Lexis. The name used in the docketed version of the case may vary from the name in the published version, so if the fielded name search comes up empty, you should try both whatever names you have and the docket number itself as search terms in the appropriate full text case law databases. For recent cases, you can see if the court's own web site or a clearinghouse web site like Pacer has the case listed by docket number. If all else fails, you can call the court to see if you can obtain a copy of the case from the court's records. If the court cannot provide the records, ask who was the winning attorney, and try to contact them for a copy **(see Table 14.A)**.

5.14   OTHER CITATION WRINKLES

Occasionally you may find a citation to a case published in a non–legal newspaper. Since in the United States this is almost never the only place that a case important enough to warrant such placement will be published, you should always check to see if the case has also been published in a reporter. Other much more common non–reporter citations include generic Westlaw or Lexis citations, and medium–neutral citations, all of which are designed to identify materials without respect to where they appeared in print. You can work directly with the former only in the database for which they were devised, although if the case is not that new you can try to pull up a parallel cite in a law review database by using the citation that you do have as a search term in a full text search. The medium–neutral cites should be retrievable in both systems, and also in the court's own website or the web site for the state law library of the state in which the court sits.

A few other tricky points can arise with respect to even standard citations. Sometimes more than one case will begin on a given page of a reporter. When this happens, you will get multiple hits with the same citation when you use the citation–based retrieval feature in the legal databases. When it comes time to run the case through a citator, you need to be sure to pick the right set of citing references. Electronic citators will point out the situation to you, and ask you to specify (by choosing from a list of names) which case you want researched. In the print Shepard's citators, this situation is handled by having two separate lists of citations, each of which sports the same page number, but with a distinguishing case number and/or name at the head of each list.

If a cite is faulty or incomplete, electronic searching usually will enable you to overcome the deficiency. If some component of the citation is missing, use what you have as a full text search term, in conjunction with any other information you have about the case. One common error in citation is transposition of the numbers, so if you don't have anything except a string of numbers, try them in differing positions. Also, check to see if all elements of the citation are consistent (e.g., volume number with date, reporter with jurisdiction).

5.15　USING INDEXED AND FULL–TEXT SEARCHING TOGETHER: THE HEART OF THE CASE RESEARCH PROCESS

The single most common fault in case law research is the failure to pursue leads from one search method into another. The optimal process for doing case law research from scratch will usually involve going back and forth repeatedly between full text searching and the use of subject indexes. When you first start out and have no idea what indexing terms apply to your situation, a fishing expedition in full text is an excellent way to get started. Use a subject–targeted subset of the case law database, if you know enough to select the appropriate one.

Once you have found a good case via any method you should examine its subject headings (the Key Numbers or concepts assigned to it) and look at other cases under those headings. Those cases are likely to have additional subject headings, some of which may be relevant, and should be pursued in turn. For some sources that are indexed by more than one publisher (e.g., the *Supreme Court Digest* and the *United States Supreme Court Digest Lawyers' Edition*), you can proceed within one system from a subject heading to a case with that subject heading, and then jump to that same case in another system, and follow up on the different subject headings it has been assigned in the second system. Within the cases that you find, you will learn of other terms and phrases that you should use as new full–text search terms. And for every case that you find during this multi–stage process, you can proceed to look both at the cases which it cites (simplified by automated functions on both Westlaw and Lexis), and at the cases that cite to it.

Throughout the process you should use one method as a way to enlarge upon and to verify the completeness of the work done via another method. When you do a full text search, are you coming up with the same (and *only* the same) indexing terms in the cases that you retrieve? When you do an indexed search, are you coming across new language to use as search terms in full text searching? Remember that indexing takes some time, so to ensure the currency of your research you should as a final step do a date limited full text search, based on everything you have learned, since it will include as yet unindexed material. The multitude of ways that you can find cases, and the myriad trails that can lead out from any case as a starting point, can confuse you mightily unless you keep track of where you've been. A research log is more vital here than anywhere else in the research process!

5.16　RESEARCHING THE AUTHORITY FOR WHAT SEEMS LIKE A HOARY OR EVEN SELF–EVIDENT WELL–ESTABLISHED PRINCIPLE

Seeking authority for a legal chestnut can sometimes be challenging, because of the sheer volume of cases relying on the principle or because the origins of the doctrine are shrouded in the mists of legal time. One way to address this problem is to find an early Supreme Court or a landmark Court of Appeals case, plus a recent case: this puts you into a position to say that the doctrine has been upheld "... at least from [old case] to [recent case] ..." Full text searching should include the exact phrase in which the well–established doctrine is optimally expressed.

Other ways to approach this task are to resort to secondary sources which offer summaries of the law, backed up with case authority. Restatements, treatises, and encyclopedias (see Chapter Six) will be helpful here, as collections of maxims may be. *Black's Law Dictionary* supports some of its legal definitions with case citations. When, on the other hand, it falls to you to argue *against* such a well–established principle you will need first to establish the authority for the principle (in order to delimit it), and then to distinguish it. Your goal will be to find multiple cases that resemble your facts, and where the judge decided that the hoary principle does not apply.

5.17   PROVING THE NEGATIVE

The person in charge of evaluating a potential case, advising a client prospectively, or devising a defense needs to know what is *not* out there. Background defensive research, for instance, needs *always* to be thorough. When proving a negative, the research log (in conjunction with your professional conclusion) is your main contribution to the enterprise. It enables you to convey concisely and logically where you looked and for what, which provides the building blocks for proving the negative. As you proceed with your research, maintain a list of cases distinguished, and the grounds on which you distinguished them.

5.18   WHEN TO STOP

As you approach the completion of your case law research, you should feel like you are at a cocktail party, scanning the crowd for new faces. You should keep at it until all the case names you meet that are still pertinent to your situation in terms of fact or law are like old friends (or enemies). Actually, coming yet again upon cases that you've known about for a long time through their mention in a fresh case can also be illuminating, as when a new acquaintance tries to introduce one of your own old friends to you. It's always interesting to compare others' perceptions against your own. At first it's probably safer if you think "My goodness, all this time I had no *idea* that you were really a Syldavian prince in exile ..." But as these encounters multiply, you'll start to know when to give in to your initial impulse when confronted with a familiar mug: "Ah, he's pulling your leg—he's no prince, he's only Joey from next door!" Once you find that each new case you are turning up is too remote from your research problem to be considered relevant, you should review your research log and your research plan, to make sure that all the paths you planned to go down have been thoroughly explored. Now it's time to evaluate and work with what you have found.

5.19 FEDERAL CASE LAW

Our federal system, with all its layers of courts and its different claims to jurisdiction, makes working with case law uniquely complex. All the different types and layers of judicial expression have their uses, and the legal researcher needs to keep in mind when to focus on what. In the remainder of this chapter, we will focus on the federal court system as an example, with remarks on state case law only as significant differences make it necessary to do so.

5.20 SUPREME COURT CASES

Since the decisions of the Supreme Court of the United States are definitive and binding on all federal courts, every researcher must ascertain the very latest position taken by the Court on all issues pertaining to the subject of the research. Old Supreme Court cases are also vitally important, even where they vary from the current position, since they show trends in the development of the Court's doctrine over time, providing fodder for analysis and for predictions of further future developments.

Sometimes old cases are all there is to find. Many subject areas of the law rarely reach the Supreme Court level of deliberation, e.g., commercial sub–areas that typically involve small monetary stakes, the kinds of cases that are too time–sensitive to wait for Supreme Court action, or areas that rely only on well–settled legal principles. For these areas (as well as for very narrowly defined issues that do not come up often), the leading Supreme Court case can be a century old. The problem for the researcher in these areas is to work with the huge body of progeny engendered by old but still valid Supreme Court cases. One solution which often works is to start at both ends and meet up in the middle, i.e., use that old Supreme Court case and a new local case relying on it, without necessarily referring to much or anything in between.

The Supreme Court's position of authority makes any indication of its thinking useful to the researcher. Most important, of course, since they invoke *stare decisis* as well as an indication of the court's thinking, are the Court's opinions **(see Table 5.C)**. The best support you could possibly find for your proposition is a unanimous Supreme Court opinion in your favor from a currently valid case. Second best would be a majority opinion. An opinion joined by a plurality of the justices is pretty good, too! You can still make some hay from a concurring opinion, and even (depending on the identity of the dissenter and the subsequent development of jurisprudence on the matter) from a dissenting opinion. *Per curiam* decisions, unsigned and usually short (although not always unanimous) appear in the same places that publish full dress opinions and are useful if nothing else as a full stop to the appellate controversy below, as is also the case with denials of certiorari and other unsigned memorandum orders.

In all print and online versions of the Court's opinions, the text of each opinion is preceded by a syllabus (synopsis of the majority opinion and the court's decision) prepared for the convenience of researchers by the Court's Reporter of Decisions. Since these syllabi are in the public domain, unlike the headnotes commonly prepared for published (and some unpublished) court opinions by commercial publishers, they have been taken up by the online legal research community as a useful set of data which can be freely and efficiently searched for subject access to Supreme Court cases, with many sites linking to the Legal Information Institute of Cornell Law School (http://supct.law.cornell.edu/supct/) to do so. Commercially–edited versions of the Court's opinions are preceded by an editorially–produced summary and headnotes, as well as by the official syllabus. The *United States Supreme Court Reports (Lawyers' Edition)* and the Lexis version of the opinions based on it (library and file = GENFED;USLED) includes summaries of each concurring and dissenting opinion, as well as of the opinion of the Court. Other publishers of the Supreme Court opinions simply note the existence and authorship of these minority opinions.

The headnotes, next in the prefatory material, are consecutively numbered editorial summaries of legal points discussed in the case, couched to a great extent in the language of the opinion itself; their numbers are inserted into the case to permit location within the opinion of each point discussed. Each headnote is assigned a subject heading (e.g., a West key number in the *Supreme Court Reporter*) and the headnotes then constitute the basis for the subject indexing of the case. As with the syllabi, the condensed and summarizing nature of the headnotes makes them an excellent field for online searching for legal concepts.

The opinion itself begins with the opinion adopted by the court. This opinion is the only one that receives headnotes in the commercially–edited versions of the reports; neither concurring nor dissenting opinions receive any subject indexing. Looking for treatment of a topic in these minority opinions requires doing a field limited full–text search restricted to concurring or dissenting opinions.

Table 5.C: Sources of SCOTUS Opinions

As befits their importance as a seminal source of the law, SCOTUS output is readily available from a variety of sources.

Standardly–cited report series:

1. *United States Reports*. Washington, D.C., U.S. Government Printing Office

   The official reports, citation to which is required (if case appears therein) by *Bluebook* T.1. All but the few most recent volumes are available as .pdf files in Hein Online's U.S. Supreme Court Library (a web subscription database).

2. *Supreme Court Reporter*. St. Paul, Minnesota: Thomson/West

   The reports with Key Numbers, tied into the West American Digest System. Also on Westlaw (Database = **SCT**).

3. *United States Supreme Court Reports, Lawyers' Edition*. Charlottesville, Virginia: LexisNexis

   Also on Lexis (Library and File = **GENFED;USLED**).

4. *United States Law Week*. Washington, D.C.: Bureau of National Affairs

   In addition to the complete text of opinions (often the first print version to appear), has docket information and status reporting on pending cases. Also on Lexis (Library and File = **BNA;USLW**), on Westlaw (Database = **BNA–USLW**), and as a subscription database accessed via the Web (http://www.bna.com/).

   Other access:

5. Findlaw: Supreme Court Opinions (free searching of opinions back to 150 U.S.–)

   http://www.findlaw.com/casecode/supreme.html

6. Loislaw: U.S. Supreme Court Reports

   http://www.loislaw.com/   or   http://www.loislawschool.com/ (for law students)

   Lots of fields to which you can restrict your search.

7. LexisOne: U. S. Supreme Court Opinions (free searching of opinions back to 1790)

   http://www.lexisone.com/

8. Supreme Court of the United States, Opinions.

   http://www.supremecourtus.gov/opinions/opinions.html

   This web page also has a link to a .pdf document entitled "Where to Obtain Supreme Court Opinions," which gives additional sources. The Court does not consider its electronic opinions official.

Because of the broad significance of Supreme Court jurisprudence, materials other than the Court's actual judicial opinions are quite widely available. The records and briefs filed with the Court **(see Table 5.D)** may be significant to the legal researcher for a number of reasons. The information they contain may illuminate the Court's decision or its reasoning, and thus be helpful in interpreting the significance of a particular opinion. The same could be said of the oral arguments heard by the Court **(see Table 5.E)**. More fundamentally, the record filed with the Court may contain the only version of the trial court's opinion outside the unpublished courthouse records of the court below.

The legal researcher will also want to ensure that she understands the jurisprudential context of any Supreme Court case, e.g., what circuit splits preceded Supreme Court action, or what other reasons prompted the Court to take the case. Other background information to particular cases that would be of interest to the legal researcher would include the political background to the case (think of the Nixon cases, or the Election 2000 case), and where the case fits in to the personal background of individual justices. A wealth of such information is available, e.g., in books about individual justices and on the websites of various watchdog groups, but it does start to exit the realm of legal research.

5.21   THE UNITED STATES COURTS OF APPEALS

At the next level down from the United States Supreme Court, the cases are more numerous and less authoritative. Since there can be disagreements between courts at this level, the researcher needs to be prepared to argue on various levels for the correctness of one court versus another. You will want to take into account that not all circuits are created equal for all purposes. There are subject–specific circuits, whose expertise is respected above that of other circuits in a given legal area. For example, the Fifth Circuit, which includes prominent maritime ports and industries, takes a more prominent role in the definition of admiralty law than does the Tenth Circuit. There are also powerhouse circuits, whose general volume and level of work enhances the level of jurisprudential prestige attached to its decisions (the Second Circuit comes to mind). Note also that the Federal Circuit, created in 1982, has subject–defined jurisdiction, combining the jurisdiction of the former U.S. Court of Customs and Patent Appeals and the U.S. Court of Claims with authorization to hear appeals of patent cases tried in the federal district courts and appeals from certain federal administrative boards.

Table 5.D: Selected Sources for SCOTUS Records and Briefs

1. Findlaw: Supreme Court Briefs. Coverage begins with 1999–2000 Term.

   http://supreme.lp.findlaw.com/supreme_court/briefs/index.html

2. Westlaw: All Databases > U.S. Federal Materials > Federal Cases & Judicial Materials > United States Supreme Court Briefs Multibase (Database = **SCT–BRIEF–ALL**). "All" means all briefs present on Westlaw, which is a selection beginning in 1870.

3. Lexis: Legal > Cases–U.S. > U. S. Supreme Court Briefs (Library and File = **GENFED;BRIEFS**). Coverage begins in 1979.

4. The Making of Modern Law: U.S. Supreme Court Records and Briefs, 1832–1978.

   Fully searchable text and image database, produced by Thomson/Gale, distributed by subscription to libraries.

5. *Landmark Briefs and Arguments of the Supreme Court of the United States.* Gerhard Casper and Kathleen M. Sullivan, editors.

   Coverage begins in 1793.

   Additionally, many large law libraries have collections of Supreme Court Records and Briefs on microfiche, and some may have bound collections in hard copy. Consult library catalogs for details.

Table 5.E: Selected Sources for SCOTUS Oral Arguments

1. The Oyez Project. Audio files of oral arguments before the United States Supreme Court.

    http://www.oyez.org

2. United States Supreme Court. Argument Transcripts. These are produced by the Alderson Reporting Company under contract to the Supreme Court. Coverage begins in October Term 2000.

    http://www.supremecourtus.gov/oral_arguments/
    argument_transcripts.html

3. Westlaw: All Databases > U.S. Federal Materials > Federal Cases & Judicial Materials > Judicial Materials > Transcripts of U.S.Supreme Court Oral Arguments (Database = **SCT–ORALARG**)

    Coverage begins in October Term 1990.

4. Lexis: Legal > Federal Legal–U.S. > Supreme Court Cases & Materials > United States Supreme Court Transcripts (Library and File = **GENFED;USTRAN**)

    Coverage begins in October Term 1979.

5. *Landmark Briefs and Arguments of the Supreme Court of the United States*. University Publications of America. Gerhard Casper and Kathleen M. Sullivan, editors.

    Coverage begins in 1793.

6. *Oral Arguments of the U.S. Supreme Court*

    Microfiche set published by CIS/LexisNexis. Coverage is comprehensive from the most recently completed term back to 1969–70 term, and includes all arguments that were transcribed from 1953–54 term through the 1968–69 term.

Moreover, neither are all types of decisions created equal. While the Supreme Court justices all weigh in on each case for which an opinion is issued, most cases in the Courts of Appeals are heard only by a three judge panel. Occasionally a case is brought before a larger conclave of judges (in most circuits, all court of appeals judges for that circuit) for hearing or rehearing *en banc*, and that fact should be indicated parenthetically (see *Bluebook* Rule 10.6.1. for other factors which structurally affect the weight of a decision's authority). And, of course, different judges have different judicial histories, making for different reputations and different levels of prestige and influence.

The opinions of the Courts of Appeal are widely available **(see Table 5.F)**, but not to the duplicative extent that Supreme Court opinions are available. In print they are published unofficially only, by West. The courts select less than 25 percent of their opinions for publication; those cases selected currently appear in the *Federal Reporter, 3rd Series*. These published cases are the ones singled out by the courts as cases which can be cited unreservedly as precedential. Other opinions released by the Courts of Appeal but not so selected, which in earlier years would have been unpublished, are now "reported" by West (though still unpublished by the courts) in their *Federal Appendix*, and appear in Westlaw and Lexis. They are covered by both KeyCite and Shepards. The *Federal Appendix* cases, like the published cases, get headnotes and key numbers assigned to them, and appear in the *West's Federal Practice Digest 4th*. While in 2006 the Supreme Court promulgated a rule obliging all federal appeals courts to permit citation of unpublished opinions, the precedential value accorded these cases varies as to circuit. If you find such a case to be significant to your situation, you will need to research the current status of this issue in your jurisdiction.

Court of Appeals opinions, since they review a lower court action, accompany a decision to uphold, reverse, or remand that lower court action. Even more often than with the Supreme Court, a published Court of Appeals case can involve review of a case below that was not itself selected for publication. For that reason, as well as for explicative background, you may wish to obtain the records and briefs filed with the Court of Appeals. However, the records and briefs at this level of the court system **(see Table 5.G)** are nowhere nearly as readily available as are Supreme Court records and briefs, and you may be just as well off going back to the trial court for a copy of the opinion below as seeking it out via the Court of Appeals record. Other relevant background information would include circuit splits over the issue at hand. Until 2004, BNA's *U.S. Law Week* offered a helpful "Circuit Split Roundup" as a periodic feature of its Legal News section. Currently you can search the text of the electronic version for the words "circuit split" to get at this handy information. For progeny of a Court of Appeals case, refer to KeyCite or Shepards (*Shepard's Federal Citations*, in print).

Table 5.F: Selected Sources for Federal Courts of Appeal Cases

1. *West's Federal Reporter, Third Series,* and its predecessors (See *Bluebook*). St. Paul, Minnesota: Thomson/West.

2. *West's Federal Appendix.* St. Paul, Minnesota: Thomson/West

   Cases not selected for publication by the courts.

3. Westlaw: All Databases > U.S. Federal Materials > Cases & Judicial Materials (Databases: various)

4. Lexis: Legal > Cases–U.S. (Files: various)

5. Lois: Search within circuits or recent Court of Appeals cases.

   http://www.loislaw.com/ or http://www.loislawschool.com/ (for law students)

6. Administrative Office of the U.S. Courts: Court Links (takes you to the websites for each Circuit).

   http://www.uscourts.gov/links.html

Table 5.G: Selected Sources of Court of Appeals Records and Briefs

1. Westlaw: All Databases > U.S. Federal Materials > Briefs > Briefs by Circuit

    (Database = **CTA–BRIEF** and subsets)

    Coverage varies between circuits.

2. Michael Whiteman and Peter Scott Campbell, *A Union List of Appellate Court Records and Briefs: Federal and State.* Littleton, Colo.: F.B. Rothman, 1999.

3. Pacer: Public Access to Court Electronic Records.

    http://pacer.psc.uscourts.gov/

    Pay as you go access to the electronic records systems of individual federal courts.

5.22 UNITED STATES DISTRICT COURTS

When we get down to the trial level of the federal District Courts, the cases' greater abundance and lesser authority both contribute to a smaller proportion of them being published than with the decisions of higher courts **(see Table 5.H)**. Because of the multiplicity of judges and cases, you may well have to limit your search by criteria other than subject and jurisdiction at the outset. Ideally, you would like to find decisions by a particular judge, your judge. This can readily be done in Westlaw, Lexis, and Lois by including a name limitation in the judge field.

Additionally, many case reporters devoted to specialized subjects include district court opinions that are unreported in the Federal Supplement. These include some reporters which appear online as well, on Westlaw and/or Lexis and/or a freestanding web–based product, such as BNA's *United States Patent Quarterly*.

Even if you can't find an appropriate opinion written by the judge assigned to your case, you can pick out a case from that judge's pool of colleagues, by sorting your results by subdivisions of jurisdiction not evident from the reporter title (e.g., individual Districts, in the Federal District Courts). This information occurs in the case citation, so adding a distinctive term from the jurisdiction name as a further restriction to your retrieved results should achieve the desired results. In print digests, the cases are listed in subdivision order within each jurisdiction, so scanning the results can achieve the same ends as the electronic sorting does.

Your interest may focus on trying to find cases by your judge (or one of her near colleagues) that concerned a procedural posture similar to your own. A recitation of the case's procedural posture usually occurs toward the beginning of the opinion, so doing a proximity search requiring a maximum distance between a key word or phrase from the posture (e.g., summary judgment) and a key word from the citation (e.g., a distinctive word from the name field) should do the trick. Since a field may have been added at the beginning of the case specifying the procedural posture (e.g., a Key Number or Core Concept), you should also do a search of that field.

Another way to narrow down your selection of cases is to consider the subject expertise of individual judges. This can be determined by, for example, their contributions to the secondary literature, and by their citation as expert by the Court of Appeals, both of which can also readily be determined by electronic searching. Sometimes you may be able to obtain statistical information about a judge's affirmance rates on a particular issue. You may also wish to consider whether an opinion was written by a Senior Judge, or a judge in some other way not in the mainstream of the district's judicial activity.

The volume of cases produced by the federal district courts means that you will want to try to find a case that's ideal on your very particular set of facts. In the fact–rich set of data that comprises the output of the federal district courts, you can begin to look by executing a Boolean search with key words from your fact pattern (e.g. "banana peel" and "grocery store" and "slipped"); you don't even have to supply the legal term "negligence", but will learn it from reading the cases this search brings up. As with all case law searching, you will want to select distinctive words, especially terms of art, once you get to the point of including legal concepts in your search.

Even though there is a general reporter for federal district court cases (currently the *Federal Supplement 2d*, published by West), subject–specific reporters play a larger role in the reporting of district court cases than they do for higher courts. Inclusion in specialized reporters permits the publication of cases involving many different fact patterns within that special area, even with little variation in the legal concepts expounded.

5.23   STATE CASE LAW

For the most part, the states mirror the federal court system in having more elaborate reporting available of the output of the highest courts, and less coverage of the lower courts. With fifty state jurisdictions (and the District of Columbia), some sort of road map to the structure of the state courts will prove invaluable in research into the case law of unfamiliar states. Not only can the names of the courts vary wildly between states (e.g., in New York the "Supreme Court" is a trial level court), but the court system structures vary as well (e.g., some jurisdictions have appellate courts of limited jurisdiction, such as criminal appeals). Useful comparative sketches of those structures are available in print reference guides (such as the annual *Want's Federal–State Court Directory)*, and a wealth of information about state courts is offered on the courts' websites. The *Bluebook* itself is a handy source for information about the reports of different states, and research guides for individual states can offer more detail than you are likely to need **(see Appendix)**.

One aspect of state case law research that occasionally requires attention is to discern which reporter amongst the several which may be available enjoys "official" status for *Bluebook* purposes. The current *Bluebook* (18th edition) mandates different rules on state case law citation for practitioners citing state cases to courts in the cases' state of origin than it does for all other legal writers. The former group are referred to local citation rules, which may require a parallel citation to the state's official reporter. The latter group is obliged to cite to the regional reporter, and to a medium–neutral citation (a citation based on court of origin and filing order, rather than on publication in a reporter)

Table 5.H: Selected Sources of Federal District Court Cases

1. *West's Federal Supplement, Second Series,* and its predecessors (see *Bluebook*). St. Paul, Minnesota: Thomson/West. Note that before the inception of the first *Federal Supplement,* district court cases were published in the *Federal Reporter.*

2. *Federal Rules Decisions.* St. Paul, Minnesota: Thomson/West.

3. Westlaw: All Databases > U.S. Federal Materials > Federal Cases & Judicial Materials (Databases: various). You can choose between reported and unreported decisions, between older and newer cases, and so forth.

4. Lexis: Legal > Cases—U.S. (Files: various) You can search for district court cases by circuit, and choose between different date ranges.

5. Administrative Office of the U.S. Courts: Court Links (takes you to the websites for each District, some of which have opinions posted).

   http://www.uscourts.gov/links.html

6. Pacer: Public Access to Court Electronic Records

   http://pacer.psc.uscourts.gov/

   Pay as you go access to the electronic records systems (some including opinions) of individual federal courts.

if available in either of those. If not, the researcher is to follow the detailed order of preference set out in Rule 10.3.1 and in the Table T.1, which usually gives preference to official sources in those instances where neither a medium–neutral nor a regional citation is available.

Some jurisdictions publish their own case reports, especially for the state's top court. Others contract this job to a private publisher, designating that publication as official. In some cases, where the state has designated the West reporter as official, this means that the West regional reporter is the only physically published source for a state's case law. As more states turn to medium–neutral citation and publish their own cases on their websites, the same issue that we saw in connection with physical distribution of session laws comes to mind. Without wide distribution of a physically fixed text, how can the authenticity and reliability of the cited text be assured? It will be interesting to see how this concern plays out as medium–neutral citation becomes more widespread.

Where there is a state–specific reporter, you should be aware of its relationship to the West regional reporter that covers that jurisdiction. Aside from Bluebooking requirements, your choice of reporter will have consequences for your follow–up work if you will need to work with Shepard's in print. Since the different versions of a report are covered separately in print Shepard's, the different coverage in terms of citing sources and the different cutoff dates at any one time of the Shepard's for the different versions of your case mean that you must Shepardize all parallel versions of your case to ensure the maximum number of results. Happily, the electronic citators have eliminated this issue by merging the citations for all versions of a cited case. You would still need to consider using both KeyCite and the online Shepards to ensure the maximum possible coverage of citations to your case, since results lists can vary between the two services.

Although proper citation form has long required citation to the regional reporters, it may happen that a citation you come across is lacking that mandatory component. The non–electronic researcher in state law may need to be able to get from an official citation to a regional citation, particularly when tracking down a case from another state, so as to be able to use the more widely–owned regional reporter. One way to do this is through the initial listing of the case in Shepard's (print) Citations. If the Shepards covering the official reporter in question is not available, you can use the *National Reporter Blue Book*, published by West since 1938 (and unrelated to the *Bluebook* of citation). Within its pages (blue in the original volume, but, alas, pedestrian white in the supplements) are strictly numerical tables which translate official reporter citations into their parallel citations in West's National Reporter System (the regional reporters plus the *New York Supplement* and the *California Reporter*).

For state cases that fly below the radar of the official reporters and the National Reporter System, a variety of local publications sometimes step in to fill the breach. Typically, by virtue of the courts generating these cases, these will not appear in the general state case law databases on Westlaw and Lexis unless specifically selected for publication by the courts. Legal newspapers in the major markets often publish cases deemed of local interest only; these are sometimes indexed in separate digests and are sometimes accessible via the newspaper's website or through its file on Westlaw or Lexis. Specialized local reporters have also emerged in some high volume or highly remunerative areas of practice, such as New York City residential real estate. See the individual state research guides for details **(Appendix)**. As with the federal courts, the uses to which cases not selected by the courts for publication may be put varies between jurisdictions. The specific rules of the jurisdiction should be investigated if you are interested in citing such a case.

5.24   UPDATING CASE LAW RESEARCH

The text of a case is not dynamic, but its significance is. As with statutes, you must make sure that no development subsequent to the issuance of an authority upon which you are relying has undercut that authority. In the statutory context, that means repeal, amendment, or replacement. In the case law context you are required to ascertain whether your case is still good law. This involves not only the direct subsequent history of your case, but also what developments in the case's subject matter are going on around it. Subsequent developments affecting your case can emanate from the legislature, the executive, or the judiciary, and the legal researcher should investigate each of these.

The most overt judicial action would be for a superior court to override or uphold the case. This kind of direct history is readily researched by using a citator (i.e., KeyCite or Shepards). Less overtly, the case could be either criticized, cited or ignored. This group of less-directed actions covers a broad spectrum, which can be discerned but not necessarily pinned down precisely by the citators. The case could have been cited a lot—but with what level of enthusiasm? The case could have been left behind, remaining uncited as case law goes off in another direction—but that could merely indicate some factual anomaly that made it an inconvenient vehicle for a doctrine on a roll. The citators are indispensable, but they only get you to where your hard labor of skimming the citing cases begins.

The legislature's most overt act would be to countermand the case by statute. This could have come up in the course of the statutory research with which you began your work. Less overtly, the statutory landscape in which the case originally was born may have changed so much that the facts giving rise to the doctrine which the case announced are no longer likely to occur. This lessens the persuasiveness of the case for modern purposes, and is one reason that recent cases are generally to be preferred.

The executive branch of the government can undercut the effectiveness of a case by not complying with it, or not carrying out the actions it mandates. While in principle these executive actions would be illegal, they are sometimes used as the basis of arguments that the case result is untenable. If there is a case that undercuts your position, research into the real life consequences of that case may cast doubt on that case's vitality as authority.

Your initial indication of a problem with your case (or, on the contrary, its robust good health) could be the status flag that cases now bear in the commercial databases. In print, the only comparable flags have been the "do not cite" labels on California opinions designated "not for publication". Unlike the California labels, however, the status flags in Westlaw and Lexis are dynamic, changing with the advent of new cases or statutes affecting the significance of your case. More detailed information about any judicial or legislative action affecting the case are obtained by using the electronic citators KeyCite and Shepards, or by using Shepards in print.

Some of the citing cases are listed with specific signals about the nature of their citation to your case (see also the discussion of citators as subject research tools in section 5.9 above). These signals are variously assigned by programmed language analysis or by a human reader, and in all cases should not be relied upon. They can be helpful as a starting place for deciding which cases to look at first, but thorough research will have to encompass all cases cited. Some of the signals denote the length of the citing reference (KeyCite's star signals), and some denote the purpose of the citing reference. In the electronic citators you can sort the results so that they display in categories according to the various signals. In the print Shepards you scan the columns of citations to see the lettered signals printed alongside them.

Many citing references get no signal at all, but are merely listed. If this list is long, you will want to sort them out: you want to look at those cases most likely to be significant while you are still fresh and impressionable, not when you are tired of looking at cases and your thinking has started to calcify. Probably the most powerful way to sort them out is to limit by a particular search term within the full text of the citing cases. Adding a term related to the factual setting of your own case or the name of the judge in your own upcoming proceeding can let you start off with a bang. This kind of limiting can obviously only be done in the electronic citators.

Other limiting criteria available include date and jurisdiction of the citing case, and the number of the headnote of your case for which it is cited. All of these limitations are available in print as well as online (although the date limitation is much cruder, since it is attained merely by choosing which volumes of citations to look in). Note one point that is obvious in the print Shepards, but less so in the electronic citators: since not all the citing cases are assigned a specific headnote number as the reason for their citation, limiting a citator search by the relevant headnote will not get you all the potentially relevant cases.

In other legal research tasks, using a print source often provides greater opportunity for productive serendipity than an electronic source can offer. Not so in the use of citators. While Shepards in print offers some coverage not available electronically (see, e.g., section 2.20 above with reference to session law coverage), the electronic services offer so many additional features and so much added convenience that where coverage is not an issue, you will be better off with the electronic option. However, there is one small area in which print Shepards does offer more precise information. When trying to pin down the currency of the information on citing cases, Shepards in print offers a stop cite, akin to that mentioned in section 5.8 above in the discussion of digests. The online citators, by contrast, while usually more up to date than the print, do not offer any specification of the latest date through which citations have been noted. That slight specificity edge of the print product seems unlikely to come up as a significant factor, and the countervailing advantages of the electronic products make them the obvious first choice, in the absence of concerns about budget and cost allocation (and probably even there, given the dramatic time savings they can offer).

Citators do cover a wide range of courts and cases, but where your case is not covered by a citator (e.g., a case from a foreign jurisdiction) you can do a full–text search for its citation in the appropriate case law databases. This search should be done in Boolean mode rather than by using a relevance–based search. Searching the case law databases using a citation as a search term can also be used as a double–check on citator results, especially with regard to date–limited searches for very recent citations which may not yet have been added to the citator.

Chapter 6

INTRODUCING SECONDARY SOURCES: TREATISES AND OTHER OVERVIEWS

6.1 TREATISES

Legal treatises offer narrative exposition and analysis of a whole area of law. While this sounds like (and can indeed often prove to be) a gift from the legal gods, the use of treatises comes with at least a small price. That price is the particular authorial stance of the analysis, an explicit feature of many treatises. Treatises proper are usually the product of an individual, a group of individuals, or a series of individuals, and they generally eschew neutrality about the subjects whose mastery they display in their work. However, the marketplace abounds in treatises and if you don't appreciate or can't use the dominant treatise in your area, you can always look for another one. Unlike relevant primary sources like statutes or cases, you are under no obligation to cite to a treatise. Just don't ignore what a preeminent treatise author has said against your point, since your opponent will not!

The usefulness of treatises resides in the combination of broad scope and scholarly detail that they provide. While law review articles explore a narrow legal topic in depth, treatises cover the field within a substantial area from the most fundamental principles through the most complex and troublesome problems. Many important treatises track a major statute, combining textual and historical analysis of the statute itself with discussion of case law interpretation of each section. Others cover a broad common law subject, typically including analytical comparisons of the law in different jurisdictions **(see Table 6.A)**.

While some treatises include auxiliary practice features such as forms or reprinted selections of primary materials, the main body of the treatise concerns legal researchers in a different way, since it can itself be cited to and by a court. The only way to determine if a treatise has been cited by the courts is via a search of the full text case law databases. To evaluate the esteem in which the courts hold a particular treatise, search on the author's last name (perhaps in proximity to a word from the treatise title) to see how many times the work in question has been cited, and by which courts, and in what fashion. Did the court refer to the treatise as authoritative or otherwise rely on its statement of the law? Add a search term pertaining to your legal issue to see if a court has actually cited the treatise on a point pertinent to the subject of your research.

Westlaw, Lexis, and Lois all offer numerous treatises online, including some of the biggies, e.g., Williston, Nimmer, and Wigmore, respectively. One of the great assets of the Westlaw and Lexis treatise collections is the ability to click through to many of the cited sources. That said, however, print treatises, like so many print sources, make it much easier to see a particular treatise section in its surrounding context. The majority of current treatises are published in print only. Occasionally an older treatise may be useful, and many thousands of them have been digitized in a fully searchable text and image database called The Making of Modern Law: Legal Treatises, 1800–1926, produced and distributed on a subscription basis to libraries by Thomson/Gale.

Print treatises take a number of forms, with particular formats enjoying bursts of popularity at different times. Huge multi-volume treatises tend to be either looseleaf format or hardback with pocket part supplementation. When an individual volume becomes substantially outdated before the others do, it gets replaced. When the whole treatise undergoes a major revision, volumes of the new edition are frequently issued piecemeal, often with completely renumbered contents and volume numbers. As with digests, you will need to find the tables provided by the publisher which convert old citations to the new numbering scheme.

Shorter multi-volume treatises are increasingly published in looseleaf format, and single volume treatises can be either looseleaf, hardback with pocket part, or (especially those with institutional authorship) an annually–revised soft cover book. The "portfolio" format used by, e.g., Tax Management, Inc. treats each topic in a separate pamphlet publication, replacing each one individually as new developments warrant. Each of these formats has its good and bad points from the researcher's point of view. The looseleaf format, for instance, is a problem for someone wanting to investigate what the prevailing view of the law was at some earlier date, a date for which the relevant looseleaf page has already been replaced and tossed in the garbage. Since each update can include changes to the text as well as citations to new cases on old points, looseleaf supplementation makes it all but impossible to track the evolution of this commentary.

The electronic treatises all offer table of contents access as well as full text searching. The print treatises also have tables of contents, of course, and indexes that unfortunately vary quite a bit in their quality. Nonetheless, using a print index, especially one which includes subheadings under index entries, can let you pick your treatise section on the basis of more information than if you had to examine each section that came up in response to a full text search.

Both the tables of contents and the indexes of an increasing number of print treatises are incorporated into a searchable subscription database called IndexMaster (reachable at www.indexmaster.com). Searching this amalgamated index for a search term can get you to an index of a particular treatise, and show you where your term appears in that book, giving you a starting point for your treatise research without looking through dozens of books. One issue when using amalgamated indexes of any sort, including this one, is whether varying terms for the same concept have been pulled together (at least by cross–references) to make the index easier to use and thus more reliable. You should always examine any such index to see if you will need to come up with a lot of synonyms on your own. Another issue is the coverage of the index, in terms of what books are indexed. Index Master, while it lacks the books of a few major publishers like BNA, does contain works from the major treatise publishers.

6.2   RESTATEMENTS OF THE LAW

The Restatements of the Law, introduced to every first–year law student via at least the Restatement of the Law of Contracts, might be described as quasi–institutionally authored treatises. They combine the prestige of their individual editor (the "Reporter") with the leg work and peer–reviewed imprimatur of the American Law Institute. Restatements all contain narrative text synthesizing black letter formulation of the law from the best cases nationally. However, they vary in the degree to which they aim to be normative. In the beginning, way back in 1923, the first Restatements started out to be plain old descriptive of "what the law was". The original undertaking was to be descriptive of the actual prevailing judicial consensus on the matters covered. Subsequent Restatement Second and Third projects, however, have embraced a more prescriptive intention by focusing on those cases considered by the Institute to reflect the "best" interpretation of the law.

Restatements were designed to be persuasive authority: court citations to them can by found in the Appendices to each of the Restatements (and in the predecessor publication to the Appendices, the *Restatement in the Courts*), and in *Shepard's Restatement of the Law Citations*. Since the courts of a particular jurisdiction may have adopted the doctrine announced in an earlier Restatement and then not followed up later by adopting the subsequent Restatement's different doctrine on that point, you should not regard the earlier series as necessarily being superseded.

Table 6.A: Sources for Lists of Prominent Treatises

Kendall F. Svengalis, *Legal Information Buyer's Guide and Reference Manual*. Annual. Westerly, Rhode Island: Rhode Island Lawpress.

Chapter 27, "Legal Treatises & Other Subject Specialty Materials," includes an excellent introduction on the different kinds of treatises, followed by more than 250 pages of evaluative descriptions of treatises grouped under 61 different legal subjects. Includes detailed information on pricing and supplementation, as well as suggestions for alternative ways to update the information in many of the treatises.

Kent C. Olson, *Legal Information: How to Find It, How to Use It*. Phoenix, Arizona: Oryx Press, 1999.

Chapter 4, "Law Books," has a section on treatises that starts out with an engaging history and overview of the world of treatise publication, and goes on (in Table 4–1) to list the real multivolume superstars in the treatise heavens. Highly selective list that truly hits the high points as of 1999, still very helpful in 2006. These are the treatises you will almost certainly be asked if you checked. No descriptions.

Harvard Law School Library, "Legal Treatises by Subject".

http://www.law.harvard.edu/library/services/research/ guides/united_states/basics/legal_treatises_subject.php

Part of a series of research guides, this is another selective list of legal treatises, arranged under 30 major subject headings, many of which differ from Olson's. A few idiosyncratic omissions (e.g., no Williston on Contracts, no Wigmore on Evidence). No descriptions.

William P. Statsky, et al., West's Legal Desk Reference. St. Paul, Minnesota: West Publishing Company, 1991.

This multi–purpose reference book includes more than 450 pages on research sources for particular subjects, including for every subject a very nicely chosen (although obviously at this point not up to date) list of treatises. Still useful for identifying the classics. No descriptions. One peculiarity (for this sort of reference work) is that for each treatise only the author's first initial is given. Some of the subject headings used are a little unexpected, and the cross-references even more so, so do scan the list of them at the beginning of the sequence.

As with any joint legal utterance, the adopted texts of the Restatement were preceded by deliberations; these tentative drafts and other historical underpinnings are available in a variety of formats, and can be used after the fashion of legislative history.

6.3 ENCYCLOPEDIAS

Encyclopedias can be viewed as the stepchildren of treatises. They perform many of the same functions as the latter, but are not accorded the same position or regard. Like treatises, encyclopedias offer narrative exposition and analysis of the law, replete with a full arsenal of statutory and case citations. Unlike treatises, however, they are not the product of a recognized or budding authority, flowing instead from the anonymous editorial staff of a commercial publisher. Encyclopedias do not offer the extensive coverage of any subject that a treatise can, because their scope is broader. Although they point with pride to the number of times they have been cited in judicial opinions, you should not think of the encyclopedias as citeable, but as tools to help you find citeable material.

As with treatises, encyclopedias are produced on a number of different scales. The enormous multivolume general legal encyclopedia, a tremendously popular format in the pre–electronic past, is represented today by two titles: *Corpus Juris Secundum* ("CJS") and *American Jurisprudence, 2d edition* ("AmJur 2d"), both of which are available on Westlaw as well as in print. AmJur2d is also available on Lexis, but sometimes there is a delay in its updating. Each of these two encyclopedias contains articles on legal topics, covered nationally, studded with footnotes, and updated annually with additional references.

Historically, one difference between these two encyclopedias was that AmJur tended to be more selective in its case coverage, while CJS aimed at being more generous with its citations. The relationship between the two has changed recently, however, since they are now both published by West, and it remains to be seen whether these distinctions will continue to hold true. Previously, and throughout most of their run to date, the two sets were produced by rival publishers. That historic rivalry still has consequences for today's legal researcher: prior to 1996, when the owner of AmJur's publisher merged with the publisher of CJS, cross–references in many legal materials to secondary sources like these encyclopedias were limited to citations to that publisher's own products. The *U.S.C.A.*, a West product, would follow a code provision with a section of Library References that included only other West products, like CJS. The *U.S.C.S.*, similarly, would cite to AmJur but not to any West products. Even though the ownership picture has shifted dramatically over the last ten years of American legal publishing, the researcher who wants a full spectrum of secondary cross–references, or one who prefers to use a particular secondary source, needs to be aware of who publishes what. When the interrelationships between the different publications is understood, you will have a clear picture of where to look for citations to which research tools.

Look (e.g., in the sources listed in the **Appendix**) to see if a local encyclopedia exists for the jurisdiction whose law you are researching. Like the national encyclopedias, these multivolume publications offer narrative expositions of state law, integrating discussion of statutory and case law. Some local encyclopedias specialize in a particular area of practice. Shorter, one–volume encyclopedias take a categorized survey approach to particular legal topics.

When starting to use an encyclopedia unfamiliar to you, you should take a moment to evaluate the nature of its editorial stance. Pick a legal subject about which you know a fair amount, and see how you would characterize the way the encyclopedia handles its treatment of that subject. Would you call the treatment simplified? Cautious? Bear your observations in mind when you turn to read what the encyclopedia has to say about matters where you are relying on it for your initial orientation.

6.4 AMERICAN LAW REPORTS: THE ALR

Despite its title, the hybrid *American Law Reports* series ("ALR") is more like an encyclopedia than it is a case reporter. You might think of it as an encyclopedia published in chronological order, as issues arise, rather than in an alphabetical arrangement as are CJS and AmJur. Since 1919, ALR (and before that, its predecessor *Lawyers' Reports, Annotated*) has selected recent cases of significant legal interest and published them each in connection with an essay (by a journeyman author) surveying the law in the area raised by the case. Subject access to the essays is gained by full text searching (on Westlaw and Lexis) or by an elaborate system of index volumes in the print sets.

The ALR essays, called Annotations, usually go into considerable depth in their presentation of the decisional law on the topic covered. A recent Annotation devoted 71 pages and 118 case citations to the subject of damages payable for injury or death of a dog (see 61 ALR5th 635). By contrast, Am Jur's closest comparable entry (4 Am Jur 2d, Animals 165: Liability for Injuries to Animals—Damages Recoverable—Injuries to Dogs) takes up less than a third of a page and includes 15 case citations; the CJS entry (Animals 471: Injuries to or Killing of Animals—Civil Liability—Actions and Proceedings—Damages—For dogs) is four sentences long and has 10 case citations. If you can find a recent ALR Annotation that touches on (or, best of all possible worlds, is devoted to) the topic of your research, it can save you a lot of time and definitely get you pointed in the right direction.

The Annotations do get updated regularly with new case citations. On Westlaw and Lexis the new cases are added to the existing "Jurisdictional Table of Cited Statutes and Cases", even though they are by definition not cited in the annotation. In the print ALR the new cases are of necessity (and more logically) segregated from the annotations:

they are provided via pocket part supplementation in those parts of the series that are currently being updated.

The problem with this updating is that the new cases are being cited to support an idea that might have become beside the point. Annotations go stale, even if they sport updating cases from last week. Each annotation's text is like a snapshot of the current state of decisional law, and, like all snapshots, their freshness starts to fade away immediately. Find out just when the Annotation you are reading first appeared. Since an ALR Annotation, like any secondary source, is only used to get you started on what must eventually become your own professional investigation of the primary legal sources, even a faded Annotation can sometimes still give you a good head start. The problem arises when the law has veered sufficiently away from what it was at the time the Annotation was written to make the whole thrust of the analysis dated. You are generally better off starting off with a fresher viewpoint, either a newer ALR annotation, or perhaps a recent law review article.

Chapter 7

INTRODUCING SECONDARY SOURCES: FORM BOOKS AND JURY INSTRUCTIONS

7.1 FORM BOOKS

In the practice of law, it is often necessary to draft certain kinds of documents over and over again during the course of one's career. If a real estate lawyer wants to work efficiently, he or she develops a collection of forms that can be reused in different but similar transactions. One can reuse the standard organization and clauses, modifying the text with the specifics of each individual transaction. This saves the lawyer a great deal of tedious labor. For an inexperienced lawyer, using a standard form drafted by a more senior lawyer serves to ensure that mistakes are far less likely to be made. Because of the elimination of repetitive work and the confidence that comes from working with a document already successful in another transaction, form books have become an indispensable part of the lawyer's arsenal, and a resource with which every law student should become familiar. Moreover, they can alert the newcomer to some of the legal issues that need to be researched in an unfamiliar kind of transaction.

The publication of legal forms has a long and venerable history in Anglo–American law. In England, one can find centuries-old examples of legal forms. By the time of the reign of the Tudors, the publication of books of forms, or of the inclusion of forms in legal treatises, was widespread and common. Lawyers, practicing as, for example, conveyancers of land or drafters of wills, relied heavily on form books to obviate the need to begin anew for each transaction or document. In America, even during the colonial era, lawyers, justices of the peace, sheriffs and others used printed legal forms for a wide variety of transactions and pleadings.

Today, there are a variety of ways to find and use forms. As we will discuss below, there are a few standard, multi-volume form books in print which cover every aspect of legal practice imaginable, although in a

144

very general way. There are also commercially available electronic collections of forms that serve as word processing templates for the practitioner. Law firms often collect a selection of forms and pleadings their lawyers have drafted over the years. In addition, the web is increasingly becoming a good resource for locating forms, although as with anything found on the web, you have to be very careful to check the reliability of the source.

7.2   A WORD OF CAUTION ABOUT FORMS

Although forms are, and have always been, a great boon and an important labor–saving device for lawyers, a word of caution is in order. Remember that forms are written in response to the requirements of the law in a specific transactional or procedural setting. No matter how seemingly official the source of a form on which you want to rely, you must always check to see that the form comports with all of the requirements of the jurisdiction in which you are practicing. Moreover, you must always investigate to ensure that the form you plan to use is still current. In other words: laws change, rules change, and you have to ensure that the form you intend to use meets the needs of the current version of that law or rule.

No matter the source, you can never substitute reliance on forms for your own research and investigation. Even in a law firm setting, where senior lawyers have drafted the pleadings or forms you want to use, it is incumbent upon you to make sure that you are satisfying the subject matter, currency, and procedural requirements of the situation you currently face.

7.3   GENERAL COLLECTIONS OF FORMS

While it is possible to find collections of forms on even the narrowest of topics, many lawyers prefer to consult the handful of general form sets. These often contain several dozen volumes and are kept current with pocket parts. Each form within such sets will usually be annotated with citations to cases construing the actual language or situation addressed by that form. Most law libraries of any size own one or more of the large sets described below. Most sets focus on either transactional forms (wills, leases, sales of real property, etc.) or on procedural forms (complaints, interrogatories, motions, and other pleadings), and a few of the major sets maintain this distinction, publishing two different collections, divided into a transaction set and a procedural set.

For example, the encyclopedia *American Jurisprudence 2d (AmJur)* (see section 6.3, above), has spun off a number of complementary titles, including two large collections of forms. *American Jurisprudence, Legal Forms, 2d*, is the *AmJur* transactional collection of forms. This set covers a wide variety of transactional topics in more than twenty volumes. The *AmJur* procedure collection is called *American Jurisprudence, Pleading and Practice Forms*. Also more than twenty volumes, this set contains examples of all manner of pleadings and motions forms. Both sets are carefully indexed and annotated. Some portions are available on Westlaw.

A competitor collection is commonly known overall as Nichols Forms. Again consisting of a transactional title and a procedural title, Nichols forms are annotated, kept current with pocket parts, and attempt general coverage of all common forms. The procedural set, *Nichols Cyclopedia of Federal Procedure Forms*, contains annotated forms for motions and pleadings according to the rules of procedure for federal courts. The transactional form set, called *Nichols Cyclopedia of Legal Forms, Annotated*, is probably the better known of the two. This set, which dates back to the 1930s, contains a wide variety of forms for common legal transactions such as wills, deeds, leases, and so on. It is also available on Westlaw.

A newer entrant to the field is *West's Legal Forms, 2d*. This set of mainly transactional forms contains more than thirty volumes, is annotated (by West, and therefore coordinated with other West primary and secondary sources), is thoroughly indexed, and supplemented with pocket parts. Again there is an associated procedural set, *West's Federal Forms*. Unsurprisingly, both of these are also available on Westlaw.

On the web, there is a burgeoning list of free sites where one can find general legal forms. Again, it is absolutely vital to make sure that you can trust the source from which you are getting your forms. One of the better known (and most trustworthy) is Findlaw Forms, at http://www.findlaw.com/16Forms/index.html, which contains state and federal forms (and links to them on other websites) for both procedural and transactional subjects. Another is the 'Lectric Law Library's Law Practice Forms, at http://www.lectlaw.com/form.html. This site contains a wide variety of forms of both major types. A number of law school and university libraries have also begun to collect links to forms, from both official and unofficial sources. One good example is the Forms From The Feds website at the University of Memphis, at http://exlibris.memphis.edu/resource/unclesam/forms.html. This website lists links to dozens of government websites that contain downloadable forms. Not all are relevant to the lawyer, of course, but collections like these can prove very useful. There is no doubt that as time passes more legal forms will be distributed electronically.

7.4   SUBJECT–SPECIFIC COLLECTIONS OF FORMS

In addition to the collections of general forms described above, there are many specialized form books containing forms for use by practitioners in areas as diverse as elder law (*ElderLaw Forms Manual*), securities (*Securities Regulations Forms*), and environmental law (*Environmental Law Forms Guide*). There are dozens more like this, in nearly every area of practice you can imagine. The reliability, currency and authority of these forms is, of course, always a question on which you will have to satisfy yourself before using any of these books.

Do note that there are also collections of forms found as part of many legal treatises. Often, a scholarly treatise will contain an appendix with representative forms. Examples include *International Child Abduction: A Guide to Applying the Hague Convention, with Forms* and *Land Use Practice and Forms: Handling the Land Use Cases*. Often, treatises containing forms will say so in the title, but not always. It is wise, when examining treatises in an area of the law in which you need to conduct research, to note which ones contain forms that might be useful to you later.

7.5 JURISDICTION–SPECIFIC COLLECTIONS OF FORMS

Many specific jurisdictions, usually states, have collections of forms tailored to that jurisdiction's law. Most common are state-specific collections of procedural forms. Among the leading examples are *Carmody-Wait 2d Cyclopedia of New York Practice, With Forms*, a very important encyclopedia of New York procedural practice, and *West's Texas Forms, 2d*, widely used by Texas practitioners.

There is also a wide variety of collections of forms specifically focused on federal procedure. These form books track the federal court rules described in Chapter 10 of this book. Many lawyers rely on these form books to help in drafting motions and pleadings when appearing before federal courts.

7.6 PATTERN JURY INSTRUCTIONS

One last category of form book merits a mention here. In civil and criminal jury trials, part of the judge's task is to instruct the jury on the applicable law before the jury retires to deliberate. It is often the case that the lawyers submit suggested jury instructions to the judge, from which he or she may fashion the instructions to be read. To help facilitate this process, collections of instructions that have already met with judicial approval have been published for many decades. It is now the case that there are pattern jury instruction sets for federal civil and criminal trials, as well as for virtually every state.

These pattern jury instructions can help lawyers and judges craft acceptable and appeal-proof jury instructions. It is the wise litigator who is familiar with the pattern jury instructions in the relevant jurisdiction and subject matter before beginning case preparation. In some sense, the outcome of trials often depends upon how the judge instructs the jury, and the careful lawyer prepares for this phase of the trial from the beginning.

Chapter 8

SOURCES OF ADMINISTRATIVE LAW

8.1 INTRODUCTION TO ADMINISTRATIVE LAW RESEARCH

Traditionally, administrative law has been known as a highly complex field, difficult for the researcher. In this chapter we will discuss the sources of administrative law, the publication patterns of regulations and other documents related to the act of regulating, and show the ways lawyers practicing in heavily regulated areas conduct research and stay current with recent developments. Despite its reputation, research in administrative law is not particularly difficult; however, it does require mastery of techniques not usually taught in the typical first year legal research curriculum.

Broadly speaking, Congress is empowered to do two different things, make laws and delegate lawmaking power to other bodies. That delegated lawmaking is regulation. And to whom is this lawmaking (or, more properly, rulemaking) delegated? Congress delegates this power to executive branch agencies. In fact, several hundred of these agencies are empowered to make regulations. Some agencies are familiar, such as the Internal Revenue Service, the Food and Drug Administration, and the Department of Agriculture. Others are rather more obscure: the Construction Industry Collective Bargaining Commission, the Local Television Loan Guarantee Board, and the Office for Micronesian Status Negotiations, for example.

Congress grants to each of these agencies the power to make and enforce rules on specific and limited topics. As we begin looking at the primary sources of regulation, notice that each unit of regulation contains something called an authority note, a citation to the particular place in the *United States Code* or *United States Statutes at Large* where that agency's authority to regulate on that specific topic was authorized by Congress. This will be discussed more fully in section 8.13 below.

148

Agencies are not free to regulate as they please. It may seem strange to think of representatives of the executive branch performing what is essentially a legislative function. Surely, you might think, our general principle of separation of powers prohibits the executive branch from taking action that is essentially legislative. Constitutional problems, however, are avoided by the fact that Congress retains power to approve, reject or amend any regulation put forward by the regulating agency. In that way the agency is acting as the proxy of Congress, and Congress adopts and approves the regulation as if it had passed through the normal congressional lawmaking process. It may be a strange state of affairs, but this arrangement is a practical solution to an increasingly complex world in need of more oversight and detailed regulation than Congress can provide by itself.

What kinds of rulemaking does Congress delegate to executive branch agencies? What is the difference between the subject matter of federal laws and federal regulations? Can you tell whether a specific subject will be treated in the *United States Code* or the *Code of Federal Regulations*? These questions have no simple answers. In theory, Congress passes laws outlining principles, desired outcomes, general prohibitions and the like, and delegates to agencies the power to make rules to help implement Congressional will. In practice, the division is not so neat. In fact, it is not too much to say that there is no way to know whether any given topic will be dealt with by Congress, by an agency, or both. There are a variety of political, practical, economic and other reasons why Congress makes the choices it does. For the researcher, it is enough to know that in order to thoroughly research any area of federal law it is necessary to look for both federal statutes and federal regulations.

In the following pages we will examine the *Federal Register*, the *Code of Federal Regulations* (or "*CFR*") and other related publications that make up the primary sources of the administrative law world. The patterns of publication in this field should be familiar to you by now. First, there is a publication which tracks the developments of the field in chronological order. In administrative law this chronological publication is the *Federal Register*. Next, owing to the difficulty for the researcher in using the publication of record (with its chronological rather than topical arrangement) to determine what the law is on any topic, someone has to come along to rearrange that chronological material into subject order. In administrative law that subject arrangement is the *Code of Federal Regulations*. Next, there are judicial or quasi-judicial proceedings used to determine the meaning or application of the laws in specific factual situations and/or cases in controversy. Hundreds of executive branch agencies hold such administrative hearings, and the federal courts can review their decisions in certain cases. Finally, there is a wealth of secondary publication used to explain the primary sources, advocate for particular interpretations or changes, serve as student or researcher aids, and so on. Thus, the materials the researcher has at his or her disposal in this field are exactly parallel to the materials used in the legal research subjects we have discussed up to this point. In fact, there are only a small number of ways to arrange and present legal information no matter what the subject matter may be. Administrative law materials, although facially different from more familiar federal statutes and cases, in fact follow the same publication patterns.

With that short introduction as background, let's look at administrative law sources and their use in more detail. First, we will examine the primary sources themselves, dissecting them with an eye toward those specifics which experienced researchers seek out when faced with previously unfamiliar sources. Next, we'll discuss the methods of using those sources to determine what regulations exist, what they mean, how they fit together, and what impact they have on the research at hand. Finally, we will discuss how experienced practitioners in heavily regulated fields actually conduct legal research in their areas of administrative law, how they keep current, and what sources exist to help. That final topic of discussion will introduce you to the looseleaf, the subject of the following chapter, arguably the crowning achievement of the legal publishing world. By the time you've worked through this chapter's primary sources and the methods of their use, you will understand how critically important looseleaf publications are and why they arose in the form they did.

8.2 SOURCES OF ADMINISTRATIVE LAW: THE *FEDERAL REGISTER*

Regulations have been part of the legal landscape from the country's earliest days. Recognizing the need to enlist the executive branch in some facets of rulemaking, Congress delegated certain rulemaking to its sister branch as far back as the 18th century. Until the early decades of the 20th century, however, the publication of executive agency regulations was haphazard and irregular. While this had been no more than a small inconvenience before the New Deal era, at that point the lack of reliable, timely and accurate publication of regulations quickly escalated into an intolerable situation. In several oft-told stories of outrageous lack of governmental oversight, the government itself was unsure of the current state of regulation in particular areas. As currently with the issuers of much municipal regulation (e.g., most city and county building codes), federal agencies before the middle 1930s were under no obligation to publish their regulations. Often, the only accurate copies of regulations then in force were held at the agency offices themselves.

When it eventually became apparent that this state of affairs could not be allowed to persist, Congress passed the first of several acts intended to make the texts of all federal regulations readily available and the patterns of publication transparent to all. The first legislative response to the need for publication of rules, the Federal Register Act, c. 417, 49 Stat. 500 (1935), required the timely publication of all federal regulations.

The resulting publication, the *Federal Register*, has undergone a slow evolution into the publication of today, as the government worked out the details of just what should be published, in what format, and according to what arrangement. The story of this development has been told elsewhere, and is in any case not entirely pertinent to our purpose here, so we will jump ahead a few decades to what might be considered the modern era of the *Federal Register*. Researchers who find themselves conducting research in older regulations can consult Richard J. McKinney's web page "A Research Guide to the Federal Register and the Code of Federal Regulations," at http://www.llsdc.org/sourcebook/fed-reg-cfr. htm. There is nothing particularly difficult about researching older regulations, but one must be prepared to commit a little time to become familiar with older usages and patterns.

The form of the *Federal Register* of today reflects its beginnings and a number of important evolutionary steps along the way. Several other federal laws, aimed at increasing the transparency of the regulatory process, have changed the substance and methodology of the *Federal Register*. Probably the most important piece of legislation in the area of administrative law is the Administrative Procedure Act, c. 324, 80 Stat. 237 (1946). This milestone legislation established the framework for modern administrative practice. The effect of this statute on the publication of federal regulations was profound; most notably, this law required agencies to publish notices of proposed rules in the *Federal Register* in order to give citizens a clearer understanding of the actions of agencies and a better opportunity to participate in the rulemaking itself. The Freedom of Information Act, P.L. 84–487, 80 Stat. 237 (1966), required agencies to publish much more detail about their structures, their activities, their rulemaking, and other information. The Sunshine Act, P.L. 94–409, 90 Stat. 1241 (1976), required agencies to hold open meetings and to publish notices about those meetings. Together, these Congressional acts and the resulting practices of agencies, lawyers and the citizenry at large have resulted in today's *Federal Register*.

The *Federal Register* is published every business day of the year. In it, every federal agency empowered by Congress to make rules of general application must list every action they take, or plan to take, that might add, remove or change regulations. As we will see, this description is only a partial one because a number of things find their way into the *Federal Register* apart from those described above. We will look at the constituent parts of each day's issue in order to understand this most important publication.

In recent years, the publication of the *Federal Register* has been overseen by the Office of the Federal Register, part of the National Archives and Records Administration. Early in the morning of each business day, that current day's *Federal Register* is made available electronically at http://www.gpoaccess.gov/fr/index.html. For sources where the *Federal Register* can be found, **see Table 8.A.** Note that federal law specifically states that this electronic version is as official as the printed version. Only in a very few select places is the current day's printed *Federal Register* available (think of mailing times, for example) so for most researchers, today's *Federal Register* is only available online.

Table 8.A—Where to Find the *Federal Register*

1. *Federal Register*, Government Printing Office (1936–)

    Available in microfiche as well as paper.

2. Westlaw:

    Database name: **FR** (1980–) (Files are in star-paginated text format. The *Federal Register* indexes are not included.)

3. Lexis:

    Library; Filename = **GENFED;FEDREG** (1980–) (Files are in star-paginated text format. The *Federal Register* indexes are not included.)

4. HeinOnline, Federal Register Library (1936–) (Subscription-based web database. Files are in .pdf format. Includes all *Federal Register* indexes.)

5. GPO Access, http://www.gpoaccess.gov/fr/ (1994–) (Files are in .pdf and html formats. Indexes are not included.)

The website of the online *Federal Register* contains a number of other useful features as well, including the full text (in .pdf format) of the *Federal Register* from 1994 (Volume 59) forward. The site also offers a number of different ways to search for specific citations or terms. Recently added is an email service for each day's Table of Contents, which some practitioners might find useful. Later in this section we will discuss the Unified Agenda. It, too, can be found online at this website.

Each day's *Federal Register* contains several different parts. It is critically important to understand the purpose of each section and the related finding aids and other user aids. It is our belief that it is very difficult, if not impossible, to effectively use the online versions of administrative law sources without achieving some fluency with the printed versions from which the electronic versions were derived. With that in mind, what follows is a short overview of the basic structure of the *Federal Register*, with an emphasis on the uses to which each section can be put.

The first thing to examine is the cover itself. Note the date and volume number. Each year begins a new volume, starting with the first business day of the year. In 2006, for example, the *Federal Register's* first issue of the year was January 3, which is Volume 71, Number 1. The page numbering is also worth noting. Each volume is through-paginated, meaning that each year (or each volume, which amounts to the same thing) the page numbering begins with issue number 1 and continues until the last page of the last issue of the year. In recent years, the *Federal Register* has run to approximately 80,000 pages annually. Why bother telling you about page numbering? The reason is that most finding aids (indexes, cross-references from other sources, and so on) will cite to a specific page of the *Federal Register*. But since the *Federal Register* is published in daily pamphlets, it is natural when standing in front of a shelf of print *Federal Registers*, or browsing through the online versions, to think in terms of dates, not page numbers. We will see in section 8.17 below that there are a number of aids to help you easily translate pages numbers into dates.

Each day's *Federal Register* contains a Table of Contents. The *Federal Register* prints information from a variety of executive branch agencies; sometimes any one issue contains submissions from dozens of different agencies. The Table of Contents, in alphabetical order by agency, allows the researcher to quickly scan to see whether the agency he or she is concerned with has included any information of any sort in that day's *Federal Register*. To facilitate this current awareness use of the *Federal Register*, the Office of the Federal Register has instituted an email listserve (see the main GPO List Archives page at http://listserv.access.gpo.gov/ for subscription and other information) that each morning distributes that day's Table of Contents to subscribers. As of this writing, nearly twenty thousand subscribers receive this email every day. Presumably, the vast majority of these subscribers are lawyers, legislators, researchers, non-profit organizations and others who need to stay current with the doings of one or more agency. There are other ways to keep current with the rapidly changing world of federal regulation, methods to be discussed later in this chapter.

Near the beginning of each day's *Federal Register* is a chart titled "Parts affected in this issue." The "parts" referred to are divisions of the *Code of Federal Regulations*. Although this concept, and the particulars of how to use lists of parts and sections affected, will be discussed fully in the section on the *Code of Federal Regulations* which follows, it is important to note here that this section exists. The reason is fairly obvious; if a practitioner is concerned with a narrow area of regulation as found in a particular part of the *CFR*, one way that practitioner might keep himself or herself current on any changes made or contemplated by the regulating agency would be to scan the list of parts affected each day to see if there is anything in that issue which pertains to the matter in which the practitioner is interested. At the back of every day's *Federal Register* there is a similar table listing the parts affected during the current month. This list is cumulative, building each day of the month until starting over on the first day of the next month. The use of this table should also be clear; that same practitioner can quickly determine if anything has been issued this month that affects the issue or issues with which the practitioner is concerned. It may be that a once or twice monthly check is sufficient. This cumulative list of parts affected is also a useful tool for the all-important task of updating sections of the *Code of Federal Regulations*. More on that in the *CFR* section that follows.

After the preliminaries, the main body of each issue consists of agency information, divided into the different kinds of texts the agencies produce. A web of federal laws establishes the reporting obligations of rulemaking agencies, and it is these obligations that give the *Federal Register* its form.

8.3 RULES AND REGULATIONS SECTION OF THE *FEDERAL REGISTER*

The most significant section in each day's *Federal Register* contains the texts of new regulations, and is titled "Rules and Regulations". These new regulations have been proposed by the agency, undergone the public comment period, there may have been one or more open meetings or hearings to discuss public opinion about the regulation, and so on. That process complete, the regulation is printed in its final form, complete with its effective date, its *CFR* citation, and other pertinent information. Final regulations are usually printed well in advance of their effective date.

Note that final regulations (as well as proposed regulations, discussed next) are written with reference to the *CFR*. They either contain a new *CFR* section number (if an entirely new section is being added) or the citation of an existing *CFR* section which is being altered or amended. Contrast this practice with the far less orderly practice of internal numbering within Congressional session laws, discussed in section 2.23 above. Statutes amending code sections in Titles which have been enacted into positive law cite code section numbers just like new and proposed regulations do. However, in statutes affecting code sections in Titles not enacted into positive law, the practice is quite varied. Sometimes a bill is written with reference to the code section which may be affected, but often this is not the case. It is frequently the case that the text of the bill is numbered in outline form with no reference to the code structure at all, leaving it to the Office of the Law Revision Counsel to determine the impact on the code should that bill become law. The fact that new and proposed regulations are always written reflecting the *CFR* arrangement into which they will fit makes it easier for the researcher to evaluate the impact of a new or proposed regulation on the language currently in force.

The importance of this codification structure in the electronic era should be readily apparent. If every new regulation has as part of its language the place in the *Code of Federal Regulations* it will occupy as well as its effect on existing sections, it becomes easy to keep a constantly updated version of any particular *CFR* section. There is never any doubt about or interpretation of the current subject arrangement of regulations in any area. In fact, Westlaw, Lexis and the Office of the Federal Register itself now all offer versions of the *CFR* that are updated continuously. In section 8.18 below we will take up the advantages and potential pitfalls of online versions of the *CFR* that are updated daily and do not match the official version in print. For now it is enough to know that such practice exists, and that it is the structure of new and proposed regulations in the *Federal Register* that makes it possible.

In the Rules and Regulations section of each day's *Federal Register*, it is the text of these rules that is, obviously, of paramount importance. However, be sure to note any other items of useful information published along with the new regulations. First, be sure to read the preamble to any group of regulations, if there is one. The preamble may contain a statement of the intended scope or interpretation of the entire section, definitions to be used throughout, or other textual clues that will help the researcher. In this sense it can be said that the preambles often serve as a kind of legislative history for regulations. One danger in regulatory research is that the preambles occasionally are not reproduced in the *CFR* and thus the researcher can miss them. Similarly, it is easy when searching through online versions of the *CFR* to retrieve a particular provision and not realize that there is a preamble associated with it, a preamble one needs to read in order to fully understand the specific section retrieved. Each *CFR* part will contain a source note directing the researcher back to the original publication of the regulation in the *Federal Register*, but it is not always evident that there is any reason to double check the *CFR* text by looking up what may prove to be identical language in the *Federal Register*. Looking for a preamble is one good reason to do so.

8.4 PROPOSED REGULATIONS SECTION OF THE *FEDERAL REGISTER*

After the section containing new regulations comes the Proposed Regulations section. Proposed regulations are put forward from time to time by agencies. Usually, there is an open comment period, during which members of the public, corporations, organizations, or anyone else can comment on the proposed rule. Even the smallest and seemingly least consequential amendment to a regulation is treated as a proposed regulation, as are, of course, entirely new regulations.

Proposed regulations are always published in a stable and recognizable format. After the agency's name comes the citation of the *CFR* part or parts that will be added or changed if the rule becomes final. Then come parallel citations to other places the proposed regulation's text has been published, often an official publication of the agency itself. After that, one finds the title of the proposed regulation, then a short summary of its provisions. After the summary, the dates for submission of comments are listed, and then the address to which comments can be sent. One interesting recent development is that the government has established a new website, at http://www.regulations.gov, where comments on proposed regulations can be entered electronically. Previously, one had to send print copies of comments to a specific address. The government has recently begun making a small fraction of submitted comments available for viewing over the internet, but all comments can be viewed at one or more agency locations, which are listed in this part of the proposed regulation. (Plans are underway to make all comments available via the web by 2008). After the section related to comments comes contact names, addresses, phone numbers and occasionally an email address to use when requesting further information. Finally, there may be special or supplementary information designed to aid the reader in understanding the proposed regulation or the process of its adoption and approval.

8.5   NOTICES SECTION OF THE
FEDERAL REGISTER

After the Proposed Regulations section comes the Notices section. There are a variety of notices one can find here. Various federal laws require publication of notices for open meetings to discuss proposed regulations (called Sunshine Act meetings in the *Federal Register*). In addition, this is the section in which one can find notices of expiring or expired regulations, technical corrections or amendments to previously published regulations, announcements of a general nature, and so on. It is difficult to categorize the many types of notices found here, but it is enough to know that most of these notices are of only ephemeral interest, and thus usually have little value to the researcher.

8.6   READER AIDS SECTION OF
THE *FEDERAL REGISTER*

At the end of each day's *Federal Register* appears the Reader Aids Section, which contains many of the most useful finding aids for the administrative law researcher. After a short listing of contact information for various services provided by the Office of the Federal Register and the Government Printing Office, the researcher can find the three most important reader aids in the *Federal Register*; the *Federal Register* Pages and Dates Table, the cumulative table of *CFR* parts affected this month, and the Reminders section.

The Pages and Dates Table allows the researcher to quickly translate *Federal Register* page numbers into dates. This makes retrieval of specific passages easier because, although pinpoint cites are always made to page numbers, it is easier to find issues by date, both in print and online, since the *Federal Register* is published each business day. You should note that in each day's *Federal Register* the table that appears contains only page numbers and dates from that month. Sometimes the researcher armed with a page from previous months needs to determine the date that page number appears. To go back in time to before the first day of the current month, there is a cumulative annual table in every month's *List of Sections Affected* pamphlet, discussed in more detail in section 8.17 below.

The Table of *CFR* Parts Affected This Month lists all of the *CFR* parts affected or even potentially affected by developments contained in the *Federal Register* issues during the current month. This table is the quickest way to see whether a particular *CFR* part has been changed recently or whether there is any recent proposed rule or other agency action which would affect that *CFR* part. The *List of Sections Affected* pamphlets help a researcher update the *CFR* from the last time that title was recodified and reprinted up to the date of the last *LSA* pamphlet, but from there the researcher needs to rely on this cumulative table in order to update the *CFR* language to the current day.

Finally, at the end of every issue of the *Federal Register* is a section of general Reminders. Several types of reminders appear here: new rules going into effect soon, comment periods on proposed regulations closing soon, expiring regulations, and a list of new public laws.

8.7 HOW THE *FEDERAL REGISTER* IS ACTUALLY USED IN LEGAL RESEARCH

Now that we have dissected and described the *Federal Register*, how does one use it? What do lawyers, law students and others really do with the *Federal Register*? One obvious answer is that, like all chronological legal publications, the *Federal Register* serves as the publication of record. The *United States Statutes at Large* contains the exact texts of new public laws in chronological order as passed. The *United States Reports* contains Supreme Court cases printed in roughly chronological order, preserving the exact text the justices have written. So, too, with the *Federal Register*. Like these other chronological publications, the *Federal Register* is used primarily for retrieval purposes. When one needs to see the text of, say, a final rule as it appeared when first adopted a decade ago, the *Federal Register* is the only option. Because the *CFR* is constantly updated and amended and rearranged into subject order, just like the *United States Code*, the *Federal Register* is usually the only place to find the original text in its original form. This retrieval function is useful more often than might be supposed. Many times cross-references from other primary or secondary sources are to *Federal Register* pages, not to *CFR* parts or sections. As noted above, preambles to new regulations occasionally are found only in the *Federal Register* version, not in the *CFR* section to which it gets codified. The administrative law researcher will need to know how to find *Federal Register* provisions in order to conduct effective research.

Another use researchers make of the *Federal Register* is as a current awareness tool. As mentioned above, there are several ways to keep current on specific topics by viewing each day's table of contents, the monthly index, or the *List of Sections Affected*. Many lawyers make use of one or more of these techniques to help monitor developments in a particular field. In the discussion of looseleaf services later in Chapter 9, we will examine another, and potentially more powerful, way to do this.

A final feature of the *Federal Register* one should bear in mind is the twice-yearly publication of the Unified Agenda. Recent federal law (and a related Executive Order) mandated that each rulemaking agency publish twice each year a description of the regulations it is developing or has recently completed. These descriptions are published in the *Federal Register*, usually in April and October, and are known as the Unified Agenda of Regulatory and Deregulatory Actions (or Unified Agenda, for short.) The Unified Agenda, though not binding on the agencies, is a useful and generally very accurate description of the next six months of regulatory action by the agency. This is a very important publication, and lawyers and other researchers often consult the most recent Unified Agenda to determine if the agency has any plans in the immediate future to alter specific regulations.

As might be apparent from the preceding paragraphs, the *Federal Register*, even though it is a critical primary source, is of limited utility for the administrative law researcher. Most regular research is accomplished using the *Federal Register*'s cognate publication, the *Code of Federal Regulations*.

8.8　SOURCES OF ADMINISTRATIVE LAW: THE *CODE OF FEDERAL REGULATIONS*

The *Code of Federal Regulations* (or *CFR*) is the subject arrangement of regulations first printed chronologically in the *Federal Register*. This pattern should be very familiar to you by now; first chronological, then by subject. In this case, only a part of what appears in the *Federal Register* makes it into the *CFR*. Why is this the case? What in the *Federal Register* is not included in each year's *CFR*?

If you will recall the discussion of the several sections of the *Federal Register* from the preceding pages, the answer will be relatively obvious.

First, of course, there is no need to reprint the tables of contents, reader aids and such, as these are of only ephemeral importance. The daily and cumulative monthly lists of parts and sections affected are not reprinted in the *CFR*, but rather are printed separately (in a slightly different format which we will discuss in section 8.17 below) in monthly *List of Sections Affected* pamphlets. The Notices section, too, is of temporary interest since by the time the *CFR* is reprinted the dates and other items in the Notices section will be moot. Less obvious is that proposed regulations make no appearance in the *CFR*. This makes perfect sense on reflection, however. Unless the proposed regulation becomes final it has no legal force, so there is no need to codify it.

That leaves for inclusion in the *CFR* the final, new regulations published in the Rules And Regulations section of the *Federal Register*. All of the final rules except those of temporary duration (those that expire before the *CFR* title in which they would otherwise appear is reprinted) are considered of general and permanent application. This is not to say that they apply to everyone or that they will not soon be superseded, mooted or eliminated, but only that these regulations will remain in force until some affirmative act in the future changes their status. It is these final regulations that get arranged into subject order, added to the appropriate section or part, then reprinted the next time the title containing that section or part gets recodified. For sources where the CFR can be found, **see Table 8.B.**

Table 8.B—Where to Find the *Code of Federal Regulations*

1. *Code of Federal Regulations*, Government Printing Office (1938–). In addition to the print edition, the GPO also republishes the CFR in a microfiche set.

2. Westlaw:

   Database name: **CFR** (1984–) (Files are in star-paginated html format, with each year a separate file; e.g., **CFR92** for 1992. The current year's *CFR* is updated on a rolling basis, prior years follow the printed version. *LSA* pamphlets are not included.)

3. Lexis:

   Library;Filename = **GENFED;CFR** (1981–) (Files are in star-paginated html format, with each year a separate file; e.g., **GENFED;CFR95** for 1995. The current year's *CFR* is updated on a rolling basis, prior years follow the printed version. *LSA* pamphlets are not included.)

4. GPO Access

   http://www.gpoaccess.gov/cfr/(1996–) (Files are in .pdf and html formats. LSA pamphlets are available from 1986 to the present. This version of the CFR exactly mirrors the print and also contains the most recent Parallel Tables of Authorities and Rules, in both html and .pdf formats.)

5. E–CFR, GPO Access

   http://www.gpoaccess.gov/ecfr/index.html.   (Current year only. This e-cfr is a beta test site only. It is updated on a rolling basis, and is not official. *LSA* pamphlets are not included.)

8.9 *CFR* BASICS

The *CFR* is similar in form to other codes you have examined. It is divided into titles, corresponding to broad subjects, then further subdivided into more manageable subcategories. There is an index that helps researchers find specific sections or topics. Tables of contents and a variety of other tables help the researcher access information in different ways. Each title has a table of contents, many titles have their own indexes, and the internal structure of each title carries intellectual content. In all these ways, the *CFR* should remind you of other codes, but there are some important features to note that are unique to the *CFR*.

Specifically, the entire *CFR* is reprinted each year, according to a rolling schedule. Also, unlike many other codes, there is currently no annotated, commercially published complete version of the *CFR*, although there are several commercially published versions of the index, owing to the execrable and largely useless one volume index published with the official set. (The tables in that index volume, on the other hand, are quite useful, as discussed in section 8.15 below.) The *CFR* is bound in paper, with a different color spine for each year, rather than being hardbound and updated with pocket parts or other supplements.

There are a few key concepts to understand before we turn to a discussion of how to use the *CFR*. We noted above the peculiar publication pattern of the titles of the *CFR*. The entire code is reprinted each year, but roughly one fourth of the titles are reprinted each quarter, in accordance with the schedule found in **Table 8.C**. This means that it is vitally important to check the cover of any *CFR* volume containing a relevant regulation. The cover will tell you the date when that particular volume was last recodified and reprinted. Updating (which we will discuss in subsequent paragraphs) must proceed from the date on the cover.

A related issue is that each year the *CFR* is given a new cover color; perhaps red one year, blue the next, green the year after that. It can be distressing for a novice researcher to approach the two hundred fifty or so volumes of the *CFR*, only to see that the spines are, for example, half red and half blue. On further inspection, the red spines have one year printed on them, the blue the previous year. What's gone wrong?

Nothing. An illustration should help make things clear. Let's say that last year's *CFR* set had blue covers. Once the last of the reprinting is done, which would be after October 1 **(see Table 8.C)**, the entire current set on the shelves is blue, every volume. Then comes January 1, and the first revisions of the new year arrive in the library, with the new year's red covers. Now the first sixteen titles have red covers and the rest have blue. After April 1, the next eleven titles get reprinted with their red covers, and now the set, which is completely up to date, is roughly half red and half blue. And so on throughout the year. To make it more complicated, the new volumes tend to be published and delivered to libraries a few at a time, so it is often the case that volumes even within any single title have covers of different colors. This presents no problem for the updating tools, which track cumulative changes since the last time each particular section was reprinted.

Another peculiarity of the *CFR* is Title 3, which contains Presidential documents. (Given that the *CFR* is the place where executive branch agencies publish their regulations, it should not be surprising that at least some space should be given over to documents from the President, the chief executive.) Title 3 always has a white cover to set it apart from the other titles. It is not cumulative as are the other titles. Title 3 reprints in full the texts of all Presidential Proclamations, Executive Orders and other Presidential Documents (which include Administrative Orders, Reorganization Plans, Designations, and so on). There are also several parts which cover rules of the Executive Office of the President. Finally, Title 3 contains a number of tables which serve as finding aids to Presidential Documents. Note that all of this material is available in a variety of other locations, including the *Weekly Compilation of Presidential Documents*, the *United States Statutes at Large*, the White House website (http://www.whitehouse.gov), commercial online services, and so on, but that the *Bluebook's* preferred source is Title 3 of the *CFR*.

Table 8.C: Dates of annual revision of *CFR* titles

CFR Titles	Dates of Annual Revision
Titles 1–16	January 1
Titles 17–27	April 1
Titles 28–41	July 1
Titles 42–50	October 1

8.10 STRUCTURE OF THE *CFR*

It is important to understand exactly how the *CFR* is arranged in order to be able to use this code effectively and efficiently. It is slightly different from other codes and other subject arrangements you have seen up to this point. One major difference is the way titles are subdivided by issuing agency (more on that in the next few paragraphs.) Another difference is how the user updates a specific *CFR* section, which will be discussed in section 8.16. On the whole, though, the arrangement, the indexing, the tables, and most other features will be familiar to users who have gained some fluency with the major statutory codes, such as the *United States Code*, or one of its commercially annotated versions, or with a state code. Let's take a look at the *CFR* and its divisions; titles, chapters, parts and sections.

8.11 TITLES OF THE *CFR*

Just like the *United States Code*, the *CFR* is divided into fifty major subjects, called titles. It would be logical to assume that the fifty *CFR* titles track the subject matter of the fifty titles of the *United States Code*, making a neatly parallel set of related subjects. It would be logical to assume that, but it would be wrong. Not completely wrong, maddeningly, but mostly wrong. For it is true that a few titles of the *CFR* (Title 26, for instance, where regulations concerning taxation are found) match up with the *United States Code* (Title 26 is the Internal Revenue Code title). There are a handful of other examples **(see Table 8.D)**. It should come as no surprise, after a little reflection, that the titles don't track exactly. After all, Congress legislates and agencies regulate in some very different areas, and the titles emanating from them reflect the differing ranges of subjects that they respectively cover.

Remember from the above that each of the titles is reprinted once per year according to a rolling schedule **(see Table 8.C)**. How does this process work? It is actually simpler than one might guess, given that each year's *CFR* numbers well over two hundred volumes. An illustration should help clarify this process.

Take Title 23—Highways, as an example. It is revised and reprinted on April 1 of each year. As of this writing, the current edition is the 2005 version, which was revised as of April 1, 2005. This softbound volume is, if you will, a snapshot of the regulations in force on one particular day, April 1, 2005. Understand that a new regulation may have gone into effect on April 2 (or any date in the year thereafter) that materially changed one section or another. In fact, part of the process of learning how to use the *CFR* has to do with updating a relevant section from the date of its last revision and republishing (the procedure for which is laid out in section 8.16 below).

What will happen on April 1, 2006? Title 23 will be revised and republished. The compilers of the *CFR* will start from the text from the last printing, then revise it by taking into account any changes in the regulations made at any point during the intervening year. (These changes, of course, will have been noted in the *Federal Register* during the year). The compilers will add any new language and remove any repealed or expired language necessitated by agency (or Congressional or court) action. The resulting revision will then be printed. Remember that the April 1, 2006 revision will just be a snapshot view of the state of these regulations on that one day. On April 1 of the next year, the process will start all over again.

The only exception to the process described above is, you should recall, Title 3. This title reprints Presidential Documents, including Presidential Proclamations, Executive Orders, and the like. It is not cumulative, a completely new Title 3 is begun each year. Since Title 3 is printed each January 1, it stands to reason that the Presidential Documents included are always from the previous calendar year.

Table 8.D: Titles of *USC* and *CFR* compared

	United States Code	Code of Federal Regulations
Title 1	General Provisions	General Provisions
Title 2	The Congress	[Reserved]
Title 3	The President	The President
Title 4	Flag and Seal, Seat of Government, and the States	Accounts
Title 5	Government Organization and Employees	Administrative Personnel
Title 6	Domestic Security	Homeland Security
Title 7	Agriculture	Agriculture
Title 8	Aliens and Nationality	Aliens and Nationality
Title 9	Arbitration	Animals and Animal Products
Title 10	Armed Forces	Energy
Title 11	Bankruptcy	Federal Elections
Title 12	Banks and Banking	Banks and Banking
Title 13	Census	Business Credit and Assistance
Title 14	Coast Guard	Aeronautics and Space
Title 15	Commerce and Trade	Commerce and Foreign Trade
Title 16	Conservation	Commercial Practices
Title 17	Copyrights	Commodity and Securities Exchanges
Title 18	Crimes and Criminal Procedure	Conservation of Power and Water Resources
Title 19	Customs Duties	Customs Duties
Title 20	Education	Employees' Benefits
Title 21	Food and Drugs	Food and Drugs
Title 22	Foreign Relations and Intercourse	Foreign Relations
Title 23	Highways	Highways
Title 24	Hospitals and Asylums	Housing and Urban Development
Title 25	Indians	Indians
Title 26	Internal Revenue Code	Internal Revenue
Title 27	Intoxicating Liquors	Alcohol, Tobacco Products and Firearms
Title 28	Judiciary and Judicial Procedure	Judicial Administration
Title 29	Labor	Labor
Title 30	Mineral Lands and Mining	Mineral Resources
Title 31	Money and Finance	Money and Finance: Treasury
Title 32	National Guard	National Defense
Title 33	Navigation and Navigable Waters	Navigation and Navigable Waters
Title 34	Navy [Repealed]	Education
Title 35	Patents	Panama Canal

Title 36	Patriotic and National Observances, Ceremonies, and Organizations	Parks, Forests, and Public Property
Title 37	Pay and Allowances of the Uniform Services	Patents, Trademarks, and Copyright
Title 38	Veterans' Benefits	Pensions, Bonuses, and Veterans' Relief
Title 39	Postal Service	Postal Service
Title 40	Public Buildings, Property, and Works	Protection of Environment
Title 41	Public Contracts	Public Contracts and Property Management
Title 42	The Public Health and Welfare	Public Health
Title 43	Public Lands	Public Lands: Interior
Title 44	Public Printing and Documents	Emergency Management and Assistance
Title 45	Railroads	Public Welfare
Title 46	Shipping	Shipping
Title 47	Telegraphs, Telephones, and Radiotelegraphs	Telecommunication
Title 48	Territories and Insular Possessions	Federal Acquisition Regulations System
Title 49	Transportation	Transportation
Title 50	War and National Defense	Wildlife and Fisheries

8.12   CHAPTERS OF THE *CFR*

Each title is divided into chapters, which represent different subjects addressed within the title. In some cases, the result of this is that each of the agencies empowered to make regulations on that title's subject matter has its own chapter. For example, in Title 20—Employees' Benefits, Chapter I contains regulations from the Office of Workers' Compensation Programs, Chapter II contains regulations of the Railroad Retirement Board, Chapter III, the Social Security Administration's regulations on the subject, and so on. Of course, it is not always so simple (no surprise there, right?), but that is the basic pattern. Notice that chapters are designated with roman numerals, not arabic numbers. This graphically differentiates the chapters encountered in this context from the two kinds of "chapter" rubrics used in the statutory context (see section 2.22 above). As with statutes, very few of the finding aids that you will use actually cite to the chapters. They are really there to help organize the *CFR*, and to make clear to you the organization of each title.

8.13   PARTS OF THE *CFR*

The chapters are further divided into parts. According to the *CFR* itself, the parts are subdivisions of the chapters and cover specific regulatory areas. It is probably useful to ignore chapters when thinking about the structure of the *CFR* and instead focus on titles, subdivided into parts, then into sections. Each part has a descriptive name, then a table of contents-style listing of all the sections within that part, then the authority and source notes.

The authority note contains a citation (or series of citations) to the federal law or other action that gave that particular agency the authority to regulate on the specific subject matter with which the part is concerned. Usually, the citation is to a section of the *United States Code*, but many other kinds of things can serve as authority. As an example, it is quite common for another *CFR* part or section to be listed in the authority note in addition to the more typical federal statute. This happens because one agency has deferred to another's authority, or delegated the rulemaking authority to another, or merely incorporated part of one agency's regulation into another.

The *CFR* Index volume contains a section called Parallel Tables of Authorities and Rules. The first three tables in the section contain cumulative lists of authorities for *CFR* parts from three different parallel citations: authorities in *United States Code* section order, *United States Statutes at Large* order, and finally, Public Law number order. By using these tables, the researcher can quickly determine if a specific code section or session law authorizes any current regulations. It is important for the researcher to be able to trace the genesis of a given *CFR* part in some cases, and the authority note is the place to begin.

The source note is the same concept as the source note after each section of the *United States Code*. The source note refers back to the source of the language contained in that *CFR* part. In almost every case, the source cites the *Federal Register*, which is logical. Just as the source for a section of the *United States Code* is one or more public laws, so it is that the source for a *CFR* section is a new regulation printed in an issue of the *Federal Register*. The source citation, of course, allows the researcher to retrieve the original text of the language as printed in the *Federal Register* when it was first adopted. It is common for the source note to cite a *Federal Register* issue, then say "unless otherwise noted." That simply means that one or more sections within that part came from a different source (it was added later, for instance) than the rest of the part. The differing source will be noted after the individual section to which it applies.

8.14 SECTIONS OF THE *CFR*

Finally, we arrive at the section, the basic unit of regulation. In theory, the section represents one discrete topic, one indivisible idea or command. Researchers used to the general (or occasionally even vague) language of federal statutes are surprised by the specificity and granularity of the *CFR* section. It is sometimes hard to believe the level of detail. Regulations concerning drawbridges, for example, list each drawbridge under federal jurisdiction in a separate section, complete with information specific to that bridge. For those dying to know, the drawbridge over the Tuckahoe River will open on signal if at least 24 hours notice is given in advance. It is in the sections that the researcher will find the answers to most research questions in administrative law.

8.15 HOW TO USE THE *CFR*

How, then, to use the *CFR*? Beginning researchers may find it a little daunting, but the truth is that after mastering a few concepts and techniques even a novice should be able to conduct effective research using the *CFR*. The steps are really quite simple.

The first thing a researcher must do is locate relevant *CFR* citations. There are a variety of ways to do this. This is relatively simple when the researcher sets out to discover whether there are any regulations on a specific topic. In that case, the *CFR* Index is probably the place to start. The *CFR* Index, as discussed above, is not without its problems, but a persistent researcher who is willing to spend a little time with the index can usually find what is being sought. Alternatively, of course, researchers can make use of commercial *CFR* indexes, such as the *Index to the Code of Federal Regulations* (published by Congressional Information Service), which is vastly superior to the official index.

It is not unlikely that the researcher began by identifying a federal statute on point. If there is one, one approach for finding associated regulations would be to look in the Parallel Tables of Authorities and

Rules in the *CFR* Index. Annotations to statutory code sections often contain references to associated *CFR* sections. Or, if the researcher feels a full-text search might be effective, he or she can conduct a full-text search in the online *CFR*s available through Lexis, Westlaw, or on the web at the GPO website, http://www.access.gpo.gov/cfr/index.html.

Researchers must take care when relying on full-text searches that they don't commit a common error; the error of false precision. The danger is that one might find a section with language that seems to address the question, but because browsing is difficult online, the researcher doesn't take the time to determine where that section fits in the scheme of the entire part or chapter. One runs the risk of ignoring other sections whose meaning bears on the interpretation or application of the one found with the online search. It seems like a small risk, but that's deceptive. It is more common than most researchers think that two or more sections must be read together to completely understand the gist of the rule. This is not an exhortation never to use online *CFR*s, only a warning to take care. In statutory or regulatory interpretation and research, context is everything.

Once the specific section has been identified, its context examined, and the other textual clues and references followed, the researcher must then update the section from the date of the last revision. It is possible to update any section to the current day.

8.16 UPDATING A *CFR* SECTION

CFR sections are revised and reprinted each year. The date of the last revision is printed on the cover of every individual *CFR* volume. If the researcher is interested in, say, 23 CFR 751.11, he or she should note that (as of this writing) the current print version was revised on April 1, 2005. This section is:

Title 23—Highways

Part 751—Junkyard Control and Acquisition

Section 751.11—Nonconforming junkyards

Note also that this section is part of Chapter I—Federal Highway Administration, Department of Transportation, and Subchapter H—Right-of-Way and Environment. Remember, though, that chapters and subchapters are ordinarily contextual clues, and rarely are included in citations.

The process for updating 23 CFR 751.11 from its last revision, April 1, 2005, until today, is mechanical and simple, but takes a little explanation. If you recall from the discussion above, in each issue of the *Federal Register* there is published a list of parts affected, cumulative for the month to date. One could update our *CFR* section by looking at the list of parts affected every day from April 1, 2005 until today. A little further thought will suggest a shortcut; since each day's list is cumulative, one could look at the parts affected list in the last issue of each month since

April. Why would this work? By looking at the table in the last April issue, you can see whether anything that appeared in the *Federal Register* that month had any impact on Title 23, Part 751. Then one could check the table in the last May issue for all of May's potential changes to this part, then June, and so on. Arduous, but ultimately effective.

8.17   A BETTER WAY: THE *LIST OF SECTIONS AFFECTED*

Fortunately, there is a far easier way. Each month, the government publishes a thin pamphlet called the *List of Sections Affected* (or *LSA*). This pamphlet contains a table with citations to every *Federal Register* issue that affected any individual section of the *CFR* since the last time it was revised. Thus, the October *LSA* contains citations to every *Federal Register* issue that affected any section in Title 5 since January 1 (when it was last revised), that affected any section in Title 23 since April 1 (when it was last revised) and so on for all fifty titles. (*LSAs* from 1997 until the present are also available at http://www.gpoaccess.gov/lsa/index.html).

This means that to update 23 CFR 751.11 from April 1 until the last day of last month (when the last pamphlet was issued), all the researcher needs do is check last month's LSA. If this section isn't listed as having been affected, the regulation was still in force at the end of last month. That leaves the problem of updating from the last day of last month until today. But that's easy. All that is necessary is a check of the cumulative list of parts affected in the back of today's issue of the *Federal Register*. That will show if anything this month has affected this part.

Note that the *LSA* tracks changes to sections, and the cumulative daily list in the *Federal Register* only tracks to the level of the part. Thus the daily table is a slightly blunter instrument than the *LSA*. This usually doesn't present a serious problem since the researcher rarely has to consult multiple issues in the current month. Remember, too, that the citations in the *LSA* and in the cumulative daily tables are citations to page numbers in the *Federal Register*. One must take the additional step of translating the page numbers to dates, but there is a table to allow just this on the same page as the daily parts affected table, and inside the cover of every *LSA*. When searching online, this presents less of a problem since it is easy to retrieve any particular page or range of pages.

What does one do if, when updating, it becomes clear that one or more days of the *Federal Register* must be consulted because the *LSA* has indicated that your section has been affected? First, obviously, you must retrieve the cited issues of the *Federal Register* and read the relevant language. If, for example, the citation was only to a proposed regulation that was never made final, the *CFR* section was not really changed, so the researcher can ignore the proposed regulation and simply rely on the language in the *CFR*. What to do, though, if sometime after April 1, say in the January 3 issue of the *Federal Register*, a new regulation became final, and that regulation made important changes to 23 CFR 751.11? If that is the case, the researcher has to revise the language himself or herself. What was amended, deleted, replaced, or altered? This can sometimes present issues of interpretation, but usually the updating language makes clear exactly what changes have been made to the existing regulation.

In the online environment, there are electronic versions of all of these publications; the Parallel Tables, the *LSA*s, and the *Federal Registers* and *CFR* themselves. In Lexis, Westlaw, and at the GPO website, one can update the *CFR* electronically in precisely the same way as one would with the print equivalents. There is emerging, however, a different way.

8.18   ELECTRONIC *CFR*S WITH ROLLING UPDATES

Recently, the online services and the Government Printing Office have experimented with another way to help researchers update the *CFR*. Because of the way that new regulations are written, with specific citations to the existing *CFR* language into which they will fit, it is possible to maintain a constantly updated *CFR*. The idea here is that each day the compiler of the online *CFR* can take the new regulations from that day's issue of the *Federal Register*, and directly revise the affected *CFR* section without awaiting the next revision according to the rolling schedule of revisions of print titles.

The benefits of this arrangement are obvious. Manually updating a printed *CFR* section is simple and mechanical, but it does involve a few steps and requires the researcher to consult several different publications. With an online *CFR* with rolling updates there is no need to update at all, as long as the researcher checks carefully how currently updated that version is. It is even possible for researchers who prefer to conduct research (and read the results) in the print *CFR* to update that section online by retrieving the relevant section to see if the text has changed since the print volume was revised and reprinted.

There are a few potential pitfalls to be aware of. First, there is the problem of accuracy. It may be that this updating, unofficial as it is, may not be as accurately or carefully performed as one would like. Second, there is the problem of currency. Has the compiler of the rolling updates kept current? One must always check. Lexis states that its *CFR* is usually current within about two weeks. Westlaw is less specific, but periodic checks suggest that its updating window is about the same as that of Lexis. The GPO's currently updated *CFR* is only in the beta-test stage, but it is generally within a few days of being completely current. Third, it should be noted that, because of the rolling updates, a *CFR* section that one finds may appear in a form that doesn't match any print (read: official) version of the *CFR*. Said another way, the print version (and the .pdf version of the *CFR* available at the GPO website) are official. Any other version, especially one that features commercially prepared updates, is unofficial. That's not necessarily a problem, but one must keep it in mind.

8.19 ADMINISTRATIVE HEARINGS AND OTHER QUASI–JUDICIAL PROCEEDINGS

In addition to making regulations, administrative agencies are often empowered to hold adjudicative hearings. The hearings may be as informal as a consultation with a member of agency staff, or may be as formal as any court proceeding, with a judge or panel of judges, witnesses, depositions, briefs and all of the trappings familiar from federal court litigation. In very general terms, there are two different hearing systems commonly employed by executive branch agencies.

In one system, of which employment discrimination hearings are an example, the agency itself is the first arbiter of claims that one or another of its regulations has been violated. In the employment law instance, there is a multi-layered series of hearings prescribed by the regulations. These hearings can be investigatory or adjudicative, punishments can be meted out, settlements approved, and all of the other kinds of actions more traditional courts can undertake. After the parties have progressed through all of the layers of review (called "exhausting one's administrative remedies" by courts and commentators), parties have the right to appeal the findings to the appropriate federal court. This system is most commonly found in areas where the agency itself is unlikely to be one of the parties.

The other system, of which tax litigation is an example, provides a roughly co-equal forum along with federal courts for litigating disputes between a citizen and the government, usually the agency itself. This is far less common, as you might imagine. In the case of tax litigation, in certain circumstances, the citizen can bring suit in the United States Tax Court, in the local federal district court, or in the United States Court of Federal Claims.

Publication of administrative decisions is irregular at best. Generally speaking, there are three different ways that agency decisions are made available to researchers; on the agency's website, in official publications of the agency, or in commercial publications. It is increasingly common for agencies to make hearing decisions available on their websites. You should know, however, that often these decisions are reproduced with no indexes or finding aids, and are usually arranged by date or party name. There is rarely any kind of subject access to the decisions. A few agencies publish their decisions in official reporters or other publications of that agency. These publications often have better finding aids than web versions. When agency decisions are published commercially, often in looseleaf form, they usually have good indexes and other finding aids.

There is no comprehensive list of which agencies hold administrative hearings and where to find the resulting decisions. For researchers interested in a particular agency, by far the best first step is to examine that agency's website. Failing that, specialized legal research publications can often help. Westlaw and Lexis also have reports of decisions from a variety of agencies, and can be a useful place to search. Law librarians, of course, also have experience finding these publications and can usually help.

Why would these decisions be so hard to locate? And why are researchers so ill-served by the kind of indexing and other subject access tools that would make them easy to use? In part, the answer stems from the nature of administrative hearings. Unlike courts, administrative agencies generally are not bound by prior decisions. Lawyers doing a thorough job of researching will examine past decisions, however, and urge the agency to follow this or that line of precedent, or depart from it, as the case may be. Agencies have shown a marked tendency to consider their own decisions to be fact-specific and limited in scope to the case and the parties involved in that hearing. They are, therefore, less willing to take pains to ensure that every decision is published and made available to researchers. Since lawyers make use of this material anyway, it is wise for the researcher to be aware that the agency issuing any particular regulation may well have considered its application or interpretation in a quasi-judicial opinion and released an opinion on the subject. Thorough administrative law research requires a search of these decisions.

8.20   STATE ADMINISTRATIVE LAW RESEARCH

Just as every state has its own legislature, session laws and code, each state also has its own regulatory agencies with their resulting publications. It is often necessary for the researcher with a state law problem to consult state administrative registers and codes. The publication patterns are very similar to the federal system, but there are some important differences to know about.

State legislatures delegate rulemaking to state executive agencies the same way Congress does. In the state systems, the pace of regulation is slower, and one finds markedly less commitment to publishing everything. A few words are in order, then, about what the state administrative researcher will have available with which to complete his or her research.

There are state registers that serve the same function as the *Federal Register*. Often published monthly, these state registers typically contain the texts of new regulations along with some notices and other information. Almost every state makes their registers available at the state government website, so finding them is quite easy. They are not, unfortunately, thorough or timely enough to be very useful to the researcher.

States also take the final regulations from their registers and publish them in subject arrangement. These administrative codes, which different states call by a variety of names, serve the same purpose as the *CFR*. Some are published without any indexing at all, some are published only irregularly, some are available on the state government website, some are not; every possible practice seems to have at least one adherent. Many states now have their administrative codes commercially published, which has helped regularize the publication schedule and has improved the indexes and finding aids.

The point is that once you understand federal administrative research, you can conduct state administrative research even though the tools at your disposal are not as current, thorough, or well indexed. A researcher typically approaches the state administrative code with a topic or a state law in hand. Using the index (if there is one) or table of contents or whatever aid comes with the set, the researcher finds the relevant regulation. Updating is done by checking the state administrative register, which in most cases has nothing like the *LSA* to help. It is common for state administrative codes to contain contact information with each chapter or title. In order to be confident that you have thoroughly updated your section, it might be necessary to call or otherwise contact the person listed. This seeming informality is typical of administrative law practice in many states.

There are state administrative topics that are covered in much greater detail; most notably, taxation. State tax laws are covered by looseleafs and other publications, and it is therefore possible to conduct research very similar in scope and depth to federal tax research, without having to rely on state primary source publication.

Even though states do not expend as much time or energy publishing each day's administrative activity, it is still possible to conduct effective research in state administrative law. The researcher needs to be a little creative and a little diligent, but the tools are there, and they bear a strong resemblance to the more familiar tools of federal research.

Chapter 9

INTRODUCING SECONDARY SOURCES: LOOSELEAF SERVICES

9.1 INTRODUCTION: WHAT THIS CHAPTER IS ABOUT

Why devote an entire chapter to looseleaf services? Why do practitioners rely on them so heavily? Why are they so large, complex and hideously expensive? What kinds of legal subjects are covered by looseleafs? Good questions, all.

Looseleafs merit an entire chapter because they dominate legal research in the areas they cover. An extremely clever innovation, looseleafs gather primary and secondary sources together, arrange them in a useful way, update the material frequently, and add editorial commentary, all of which saves the researcher or practitioner a great deal of time and effort. They are a little tricky to use at first, however, and many students find themselves a little overwhelmed when faced with a twenty volume set of looseleaf binders. We will try to demystify these publications, and will argue that a few minutes spent familiarizing yourself with a new looseleaf can save you a great deal of research time later.

Practitioners rely on looseleaf services for a number of reasons and in a variety of ways. First, lawyers use the frequent (often weekly) updates to stay current with developments in their field. Second, that frequent updating means that the lawyer need not spend time worrying about the currency of every statute, every case, every paragraph of commentary he or she finds. The publisher of the looseleaf takes care of the currency issues. Also, the looseleaf service draws together relevant material from a great variety of sources; something the average lawyer has no time to do in a busy practice. Finally, the looseleaf's collocation and topical arrangement of related material from a variety of sources gives the lawyer a contextual framework from which to proceed. It would be a very foolish lawyer who would substitute a looseleaf editor's judgement for his own, but the looseleaf at least provides the background and context within which to work, imposing some order on the vast universe of primary and secondary sources on any given subject.

Looseleafs are so large, complicated and expensive because of the labor–intensive manner of their production. In order to achieve all of the benefits described in this chapter, the publisher has to commit vast resources to the retrieval, arrangement, publication, distribution, etc., of new material, often on a weekly schedule. In an interfiled looseleaf, described below, each week the publisher sends replacement pages, updating the entire set with new developments since the last release. That might include new cases, new statutes, new regulations, new editorial commentary, new index entries, new finding aid entries, and so on. It must all be typeset, new pages printed, instructions for filing produced, the entire week's issue printed, arranged, packaged and shipped. Every week. If looseleafs weren't so thorough, so complete, so timely, so useful, no one would be willing to pay the high price of production. Looseleafs are usually the most expensive titles in the law library, and for those who know how to use them, their cost is fully justified.

Not all legal subjects are covered by looseleafs. Indeed, most are not. Why not, if they're so useful? The answer has to do with the particular strengths of the looseleaf; currency and the gathering of a wide variety of primary and secondary sources. Looseleafs tend to flourish in heavily regulated legal subjects such as taxation, labor and employment law, environmental law, securities law and the like. Last chapter's discussion of administrative law should have made plain how time-consuming this research can be. The *CFR* and *Federal Register* are not especially difficult to use, nor, however, are they simple. Administrative hearings can be difficult to locate and often are published with no finding aids. Statutes and regulations interact in unpredictable and odd ways, and the relationship between the administrative hearing process and the state and federal courts can be hard to figure out. In just these areas of law are looseleafs powerful antidotes to the complex and unwieldy nature of the underlying sources. Practitioners and other researchers rely on looseleafs to help ease the burden of complex research.

All of this is not to say that looseleafs exist in only the heavily regulated areas of law. Many legal topics have at least one publication in looseleaf format. State jury instructions, for example, are often published in looseleaf form. These looseleafs, and others like them, don't really require weekly updating, are not compiled from a dozen different primary sources, and are not fifteen or twenty volumes in length. Many looseleaf publications are in that form for the simple convenience of replacing old pages with new, without having to discard volumes or pocket parts or supplement pamphlets. There are easy ways to find looseleafs by title, publisher or subject, which we will discuss later in this chapter.

9.2 WHAT ARE LOOSELEAFS USED FOR?

There are several situations in which a looseleaf can save the researcher an enormous amount of time. In fact, it is not too much to say that there are certain types of research in specific areas of law that would be so unwieldy and time-consuming to complete using only primary sources as to be almost impracticable. This may seem at first glance to be an extreme claim, but these examples are not as uncommon as you might suppose.

Looseleafs are used in situations where the particular advantages they contain can be used to greatest advantage. Knowing the ways in which the looseleaf is more convenient than the disparate primary and secondary sources from which it is made will make clear why looseleafs in several legal areas have largely supplanted traditional legal research in primary sources. Looseleafs gather the relevant primary and secondary material from different sources, present it in a meaningful arrangement, provide superior indexes and other finding aids, then update that material frequently.

Probably the most valuable thing looseleaf services offer the researcher is that they bring together a wide variety of primary sources in one place. To illustrate the value of this, imagine for a moment a research question involving an issue of federal taxation. Say that the question involves the tax treatment of a "wash sale." Without a looseleaf service available, the researcher may have to follow a number of steps to find the information. First, he or she might have to consult a legal dictionary to find out the definition of the phrase "wash sale." After determining the definition, the researcher might consult an annotated federal code in an attempt to find the provision covering this topic. The wash sale rule might be in the *United States Code*, in which case the researcher would then have to consult the *CFR* to find if there are related regulations, then look in treatises or other material for an explanation of the language in the statutes and regulations. After all that, the researcher might try to find cases interpreting the law, law review articles discussing the application of the law, pending bills or proposed regulations that might affect the law, and so on. Clearly, this is an arduous process.

Using a looseleaf service obviates the need to consult all of these different sources because the publishers have done that for you. In the case of the wash sale, the researcher would look up the words in the index, then turn to the appropriate page or paragraph number. There the researcher will find the statute from Title 26 of the *United States Code*, the regulations from Title 26 of the *CFR*, other interpretive rules or guidance from the issuing agency, explanatory or illustrative text written by the looseleaf's editors, citations to secondary sources for further explanation, and so on. All of this appears in one place in the looseleaf, making this truly "one stop shopping" for legal information.

Another advantage the looseleafs have over other sources is currency. Many interfiled looseleafs (we will discuss the different types of looseleafs below) are updated once per week. Given that most primary and secondary sources are updated much less frequently (some being literally years out of date), it is obvious that researchers can make great use of the currency of looseleaf sources. It is true that the advent of the online services has helped make updated primary sources, in particular, available to the researcher in a timely fashion, but looseleafs offer this same currency along with a host of other advantages to keep them from being threatened or readily replaced in the online era.

An often overlooked feature of many looseleafs is that the internal arrangement of the looseleaf is itself instructive. The *Standard Federal Tax Reporter* is arranged according to the Internal Revenue Code sections. Need to know something about a legal issue related to your client's 401(k) account? Turn to that section of the looseleaf; its numbering mirrors the Code's numbering. Another example is the *Federal Securities Law Reporter*, which is arranged by the different major securities acts in American history. There are tabbed sections containing material related to the Securities Act of 1933, the Securities Exchange Act of 1934, the Investment Advisors Act of 1940, and so on. Just being mindful of the arrangement of the looseleaf's sections can provide the intellectual outline of the subject matter.

Finally, looseleafs generally succeed in the goal of being extremely user-friendly. It is true that many researchers looking glumly at the twenty or so thick volumes of the *Standard Federal Tax Reporter* might initially be put off by the seeming complexity and sheer bulk of the set. However, a little diligence will pay dividends to the persevering researcher. Because of the rational arrangement of looseleafs, the exceptionally good indexing, the inclusion of a variety of other finding aids, and the nearly universal inclusion of instructions on how to use each looseleaf in the introductory matter of each set, most researchers can use a looseleaf with confidence and great effectiveness after a few minutes of familiarization with the particulars of each. Using a looseleaf is, despite initial appearances, not very difficult.

9.3   THE DIFFERENT KINDS OF LOOSELEAFS

Legal research guides have for generations divided the looseleaf world into two types; those published like newsletters and those that are the so-called interfiled style. There is no particular reason to depart from this tradition, for in fact there are really only the two different ideas about how to arrange, publish and keep updated comprehensive information on a legal subject from a wide variety of sources. One can either issue periodic updates, along with updated indexes and finding aids each time, in separate pamphlets that are housed cumulatively in binders, or one can send replacement pages periodically with the idea that pages or sections that have changed in any way since the last packet of pages were issued will be discarded to be replaced by the new pages. A deeper comparison of the two types of looseleaf will help explain how each is used.

The newsletter type is called that because updates are sent at regular intervals in the form of one or more pamphlets. In the *United States Law Week*, for example, each release contains one pamphlet with new Supreme Court opinions, one with Supreme Court docketing and other information, one with general legal news, and so on. Note that along with each release must come an updated, cumulative index, table of contents, and any other finding aids or finding lists that come with that looseleaf. You should understand that the indexes and other finding aids must be cumulative in nature or the researcher would have to consult a series of index pamphlets, which would be very inconvenient.

Along with a subscription to the *United States Law Week* (used as the example throughout this section because it is the newsletter-style looseleaf most researchers are familiar with), the publisher (BNA, in this case) sends tabbed binders into which the different pamphlets will be filed. The idea here is that all of the pamphlets from each release will be retained (with the exception of the indexes and other finding aids which, being cumulative, could be discarded as each new one is received, leaving only the most current version). With a typical newsletter looseleaf, the publisher will send new, empty binders annually, keeping the bulk manageable. This is not always the case, however. Many different schemes have been tried, and you need to be a little flexible and prepared to conduct a short examination of each new looseleaf you investigate in order to discover the retention pattern for each new title.

By the end of a volume (one year's worth of issues in the case of the *United States Law Week*) the binders will have a full set of pamphlets behind each binder. The index and the other finding aids will cover the entire year. The next release will come with new tabbed binders, and the process starts anew. This is worth relating because researchers must determine the dates of coverage of the binder on the shelves. Most libraries keep superseded binders (the *United States Law Week* has been published for many decades), and the researcher may have to consult those older volumes in order to get to information from the relevant time period.

The other type of looseleaf is the interfiled type. If you have never turned the pages of one, it might be difficult to fully visualize the description that follows. We strongly recommend that you take a few minutes to familiarize yourself with one or two looseleafs from this category. There is nothing particularly difficult about using these loose-leafs, but they are different from anything else in the law library, and may be initially off-putting.

With the interfiled looseleaf, there are no pamphlets issued like a periodical. Instead, each release (as often as each week) comes in a packet with a description of that release's contents, and a set of pages replacing the superseded or outdated pages in the set. The act of filing the new release involves discarding the pages to be replaced and inserting the new pages. At any time, the looseleaf is completely current, and none of the text is out of date. The indexes and other findings aids are updated in the same way. They, too, are always current.

Interfiled looseleafs can be large and seemingly complex. An example is the *Standard Federal Tax Reporter*, one of the premier interfiled looseleafs on the market. This looseleaf has now grown to nearly twenty volumes per year. Each year's *Standard Federal Tax Reporter* is complete unto itself, with an entirely new edition, with new binders and new contents issued each January. Its arrangement is simple; aside from a few volumes of index and finding aids and other material, the vast bulk of the looseleaf is made up of the Internal Revenue Code, section by section, along with the regulations, explanatory text, key decisions, cross references and other material associated with each section. A researcher needing to know about 501(c)(3) organizations need only turn to that section of the looseleaf and find all of the material related to this Code section. It is not hard to imagine why this collocation of related material in Code section order, along with the weekly updating of this material, makes this looseleaf so useful, and so ubiquitous in the offices of tax lawyers.

With the newsletter looseleafs discussed above, we warned that each looseleaf has its own retention pattern; that is, some start over each new year or volume with new binders, some have other ways to store older issues. The same is true for interfiled looseleafs. The *Standard Federal Tax Reporter*, for example, issues a completely new set of binders each year. Many other interfiled looseleafs, though, do no such thing. (As an aside, why do you think the *Standard Federal Tax Reporter* starts over each new calendar year? It is because, in a very real sense, each year's tax code is a thing unto itself. Someone needing to do research on a tax problem arising in 1999 needs to have a complete set of the laws, regulations and other materials as they were in that year. Very few other legal subjects have such stark temporal divisions year to year.)

For those looseleafs where it isn't critically important to begin anew each year, a variety of other retention schemes are in place. Most commonly, though, the binders are never replaced, new material is merely added for the entire life of the subscription. Since the process of updating involves replacing old pages with new, the age of the binders, the lack of a volume number or date of publication is not an issue. Picture two libraries in the same town. The first subscribes to a particular looseleaf in Year 1 and faithfully files the updated pages each week, year in and year out. The second library subscribes to the looseleaf much later, in Year 10. The contents sent to the second library in Year 10 match exactly the text in the first library, given that the first library has been keeping their copy current by filing replacement pages as they arrive. Many researchers approach a looseleaf title on the shelves of their library, note with despair that the binders seem to be fifteen years old, and conclude that the looseleaf is so out of date it can be of no use. This is absolutely the wrong assumption to make, of course: as long as the subscription is current the looseleaf is up to date. But how to tell, then, that the subscription is current, and how to tell that the library has been filing replacement pages as it should?

The last report letter (sometimes called by slightly different names) is the way to determine the currency of any looseleaf. Recall that the updates are sent periodically in a packet, complete with a description of that release's contents. That description, which resembles a cover letter or transmittal memo, is known as the last report letter. Last report letters are always retained in the looseleaf set, usually behind a tab or divider specifically reserved for them. By paging through the last report letters you can quickly determine if every release has been received and filed. Because the last report letter contains a description of the new developments contained in the pages of that release, some lawyers use it as a current awareness tool. If you examined each last report letter in your field's flagship looseleaf as it arrived, it would be like reading a quick weekly update of recent events in the field. You could decide whether any of the new pages in that release required closer review.

One other feature of the interfiled looseleaf, especially the large, comprehensive sets, is that the finding aids can often be quite complex. In the *Standard Federal Tax Reporter*, for example, the main index alone is several hundred pages long. There are also a variety of other indexes and finding aids in the set. One typical arrangement in these looseleafs is to have a large general index, along with an index of new developments. This allows the researcher to check quickly for new matter. What constitutes "new" differs from looseleaf to looseleaf. Often, these comprehensive looseleafs reprint cases from a variety of reporters that have to do with the subject matter the looseleaf covers. *Standard Federal Tax Reporter's* associated publication of tax cases, *United States Tax Cases*, is a reprint of tax cases from the primary reporters, along with descriptions of some unpublished cases not appearing anywhere else in print. The indexing in the main looseleaf usually includes a table of cases keyed to the cases volumes. One occasionally finds a table of new cases, too.

The point here is that each looseleaf has a form suited to the needs of the researcher in that particular field. Often, even in the titles produced by a single publisher, there is a bewildering variety of arrangements, finding aids, and other practices. This statement is not made to intimidate; rather, the object is to convince you to take a few minutes to examine the looseleaf's particulars before diving in, and to convince you to take the time to read the instructions for use (often found behind a tab labeled something like "How to Use This Reporter"). These short instructions can save the researcher valuable time and frustration.

9.4 USING A NEWSLETTER–STYLE LOOSELEAF

Newsletter–style looseleafs are as often used for current awareness as for actual research. Many practitioners read the releases as they are issued, and retain them in their binders for future reference if some development or case or problem calls to mind something read and remembered at some point in the past. Using a looseleaf in this way is simplicity itself, and needs no further explanation.

Using a newsletter–style looseleaf for research is different, but not necessarily difficult. Usually the researcher begins with a topic or subject to be researched. Remember that this type of looseleaf has a cumulative index, updated with each new release, so there is no need to consult any but the most recent version. There are often other, more specific indexes, which could be consulted as well. These looseleafs commonly have tables of contents, tables of cases, tables of statutes, and other aids to research. Depending upon the specific situation of the researcher, one of these tables might be the logical starting point. It is incumbent upon the researcher to investigate the available finding aids to determine which is appropriate for the current research need.

Once the index or finding aid has yielded a citation to the relevant section or sections, the researcher need only turn to the part of the looseleaf indicated. Remember that the looseleaf is constantly being updated, and that even if the search refers to a release from several months ago, it is generally true that there is no need to try to update beyond what the (updated, remember) index has referred you to.

The thing to bear in mind while researching in a newsletter–style looseleaf is that while these publications attempt to draw together all of the material relevant to specific areas of law, the periodic updating with pamphlet releases makes integrating current information difficult. In rapidly changing areas, the index may point the researcher to the main text and to a series of new matters or new developments sections. The researcher may be forced to trace his or her issue across several different locations within the looseleaf. There is nothing particularly difficult in this; it simply requires a little diligence and some organized thinking and planning.

9.5   USING AN INTERFILED LOOSELEAF

Researching an issue in an interfiled looseleaf presents the researcher with none of the updating issues of the newsletter–style looseleafs, but there are a few complications worth noting. One of the key features of the interfiled looseleaf is the indexing, which is often incredibly detailed. Researchers used to substandard indexing, such as that found in the *CFR* index, will be greatly relieved to find looseleaf indexing so granular that almost any issue can be quickly located within the looseleaf. Remember, though, that the largest, most complex interfiled looseleafs might have several volumes of indexes and finding aids. It will take the researcher new to that particular title a few minutes to understand how best to begin, and which finding aid to choose.

Another apparent complication of the interfiled looseleaf is the simultaneous use of paragraph numbers and page numbers. Why would this be the case? Imagine a case where the publisher of an interfiled looseleaf relies exclusively on page numbers. When it comes time for the next update, the new release contains a twenty page discussion of a topic that will replace a one paragraph discussion that came before. The library discards the single page, replaces it with twenty new ones. What happens, then, to the page numbers? This is an obviously unworkable situation. The solution is the use of paragraph numbers. In the typical interfiled looseleaf (we say typical because there is always an exception out there somewhere) the paragraph number refers to the smallest, indivisible treatment of a topic. It may be one paragraph long or many dozens of pages. In fact, in those looseleafs that reprint cases, each case is usually assigned one paragraph number. What, then, are the page numbers for? They are for the library's filers only, and can be ignored by the researcher (except if you suspect a page is missing or some other unusual situation). All of the looseleaf's finding aids refer solely to the paragraph numbers, not the page numbers. Novice researchers are often thrown by the paragraph numbers, but there is absolutely nothing complex or mysterious about them or their use.

The researcher using an interfiled looseleaf almost always begins with the index or another finding aid. Sometimes the arrangement can be so transparent that the researcher can turn directly to the relevant section (as in our discussion of 501(c)(3), above), but that's risky, for reasons of completeness. After the paragraph citation is found, the researcher turns to the appropriate paragraph, and finds there the statute, regulation, editorial commentary, cross references to other material, case law, journal articles, and so on. It is this drawing together of text from disparate sources that makes these looseleafs so valuable. Remember that the text is constantly updated, so it is not necessary to spend time confirming that statutory, regulatory and other text is current.

In some areas of practice, the comprehensive looseleaf is so pervasive, so thorough, and so indispensable, that it is often the only work the lawyer consults on an average day. Clearly, these looseleafs are seen to be worth their surprisingly high prices because they save the lawyer valuable time by gathering together, arranging and updating all of the relevant information on their area of law. A student graduating from law school with no experience using looseleafs, even if that student is planning to enter a practice area, like general litigation, not well served by looseleafs, is missing an important part of his or her education.

9.6   WHAT IS NOT IN LOOSELEAFS?

As thorough as looseleaf services can be, it is a mistake to think that everything one might need to find or read on a particular topic can be found in the relevant looseleaf. That is not always the case.

It is often the case that the most recent developments are only described, not reprinted in full text. Very recent opinions are an example of this, as are unpublished decisions. It is very common that the reprinting of opinions can take a release or two. New statutes or regulations are also occasionally represented only with a citation and a brief description. This is not a very big problem, of course, only a mild inconvenience.

Of more consequence is the fact that few looseleafs publish administrative hearing decisions and other possibly relevant matters. With the Internal Revenue Service, for example, the major looseleafs tend not to reprint Private Letter Rulings, No–action Letters, field manuals and the like. These materials are printed in other sources. In nearly every field of law covered by a looseleaf service there are some potentially relevant sources the researcher will have to consult other kinds of publications in order to find. There is no general advice to give here, only that researchers should try to familiarize themselves with the literature in the particular field, consult specialized research guides or the nearest law librarian for help. These omissions are not failings of looseleafs, just a practical limit on the amount of material that can be included in any one publication.

Students are often surprised at how few are the citations to law review and other journal articles in the typical looseleaf. Since looseleaf services are geared for the practitioner, however, it shouldn't come as too much of a surprise that the publishers focus on primary sources and narrowly tailored commentary on those sources rather than on academic literature. The researcher may wish to supplement looseleaf research with a search for legal journal articles using the indexes or full text databases described in Chapter 4, above.

9.7   FINDING A LOOSELEAF ON YOUR TOPIC

Once you've determined that your legal research problem is not one easily solved by other means, that it seems likely to require consulting a number of different kinds of primary sources for an answer, that your subject matter is in the kind of heavily regulated area often covered by looseleaf services, and that you don't know the names of any looseleafs that might help, how should you proceed? There are several different ways to look for a looseleaf on a particular topic.

The first thing to do is consult, if it is available, a reference work called *Legal Looseleafs in Print*. This soft-bound work, compiled by Arlene L. Eis and published annually by InfoSources Publishing, is an invaluable aid for helping locate a relevant looseleaf. The book is helpfully arranged into three different finding lists; listing looseleafs by title, by publisher, and most helpfully, by topic. Within each topic, available looseleafs are subdivided by jurisdiction where necessary. There are, for example, looseleafs focusing on the law of one state on a particular topic; such as *Pennsylvania Workers' Compensation: Law and Practice* or *Tennessee Corporations*, both published by West Group. But what if the library to which you have access doesn't have a copy of *Legal*

Looseleafs in Print? Not likely. If a library is large enough and serious enough to own more than a few looseleafs it will also have a copy of this work. If your library does not have this book, check to see if your library has access to the contents of InfoSource Publishing's website, which they call LawTRIO, which contains an electronic version of the contents of *Legal Looseleafs in Print*.

If you cannot consult *Legal Looseleafs in Print*, you might try to find a relevant product by examining the websites of the largest publishers of looseleafs. All major legal publishers have their catalogues of titles available on their websites. Although many publishers produce legal looseleafs, the list of major publishers is surprisingly small. We would recommend searching the websites of Commerce Clearing House (CCH), Bureau of National Affairs (BNA), West Group, Lexis Law Publishing, Juris, and Matthew Bender. These imprints change some over time as publishers are bought up by one another and by other large publishers, but these six imprints together account for the majority of leading looseleaf publications.

Of course, another solution to the problem of locating an appropriate looseleaf is to consult a law librarian. Law firm librarians, law school librarians, court librarians, and many others are familiar with these publications, know how to locate and evaluate them, and are willing to help. Remember that even a publication as useful as *Legal Looseleafs in Print* cannot replace the experience and advice of a librarian whose reliability you have come to trust. Within any single topic there may be several choices of looseleafs available, and comparing and evaluating the choices is something with which most librarians have considerable experience.

9.8   ONLINE VERSIONS OF LOOSELEAFS

It will come as no surprise to you that many of the leading publishers of looseleaf services have made their contents available electronically. After several years of experimentation with versions of looseleafs using a variety of proprietary software, diskette and cd-rom formats, the emerging standard now is to deliver this content to subscribers via the web. While this has greatly simplified the technical aspects of looseleaf management for practitioners and librarians, it is too much to say that the electronic looseleafs are supplanting their print equivalents. The reason for this is simple; it has proven devilishly hard to create online interfaces that are as transparent and intuitive as the print versions. Users must invest a good deal of time up front to overcome the relatively steep learning curve for each title. Also, many users of electronic looseleafs end up printing out a great many pages, choosing to print results rather than to read them online. Despite these drawbacks, which may yet prove to be soluble, the advantages these services offer make them attractive to users committed to learning how to use them.

The newsletter–type looseleafs were the first to be made available electronically, for reasons easy to discern. Since these looseleafs are published like journals, in self–contained issues, it is simple to make an electronic version searchable by release date, or keyed to the cumulative indexing. The huge advantage of the electronic looseleaf over the print equivalent, of course, is the keyword searching function. As good as the indexing and other finding aids in the typical looseleaf are, the ability to search for specific terms and phrases and retrieve every occurrence is an immensely powerful enhancement. As an example, Westlaw and Lexis have included the *United States Law Week* as part of their respective services from their earliest days. Users find this easy to understand; one can search the database containing past issues of the *United States Law Week* as easily as searching the database containing all of the opinions from the Ohio or Minnesota courts. Due to the power of keyword searching and the relative ease of use (or said another way, due to the less steep learning curve involved in using these services effectively), it is very likely that we will see more and more newsletter–type looseleafs available via the online services or on the web by subscription.

Interfiled looseleafs currently are more problematic. The interfaces have proven notoriously difficult for users to understand. In addition, the interfaces have not proven stable over time as publishers try to respond to customer suggestions, striving to make the electronic version usable (and less daunting) without the investment of time up front.

Some of these electronic interfiled looseleafs are immensely powerful, with completely hyperlinked indexing, tables (contents, cases, statutes and so on), and other finding aids and features that make following the annotations from source to source quite simple. Also, these products have keyword searching capability that allows the user to find material even more narrowly focused than that in the excellent indexes. Despite all of these advantages, researchers have proven resistant to using these resources. The interfaces put them off, the arrangement of the sections, so critical to making the structure of the subject matter clear, is harder to visualize in the electronic versions, and, as in the newsletter looseleafs, researchers wind up printing out much of what they find. In fact, many researchers limit their use of online interfiled looseleafs to simple retrieval tasks.

This situation may right itself as publishers gain more expertise in the difficult task of presenting their content on the web. Users may gain in sophistication, making the barriers to use seem lower on average, or the high costs of the print versions may convince libraries to cancel their print, leaving researchers no other choice but the electronic versions.

Our advice? Don't be daunted by the apparent complexity of the electronic looseleafs. They conform to principles that you should, by now, be fluent with. These services, like their print counterparts, gather together primary and some secondary sources from a wide variety of other publications, then arrange them in a meaningful way. They are continuously updated, with dead or moot or superseded language excised. The finding aids are state of the art, typically, and in the online environment you will also have the option of keyword searching. Remember a few key characteristics shared by all looseleafs regardless of format; they all have instructions for use, they all rely on superior indexes and finding aids. Publishers of the electronic services usually have help lines you can call or email for help, and they occasionally (and more and more frequently) have tutorials and other quite elaborate instructional material. Investing a little time before beginning research can save you a great deal of time later.

One final word about online looseleafs is in order, and the general principle will hold you in good stead with any online source you may use. It is still the case that virtually every source available in electronic format began its life in print form. In virtually every case, it is very difficult to use the online version of any publication as effectively, efficiently and thoroughly if you are not fluent with the print source from which the electronic source is derived. As true as this is for case reporters or annotated codes, it is even more the case with looseleafs, which are such hybrid and complex sources to begin with. It is tempting to log on to the electronic version of a looseleaf on your topic from the comfort of the office or from home, but without a thorough grounding in the print progenitor you will be taking an unnecessary risk.

Chapter 10

COURT RULES

10.1 WHAT ARE COURT RULES AND WHY DO THEY MATTER?

Early in our country's history, it became clear that courts needed to have the authority to make and enforce rules to ensure the smooth and fair operation of court business. The resulting court rules varied from jurisdiction to jurisdiction. There was also an ongoing question of the power of courts to make rules that were not purely procedural. By the 1930s, the federal court system required a uniform set of court rules that would apply throughout the country. The story of the passage of the first of the federal court rules, the Federal Rules of Civil Procedure, is too long a tale to relate here, but the rules represented a great step forward for both the reality and the perception of fairness that the federal courts require.

After the adoption of the FRCP, the federal courts continued to develop rules to govern the operation of the courts and to lay out orderly processes by which parties could conduct litigation. The resulting sets of rules, most notably, the Federal Rules of Criminal Procedure, and the Federal Rules of Evidence, together form the basic rules of federal litigation by which all parties must abide.

In addition to these overarching federal court rules, two other kinds of rules were developed. The first type govern procedures in particular courts: Rules of the United States Supreme Court, the Federal Rules of Appellate Procedure, Federal Rules of Bankruptcy Procedure, and so on. The idea is that each of these courts is so specialized that additional rules are needed to address issues specific to that court. The other type of federal court rule is the body of local court rules. Each federal district court and appellate court is empowered to enforce rules local to it. These local rules tend to be more focussed on the formalisms of litigation:

maximum page lengths for briefs, rules about cameras in the courtroom, or electronic filing requirements, for example.

State courts, too, have their own court rules. Usually printed as part of the state's annotated code, state court rules tend not to vary from court to court within a jurisdiction as much as the federal court rules do. Almost all states have rules that mirror the major federal rules, those related to civil procedure, criminal procedure and evidence.

Does this matter to the researcher? Definitely. It is critically important for the researcher involved in litigation to understand the procedural requirements of the court where the case will be heard. Without understanding rules related to procedure, for example, a lawyer can miss filing deadlines, have pleadings returned because of improper formatting, delivery method or timing, etc. There is an ongoing debate on where the line between process and substance can be drawn. Court rules are intended to be purely procedural, but it is true that unless the procedural rules are understood and followed, a client's substantive rights can be severely affected.

Court rules, then, can be thought of as the rules governing any piece of litigation. They are the rules of the game, and one cannot properly plan and execute a case without a clear understanding of their requirements.

10.2   FEDERAL COURT RULES

As mentioned above, the 1930s brought a movement to standardize the procedural rules in the federal courts. The first set of rules promulgated were the Federal Rules of Civil Procedure. These rules were followed a few years later by the Federal Rules of Criminal Procedure. It took another three decades and Congressional action to bring the Federal Rules of Evidence into being. The rules in these three sets have been published in many unannotated and a few annotated versions. The annotations are crucial because these rules are so often the bases of federal appeals, and the annotations track all of these opinions where the rules have been parsed, examined and applied by federal courts. In addition, there are many helpful secondary sources discussing federal rules which the researcher might consult, and the annotations provide citations to these as well.

10.3   FINDING ANNOTATED FEDERAL
COURT RULES

The three major sets of federal court rules are widely available in a number of formats. Several publishers, for example, produce relatively inexpensive, softbound unannotated sets of the rules for use by law students in first year Civil Procedure courses. The web is also an easy place to find the bare texts of the rules themselves. In one such source, the Administrative Office of the U.S. Courts maintains a website with links to electronic versions of the rules for every federal court in every jurisdiction, at http://www.uscourts.gov/rules/. (This website, by the way, also contains a wealth of information on the rulemaking process, including drafts of proposed new rules, committee reports on rules, and so on). These rules can also be found in a looseleaf set called *Federal Local Court Rules*. Whether in print or electronic versions, there are many ways to find unannotated court rules.

That, however, is almost never what the researcher needs. The language of the rule itself is tested, interpreted and applied by case law. Courts are frequently asked to rule on procedural issues and, not surprisingly, new questions are raised constantly by litigants. In addition, these rules, particularly procedural, evidentiary and jurisdictional rules, are the subject of a great deal of scholarly investigation, and a wealth of secondary sources exists to explain, to criticize, to categorize, and sometimes to influence the interpretation and application of court rules. In order to easily locate the entire universe of written material relevant to the understanding and use of federal court rules, the researcher needs annotated rules.

What is in the annotations to court rules, and why are they so important to researchers? In short, the annotated rules are like any other annotated statute. The annotations gather together relevant material from a variety of sources: the rule itself, the committee reports and drafts and other "legislative history" of the rule, cases construing the meaning and application of the rule, and secondary sources explaining or contextualizing the rule. Together, these disparate materials can tell you what the law really is, what the rule really means.

The easiest place to find annotated federal rules are in *United States Code Annotated* and *United States Code Service*. In these two commercially published versions of the federal code, the major rules sets are reprinted as appendices to relevant Titles, and annotated exactly as are the statutes themselves. There are other places where federal court rules are annotated, and in different ways. For a description of where to find important annotated versions of different federal court rules, **see Table 10.A.**

10.4 SECONDARY SOURCES AND FEDERAL RULES

While it is certainly true that consulting annotated collections of federal court rules represents a significant advantage over unannotated versions, often the researcher needs more information or explanation

Table 10.A—Selected Sources of Annotated Federal Court Rules

1. **Federal Rules of Civil Procedure**

   USCA: Title 28 Rules volumes

   Westlaw: Database, **US–RULES** (same annotations as in *USCA*)

   USCS: Rules volumes

   Lexis: Library;File = **GENFED;FRCP** (same annotations as in *USCS*)

   Moore's Federal Practice

   Federal Practice and Procedure

   U.S. Supreme Court Digest, Lawyers Edition—Court Rules volumes

2. **Federal Rules of Criminal Procedure**

   USCA: Title 18 Rules volumes

   Westlaw: Database, **US–RULES** (same annotations as in *USCA*)

   USCS: Rules volumes

   Lexis: Library;File = **GENFED;FRCRP** (same annotations as in *USCS*)

   Moore's Federal Practice

   Federal Practice and Procedure

   U.S. Supreme Court Digest, Lawyers Edition—Court Rules volumes

3. **Federal Rules of Evidence**

   USCA: Title 28 Rules volumes

   Westlaw: Database, **US–RULES** (same annotations as in *USCA*)

   USCS: Rules volumes

   Lexis: Library;File = **GENFED;FRE** (same annotations as in *USCS*)

   Moore's Federal Practice

   Federal Practice and Procedure

   U.S. Supreme Court Digest, Lawyers Edition—Court Rules volumes than can be readily gleaned from the annotated source. In that case, especially where explanation or context is what is most needed, it is to secondary sources the researcher should turn. Fortunately for the researcher, there are a wealth of useful, current and authoritative treatises available to help. In most cases, the treatises have been written by eminent scholars and are compiled in large, comprehensive, multivolume treatises. The best of these rank among the handful of brand-name treatises in the legal research world.

In a field filled with choices for the legal researcher, several titles stand out due to their authority, clarity, accuracy and explanatory value. Foremost among them is *Federal Practice and Procedure*, by Wright and Miller. Now in its third edition, this monumental work runs to several dozen volumes, is kept current with pocket parts, and covers virtually every aspect of federal civil procedure. Recognized as a leading authority in the field, this work is relied upon by lawyers and courts alike. Part of its appeal for lawyers and researchers is its detailed and strikingly clear discussions of procedural rules.

Another comprehensive treatment of federal court rules is *Moore's Federal Practice, 2d*. This multi-volume treatise, published in looseleaf form, was first published in the 1940s, beginning soon after the promulgation of the Federal Rules of Civil Procedure. Moore's provides in-depth explanation and annotation of the federal rules on civil procedure, evidence and criminal procedure, as well as other related material.

A third important source of federal court rule annotations is the *United States Supreme Court Digest, Lawyers Edition*. This digest contains several volumes dedicated to court rules. It is worth noting that the case annotations only include Supreme Court cases. This source includes Advisory Committee notes as well.

10.5 FEDERAL COURT RULES
JUDICIALLY CONSIDERED

Part of the value of the annotated sets of federal court rules and the comprehensive treatises is that they cite and discuss the many opinions which examine, interpret and apply those rules. Just as is the case with any other kind of statute (for federal court rules can be so considered), the language of the statute, the legislative history behind its drafting and adoption, and the case law construing it all work together in complex ways, combining to form the "meaning" of the law itself. One cannot answer a question of constitutional rights simply by reading the language of the constitutional provision in question, nor can a researcher adequately research a question of jurisdiction, evidence or procedure generally by referring only to the language of the rule.

In order to do thorough research on a procedural issue, then, it is necessary to find and address the case law. Finding this body of relevant cases should present few problems because there are tools at hand the researcher can use which make the process essentially a mechanical one. In addition to the normal case-finding methods discussed elsewhere in this book (see Chapter 5), there are annotated rules sets and one other specialized source, *Federal Rules Decisions* (*FRD*). Remember that federal cases are published in the *United States Reports*, *Federal Reporter* and the *Federal Supplement*. The *FRD* covers federal district court cases discussing federal court rules that are not reported in the *Federal Supplement*. *FRD* is published by West, and is part of the National Reporter System. In addition to otherwise unreported federal district court cases, *FRD* contains the texts of speeches and articles related to the federal rules.

10.6   USING CITATORS FOR UPDATING FEDERAL COURT RULES

Both Shepard's and KeyCite make it possible for the researcher to see which cases mention any particular federal rule, in exactly the same way one uses these citators to see which later cases have mentioned a particular case or statute. But why do this? Assuming that federal court rules aren't very likely to be overruled or held unconstitutional, is a researcher really trying to find out if any particular federal rule is still good law? Not really. The reason a researcher concerned with, say, Federal Rule of Evidence 1002 (otherwise known as the best evidence rule) would use a citator is to gather a list of every case that has mentioned this evidentiary rule in order to see how it has been applied and interpreted in a particular jurisdiction or period of time.

In Lexis, it is easy to Shepardize this evidentiary rule once you have determined the precise citation format required. The Shepard's report indicates that this rule has been cited in slightly more than 300 cases, and only once in the United States Supreme Court. (This search is also possible in print, of course, by using *Shepard's U.S. Citations*, but as with most situations, it is our opinion that it is vastly easier and better to Shepardize online when possible.) What use would a researcher make of this list? It might prove informative to at least look at all the recent cases from the relevant jurisdiction to how courts have interpreted and applied the rule.

With KeyCite, on Westlaw, the process is much the same. Once you have determined the exact citation form, it is easy to retrieve the full KeyCite report for the relevant rule. Unlike Shepard's, which returns results in the traditional order (descending order of court, then reverse chronological order), Keycite organizes the citing cases into subject matter divisions, an interesting innovation. One can then limit the

KeyCite search to include only cases from relevant jurisdictions and/or time periods. KeyCite also provides cross-references to many more secondary sources than Shepard's, which, depending upon your needs, is either very useful or simply a distraction.

10.7 STATE COURT RULES

State court rules operate very much like their federal counterparts. One difference is that there is less consensus on the source of authority for state rules, and practice differs from state to state. Some states consider state court rules to be entirely the province of the state judiciary; that is, that state court rules are nothing more than an example of the judiciary's power to regulate its own business. On the other end of the spectrum, some states hold that only legislative action can create or amend state court rules. In effect, these states consider court rules as just another area of state legislation. In between these two extremes, many states are a hybrid of the two theories above. In these hybrid states, court rules are considered delegated legislation. The state legislature is the source from which flows the authority to promulgate rules of procedure or evidence, etc., but the legislatures are free to delegate this authority to a rulemaking body, usually the state judiciary. This means that court rules occupy a niche in state law roughly parallel to state regulations.

For the average researcher or practitioner, these distinctions are without much significance. Whatever their ultimate source of power, state court rules have the status of state law, and are applied and interpreted, in most instances, no differently regardless of the theory under which they were promulgated.

10.8 ANNOTATED STATE COURT RULES

Finding unannotated versions of state court rules is very easy. Virtually every state has made the rules readily available at the state website, but without annotation, of course. In addition, state court rules are available in print and electronic formats in a number of other places. What one needs, however, is an annotated version. Remember, the text of the rules themselves are only one portion of the information you need to determine what the law is. You also need case law, and occasionally secondary sources as well. You need annotated rules.

Fortunately, in every state that has an annotated code available, the court rules are included and annotated. Regardless of the theory of authority under which the rules were promulgated (as discussed above), the annotated codes treat court rules as just another state statute. As with the rest of the statutes in the state code, the quality and comprehensiveness of the annotation depends in large part upon which publisher is responsible for the annotated code. It is true in most instances that the publishers do not exert the same effort as that given to annotating the federal code, but one will usually find enough in the annotation to satisfy the researcher's needs.

Chapter 11

LEGAL ETHICS RESEARCH

11.1 INTRODUCTION TO LEGAL ETHICS RESEARCH

This chapter is intended to introduce you to researching a legal topic that will have an impact on you throughout your legal career, no matter what field of law you choose. In truth, as important as legal ethics knowledge is, imparting this knowledge is only a secondary goal of the chapter. Our primary reason for including this chapter in the book is to expose students to a few new concepts. Most importantly, law students need to know about uniform and model laws, and why conducting research into any state law that began life as a uniform or model law can be different from ordinary state law research. By the end of the chapter you will see that, despite the differences, legal ethics research follows the familiar pattern; there are statutes, several varieties of judicial and other opinions that together can be considered case law, and secondary sources that are important in helping to explain and interpret the primary sources.

Another concept with which you should become familiar is the idea of the self-regulating industry. Until the 1970s, the American Bar Association considered its ethical rules to be private laws regulating the behavior of members of a voluntary industry group. Many industries have implemented some degree of self-regulation. In the case of the ABA, however, some of the ethical rules could have been interpreted to be private agreements in restraint of trade, which would have been in violation of the antitrust laws. Once it became clear that the kind of ethical rules the American Bar Association's members felt it was important to abide by might be found to be illegal, the idea of the national bar as a self-regulating industry was largely abandoned. The ABA, from that point until today, has taken the position that its ethics code and rules are models only, and that the ABA merely advocates their adoption by all of the state legislatures. And the state legislatures have, to a degree, acquiesced, but not without some important differences from state to state. Because of this history, legal ethics research should be approached first as a matter of state law, but second as a uniform or model law, with all of the research implications we will discuss in this chapter.

11.2   MODEL AND UNIFORM LAWS GENERALLY

The uniform or model law is a concept with which students should be familiar, even from first year courses. Most Contracts courses, as an example, contain at least some mention of the Uniform Commercial Code. Many Criminal Law classes discuss the Model Penal Code. But just what is a model law or a uniform law, how is it different from the laws we have already examined, and what difference does it make to you, the researcher?

In the typical case, a body of scholars, judges, lawyers, and other authorities meets to draft a model or uniform law on a subject, and to urge its adoption by the legislatures of many jurisdictions. This body, no matter how influential, is not making law in any way. In the case of the Uniform Commercial Code (and all the legal ethics strictures we will discuss in this chapter) the proposed uniform law has no legal effect at all until legislatures adopt it and make it part of the state law. It is also true that each jurisdiction is free to adopt all or part of the proposed law, or to change any part of it the legislature wishes. The term "uniform", then, applies only to the source, not to the resulting state legislation, which will probably be anything but uniform across all jurisdictions.

There are several groups taking the lead in drafting uniform and model laws for adoption by states. Foremost among them is the National Conference of Commissioners on Uniform State Laws ("NCCUSL"). Founded well over a century ago, the NCCUSL is now comprised of over three hundred scholars, judges and lawyers. These leading figures have been appointed by the various states, and, according to the Conference's website, at http://www.nccusl.org, their mission is to "draft proposals for uniform and model laws on subjects where uniformity is desirable and practicable, and work toward their enactment in legislatures." As of this writing, this highly influential group has drafted several dozen uniform and model laws, from the Uniform Commercial Code to the Model Marital Property Act, from the Unclaimed Property Act to the Determination of Death Act. The texts of all of these acts are available at the NCCUSL website, along with detailed information about the adoption of each act by state legislatures. Much of this information is also available in print in *Uniform Laws Annotated*, published by Thomson/West.

11.3   SOURCES OF AUTHORITY—AMERICAN BAR ASSOCIATION ETHICAL CODES AND RULES

The modern system of regulating legal ethics began in 1908 when the ABA, influenced by several state ethics codes and by urging from its membership, published the first national, comprehensive code of ethical lawyer behavior. The ABA Canons of Professional Ethics contained thirty-two canons, adherence to which was required for continued membership in good standing in the ABA. These canons described general rules of conduct, and although amended several times over the following decades, the need to replace them with a code better matching the complexity of modern practice became increasingly clear as the years passed.

The resulting new code, called the ABA Code of Professional Responsibility, was adopted by the ABA in 1969. Several years later, in response to the realization that this private "law" might not withstand antitrust scrutiny, the ABA changed the name of the code to the ABA Model Code of Professional Responsibility, reflecting the idea that the code was a model which state legislatures could use when drafting or revising state legal ethics laws. In fact, many states did just that, and the adoption of the Model Code became widespread in the 1970s.

This radical rethinking of the regulation of lawyer ethical behavior consisted of canons, ethical considerations and disciplinary rules. The canons and ethical considerations are "aspirational" meaning that they represent goals to which all lawyers should aspire, but there are no penalties for failing to meet one or more of them. One example is that all lawyers should spend a certain number of hours per year on *pro bono* legal work. Failure (or even refusal) to do so exposes the lawyer to no punishment. The disciplinary rules, on the other hand, are "mandatory." The disciplinary rules describe the minimum level of conduct below which no lawyer can fall without being subject to disciplinary action. It is important to be clear about the distinction between the canons and ethical considerations, which are aspirational (describing what a lawyer should do) and the disciplinary rules, which are mandatory (and describe what a lawyer must do).

The Model Code was not without its critics, however. Many lawyers and state legislatures felt that the Code placed too much emphasis on the ethical challenges facing the trial lawyer, and not enough on transactional work and other branches of law. In response to these criticisms, a commission was established by the ABA to draft a new set of ethical guidelines.

In 1983, the ABA approved the adoption of the commission's new guidelines, called the ABA Model Rules of Professional Conduct. Since 1983, the Model Rules have been amended several times, including a major revision adopted in 2002. The Model Rules are divided into three parts; the subject divisions (called "titles"), the disciplinary rules themselves, and then the commentary. The Model Rules are very much like the uniform or model laws described in Section 9.2, intended to serve as a model that state legislatures or courts can use when passing ethics laws or adjudicating ethics complaints or cases.

Within each of the titles of the Model Rules there are several disciplinary rules and their associated commentary. The rule itself is stated in simple, black-letter language. The comments seek to clarify or illustrate the meaning of the rule. The comments are usually explanatory in nature, occasionally illustrative, but are specifically designed not to impose obligations on the lawyer beyond what is found in the rule itself. You might profitably think of the comments as part annotation, part legislative history.

11.4 SOURCES OF AUTHORITY—STATE LAW

Despite the foregoing section on the history of the ABA codes and rules, you must bear in mind that these national models are models only. Regulation of lawyer ethics is almost entirely a state matter. The only important exception to the proposition that legal ethics is a matter of state law is that lawyers must follow the rules of court of federal courts in which they practice, some of which have adopted either the Model Code or Rules themselves. It is also true that certain local bar associations have some responsibility for lawyer oversight and discipline, but the instances in which local rules differ significantly from state law are rare.

The Model Rules have been adopted in whole or in part by several jurisdictions. The legal ethics laws and rules of other states still reflect their Model Code origins. Confusingly, some states have adopted parts of both, or adopted one or the other but with significant departures from the ABA language. California, by way of example, has never adopted language from either the Code or Rules, but since their laws are so similar to those of the ABA models, not even in California's case is the state completely self-contained when it comes to interpreting and applying ethical laws in specific cases. It is not uncommon for California courts to take outside practice and precedents into account. All of this causes no little confusion for the researcher, but by following the techniques described in Section 11.7, below, you will be able to conduct accurate and thorough legal ethics research.

11.5 SOURCES OF AUTHORITY—
"CASE LAW" PUBLICATIONS

In this section, the phrase "case law" will be interpreted expansively, taking in more than opinions written by judges in actual controversies in the state or federal court systems. Case law, for our purposes in this section, will include ethics opinions from a number of sources in addition to traditional case law. Why? Legal ethics is one of a number of practice areas where the advisory opinion (including the non-judicial advisory opinions by, e.g., one or another bar entity) is often used as a test case for a specific set of facts or for interpretation of a particular rule or statute. These opinions are relied upon by lawyers in their practices, and by courts and other disciplinary bodies when adjudicating claims and complaints. In this way advisory opinions are used like case law, and it is a useful fiction to consider them as such.

There is, of course, a body of traditional case law to be researched as well. Legal ethics rules are a matter of state law, and lawyers of a particular state have access to the courts to challenge or appeal a ruling made by the state bar or other entity charged with lawyer discipline. Ordinary state case law research techniques apply in the case of legal ethics as much as for any other area. State and regional digests allow for subject access to cases in specific jurisdictions. The online services allow for full-text searching of cases for specific words or phrases. The difference in the case of legal ethics is that this is only the first step in the process of case law research. There are other sources of "case law" to be investigated.

The researcher should also examine the results of disciplinary proceedings in the state. Often these proceedings are not published formally, but are summarized in the state or local bar association journal. These journals are available in print, on the web, and in the online services, in most cases. It can be difficult to isolate only those hearings or other proceedings that concern your specific issue.

There are two publications with which every legal ethics researcher should be familiar. One is the *ABA/BNA Lawyers' Manual on Professional Conduct*, which is jointly published in looseleaf format by the ABA and BNA. This invaluable resource is also available on Westlaw and Lexis and from BNA as a subscription-based web product. Among other useful features, this publication contains summaries of, and references to, disciplinary proceedings, court cases, and ethics opinions from every state. Consulting this looseleaf early in your research can save you a great deal of time and trouble. The other publication is the *National Reporter on Legal Ethics and Professional Responsibility*, published by University Publications of America, and edited by Roy M. Mersky and Norman Quist. This important resource reprints in full text selected state and local ethics opinions. A version of this resource is available on Lexis, but not all states are included (Library;File = **ETHICS;ETHOP**).

These bar association ethics opinions are the final type of case law the researcher needs to consult. The American Bar Association and the bar associations of all fifty states and the District of Columbia publish ethics opinions. These opinions are advisory in nature, that is, they are written prospectively, often in response to inquiries by a lawyer. Most states publish their ethics opinions in the state or local bar association journal, while a few states do not publish them at all. Westlaw and Lexis include state ethics opinions in their databases as well. Many states make ethics opinions available via the state or state bar association website. Finally, as noted above, the *ABA/BNA Lawyers' Manual on Professional Conduct* contains summaries of state and national ethics opinions. Wherever the ethics opinions from your state happen to be published, they are an important part of your legal ethics research. While it is technically true that these opinions are advisory in nature, state courts often find their interpretations persuasive and choose to follow their advice. In most instances, they have nearly the same precedential weight as actual cases.

Since 1924, the American Bar Association has issued formal and informal ethics opinions. Again, these are advisory in nature, but courts commonly cite them as authority when interpreting or applying a state statute derived from an ABA model. Formal ethics opinions are issued on matters the ABA deems to be of general interest to the bar. Informal ethics opinions, on the other hand, are more narrowly drawn, covering a particular situation or set of facts, and are therefore accorded slightly less authority and cited less frequently by courts. Formal and informal ethics opinions are available in specialized print publications of the ABA, on Westlaw and Lexis, and in the *ABA Journal*.

11.6 SOURCES OF AUTHORITY— SECONDARY SOURCES

A wealth of secondary sources exists to help the researcher. As one would expect, there are a great many law review articles written annually on various aspects of legal ethics. Locating and using law review articles should be a routine mechanical process to you by now. There are even a few journals specializing in legal ethics issues, (such as *Legal Ethics* and the *Georgetown Journal of Legal Ethics*), although one should search broadly since many general law reviews publish occasional articles on legal ethics as well.

There are also many treatises on legal ethics. Too numerous to list here, these works, if carefully chosen by the researcher, can help explicate difficult material, identify lacunae in the rules or case law, track differing interpretations of particular model language across jurisdictions, and so on.

There is also a Restatement that includes a treatment of legal ethics, the *Restatement of the Law*; *Third, The Law Governing Lawyers*, published by the American Law Institute in 2000 and updated with pocket parts. Like all Restatements, the Restatement of the law governing lawyers was written by an eminent scholar in the field, and reviewed and revised by a committee of expert lawyers, scholars and judges. The Restatement covers much more than legal ethics, but does include a few sections that are relevant to legal ethics research. As discussed in Section 6.2 above, Restatements have as their goal to restate, or describe in subject arrangement, an area of the law in declarative or black-letter terms, followed by commentary and illustrations. Although primarily descriptive of current practice, Restatements do urge reform in certain areas or express preferences for one practice or another. Restatements are very influential, often cited in court opinions. If the Restatement of the law governing lawyers contains a section discussing the rule you are researching, it would not be wise to ignore that analysis. Strangely enough, there is no first or second edition of this Restatement. Since the current round of revisions of the Restatements is generally the third, the American Law Institute decided to give this new publication the same edition number as the others.

11.7 HOW LEGAL ETHICS RESEARCH REALLY WORKS

How, then, does one actually conduct research in legal ethics, given its model law origins and state law adoption? Research is only marginally more complicated than any other state law research might be. In general terms, we can lay out the steps you might take when faced with a research problem related to legal ethics.

First, of course, it is necessary to identify the issue at hand. One thing worth mentioning is that lawyers in practice are subject to all of the laws pertaining to any business or professional in the particular state in which they practice, even if there is no mention of the suspected activity in the legal ethics or professional responsibility section of the state code. For example, no matter what provisions, if any, of the Model Code or Model Rules your state may have adopted, all lawyers are prohibited from committing fraud, embezzling money, falsifying tax returns, and so on. The legal ethics rules of a state are in no way an exhaustive list of the legal responsibilities and obligations of the lawyer. Assuming, though, that for purposes of this section you are faced with a question of legal ethics (as opposed to garden variety criminality), how should you proceed once you have identified your issue?

The next step is to consult your state law. Remember that the legal ethics laws in your state may have been passed by the legislature like any other state law, or they may have been adopted by the state supreme court and thus considered rules of court. Either way, they are the law of your state. The only difference lies in where you need to go to find them. If the legislature has passed the ethics laws like any other state law, your research will begin in your state's code, in the annotated code, actually, if your state has one available. If your state's supreme court has adopted ethics laws as rules of court, you will need to find where rules of court are published in your state. Most commonly, rules of court are published as a separate pamphlet shelved at the end of the annotated code. Every state's practice is slightly different, however.

Once you have located your state's ethics laws, the next phase of research involves reading the relevant sections, following any annotations that may pertain to your topic, performing the necessary updating, and all of the usual steps required when conducting state statutory research. You will follow the clues in the annotation, gathering citations to useful primary and secondary sources, which may prove to be sufficient. It may be that your issue is straightforward, making research fairly mechanical.

If, however, you are not so lucky, you will need to dive into the body of material reflecting your law's probable genesis in one or another model code. You may want to examine your law's model source, in an annotated version if available. The ABA publishes annotated versions of the Model Rules and the Model Code, although the Model Code annotations are no longer updated. You may want to consult the *ABA/BNA Lawyers' Manual on Professional Conduct* for tables showing which other jurisdictions have adopted the code or rule you are researching, which makes it possible to research cases, ethics opinions and other material from other jurisdictions to use to bolster your argument. The web is becoming an increasingly convenient and easy place to find state ethics codes and opinions, and even some secondary material as well. For a list of recommended websites, **see Table 11.A**.

After exhausting all of the statutory research resources, you should turn to the case law. This includes the state court opinions from your state as well as the related ABA and state ethics opinions to see whether your issue has been considered before. It may be easiest to do some of this research online in Westlaw or Lexis if your state's ethics opinions are included in either service.

In addition to statutory and case law research, you will also probably want to consult secondary sources. Law review articles can be helpful in certain situations. You should see if the *Restatement of the Law, Third, Law Governing Lawyers* contains any relevant discussion. Finally, it might prove useful to examine treatises and other scholarly work on legal ethics.

The process here differs only in a few details from the approach you would take to research any matter of state law. The differences have to do with the receptiveness of the state courts to arguments and precedent from other jurisdictions that have adopted the same model rule, or that have considered the ethical issue at hand. In a matter of tort law, for example, an Ohio state court judge would probably not be swayed by a decision on a similar issue from a Utah court. In legal ethics, on the other hand, as in all areas of law heavily influenced by model or uniform laws, you need to take other jurisdictions into account when framing arguments. This is not to say that there is anything like national common law on legal ethics, but there is greater attention to uniformity and consistency here than in some other areas of law.

Table 11.A: Recommended Websites
for Legal Ethics Information

The table below is by no means comprehensive. It merely lists several of the leading websites for legal ethics codes, opinions and other material. Entries are listed in no particular order.

1. **ABA Center for Professional Responsibility**— http:// www. abanet.org/ cpr/

   The ABA Center for Professional Responsibility's website contains online versions of the Model Code and Model Rules, drafts of both, and a vast array of other helpful materials.

2. **Legal Information Institute**, **American Legal Ethics Library** —http:// www.law.cornell. edu/ ethics/

   This website contains links to the ethics laws of every state, along with commentary on each state's laws governing the conduct of lawyers.

3. **Hieros Gamos**—http://www. hg.org/practic. html

   At this site you will find a vast collection of links to legal ethics websites of all types. Includes links to a wide variety of articles discussing ethics topics.

4. **The Virtual Chase**—http://www.virtualchase.com/ resources/ethics.shtml

   The Virtual Chase, now hosted by a private law firm, contains links to online legal ethics material from the ABA and all fifty states. This website has arguably the clearest arrangement and presentation of links of those listed in this table.

5. **Findlaw**—http:// www.findlaw.com/01topics/ 14ethics/index. html

   The legal ethics pages of Findlaw's website contains links to state bar associations and other ethics-related material.

6. **Ben Cowgill on Legal Ethics**—http:// www.legalethics. info

   This combination website and blog contains a vast array of links to official ethics sites, discussion lists and blogs, news sources, etc. Despite an emphasis on Kentucky law, this website is an excellent starting point for those looking for a comprehensive directory of general and national legal ethics links.

Chapter 12

FOREIGN AND INTERNATIONAL
LAW RESEARCH

With increasing frequency, lawyers in the United States are called
upon to counsel clients on matters related to foreign and/or international
law, to practice in foreign jurisdictions, and to appear before international or foreign tribunals. Lawyers in a wide variety of work settings are
expected to be generally familiar with other legal systems and with how
to solve legal problems for clients regardless of the jurisdiction. Hence,
this chapter.

Foreign law can be defined as the domestic law of another national
jurisdiction. The domestic, or internal, or national law of France, Malaysia, and Haiti are all examples of foreign law. There are only a small
number of different patterns of legal system organization found in the
world today, but with as many variations within those categories as
there are nations. However, some basic general principles are consistent
throughout the world.

International law can be defined as the law between or among
nations. International law includes the least significant trade, tax or
extradition agreement between neighboring countries, as well as the
workings of the largest and most complex intergovernmental organizations, such as the United Nations or the European Union. It is important
to understand the distinction between public international law, which is
the law among nations just defined, and so-called private international
law, which has to do with questions of which nation's domestic law
should govern a particular situation. In the United States, we would call
these latter issues choice of law or conflicts of law, which falls outside
the scope of this chapter.

Remember that only a minority of the world uses English as an
official language. Although a surprising amount of legal material has
been translated from original (and official) languages into English, you
must be cognizant of the fact that even the best translation is only
approximate, and should only be relied on within limits. An inability to
read and understand the original language of another country's legal

material does not mean that no useful research can be done. It does mean, however, that the researcher or lawyer limited to English is at a severe disadvantage.

This chapter is not intended to teach anyone to conduct thorough research in foreign or international law; there are a great many specialized works to help you do just that, works that go into far greater detail than we can in this book. Without that level of detail, it is simply not possible to ensure that you understand the legal system of the jurisdiction in which you are researching, and therefore it would be impossible to be sure that you are doing a comprehensive and accurate job of researching your problem. The intent of this chapter, then, is to introduce you to some basic concepts, give you some general approaches you can take to investigate your subject or jurisdiction, and to demonstrate that the basic kinds of sources with which you are already familiar appear in other jurisdictions as well, which should be in some ways reassuring.

12.1   INTRODUCTION TO FOREIGN LAW

Lawyers are called on to advise clients about the law of foreign jurisdictions more and more frequently. Having a basic understanding of the different legal systems of the world, and how to go about beginning research in another country's legal materials, should be part of every lawyer's arsenal of skills. It is impossible, of course, to fully describe the legal system and the publications of any foreign country, let alone all of them at once. What follows here is an outline of the basic sources and strategies you can use to begin foreign law research.

What you will find once you begin to examine the law of another country is that the patterns of the system and the resulting publications will be familiar to you. In every system there will be some sort of legislative body, some judiciary system, and so on. You will find that in most countries there are analogues to sources with which you are familiar from your study of United States law. It is too much to say that you will always find precise analogues, of course, but the similarities will be close enough to allow you to conduct effective research in another country's legal publications.

12.2   MAJOR WORLD LEGAL SYSTEMS

In one sense there are as many different legal systems in the world as there are jurisdictions. Delaware and Nebraska, as similar as in many ways they are, have different kinds of legislatures (Nebraska's is unicameral, for example), different court structures, different constitutions, and so on. However, despite the multitude of variations that exist, the world can be divided into three major types of legal systems: common law, civil law and religious law.

The United States and the United Kingdom are examples of common law countries. Virtually all of the modern common law jurisdictions have a constitution, written or unwritten, legislation, subsidiary or delegated regulations, and one or more levels of courts to review, interpret and apply the laws. There is no need to belabor this description; the vast majority of readers of this book have at least a passing familiarity with common law systems. The key attribute distinguishing this type of legal arrangement is the importance of case law to flesh out the meaning of statutes. This process is not uncontroversial, even in countries where it is well established, but the law of a common law country may fairly be said to be result from the interplay between the constitution, the legislation, and judicial opinions.

Much of Europe, Central and South America, and parts of Asia are civil code countries. A civil code country is likely to have a constitution, statutes and case law as well. The difference is that in a civil law country the case law is far less important in interpreting or applying the law. Scholarly writing is more influential in civil law countries than in common law countries, and is treated as more authoritative than ordinary secondary sources, almost rising to the level of a primary authority. Common lawyers are often surprised at the relative unimportance of case law in code countries. Indeed, there are civil code jurisdictions where one is not allowed to cite prior opinions as precedent when urging a court to rule a certain way.

On the other hand, recent years have seen the once clear distinctions between civil and common law erode somewhat. Increasingly, civil code countries are making more use of case law as precedent. Several code countries regularly publish case reporters, complete with digests and other subject-based finding aids. Also, common law countries, including the United States, are becoming steadily more regulated, resulting in elaborate systems of legislation that leave less room for judicial interpretation. These legal systems are constantly in flux, and in order to do effective research in any foreign jurisdiction it will be necessary to understand not only what kind of legal system it has, but also the particulars regarding the actual practice in that jurisdiction.

There is a third type of legal system that bears mention here. A smaller number of nations of the world have legal systems based at least in part on religious tenets. Interestingly, most of these countries have legal structures and publications that parallel those in common law and civil code countries. It is hard to generalize about countries with religious bases for their legal systems as they vary nation to nation even within a single religious tradition.

12.3 GUIDES TO LEGAL RESEARCH IN FOREIGN JURISDICTIONS

The first step you should take when beginning research into the law of a foreign jurisdiction is to consult a legal research guide for that country. In print or on the web, you will be able to find a guide that will help you develop your understanding of that country's legal publications and how they work.

One of the best and most comprehensive guides to foreign jurisdictions is *Foreign Law: Current Sources of Codes and Basic Legislation in Jurisdictions of the World*, by Thomas H. Reynolds and Arturo A. Flores. This is a multi-volume work in looseleaf format, and covers most of the world's countries. After a descriptive introduction discussing the legal system of each covered country, the editors list major primary and secondary sources, followed by a bibliography of other helpful works arranged by subject. There is a subscription-only electronic version of this work called *Foreign Law Guide*, which is essentially the same as the print. You could do far worse than to begin your foreign law research by consulting this work in either print or electronic format.

Other valuable general works on foreign jurisdictions include *Germain's Transnational Law Research*, *Modern Legal Systems Cyclopedia*, *Bibliography on Foreign and Comparative Law: Books and Articles in English*, and *Accidental Tourist on the New Frontier: An Introductory Guide to Global Legal Research*. Each of these has its own focus, strengths and weaknesses. And, of course, there are dozens more we could have listed here. The point here is not to create a bibliography of useful works, but to urge you to begin here. Unless you are very familiar with the foreign jurisdiction, you will need these works for background and context.

In addition to the print sources listed above, there are an increasing number of useful research guides on the web. One of the best websites is LLRX's collection of articles on foreign jurisdictions found at http://www.llrx.com/comparative_and_foreign_law.html. This site contains articles on several dozen major foreign jurisdictions written by various experts. As you would expect, the articles are filled with links to official country webpages, links to important legislative and judicial sites, and other useful information. There are other such sites. Findlaw, for example, has a collection of guides for foreign country research at http://www.findlaw.com/12international/countries/index.html. Many others have been compiled by librarians at U.S. law schools and can be found on the law schools' websites. As you might expect, these web guides vary in quality, but in general they tend to feature lots of helpful links. They are less rich in the explanatory material that makes the best print sources so valuable.

12.4   METHODS OF FOREIGN LAW RESEARCH

How, then, does research in the law of a foreign jurisdiction proceed? After consulting a good research guide to the country in question, you should have a fair grasp of the legal system of that country. You should know how to find the constitution, session laws (called gazettes in many code countries), codes (if any), case law, and important secondary sources. Once you have identified your issue, placed it in its legal context, and identified the primary and secondary sources that might be relevant, research proceeds much as it would for a problem of U.S. law.

Take an issue related to Malaysian income taxation as an example. Your first step would be to consult a good legal research guide for background and a description of the major primary and secondary sources. You might choose to begin with the *Foreign Law Guide* online. (See Section 12.3 above for more on this source). From it you will learn that Malaysia is a constitutional monarchy with common law traditions (it was a British Colony until the 1950s), but a legal system that is a mix of Islamic law, common law, Chinese customary law, and indigenous Malay law. Also, although official documents are printed in English and Bahasa, there is an increasing desire to make Bahasa the sole official language for legal and government publications. From *Foreign Law Guide* you will also learn about the different primary and secondary sources; statutes, regulations, court reports, and secondary sources.

In the section on Malaysian income taxation, which is the topic that interests us, *Foreign Law Guide* lists all of the revisions of the income tax law, including a website where the entire current law is available in English and Bahasa. It lists a source for tax regulations, and several treatises on income taxation in Malaysia.

Armed with all this information, the researcher does precisely what a researcher working on U.S. tax law would do. The next step might be to consult the statutes and regulations. Finally, you might consult other secondary sources for a discussion of your specific subject matter. You might also consult the Malaysian court reports and the *Malayan Law Journal*, which reprints important opinions.

Once you have examined all of the resources available to you, and followed citations and other textual clues where they lead, you have done as much as can be done without hiring local counsel in Malaysia. Can you have the same confidence in your results as you could for the same research in U.S. tax law? Probably not. First, it is highly unlikely that any U.S. library will have all of the Malaysian sources listed in *Foreign Law Guide*. Second, there is a wealth of other potentially relevant information not published at all, not published yet, not in English, or otherwise unavailable to you. Very few jurisdictions publish legal information as thoroughly as the United States does. You will, on the other hand, know a great deal more than you did before, and may have learned enough to solve the legal problem before you. This process is time-consuming and, frankly, fraught with problems and frustrations. But it can be done, and done well, by the informed, diligent, resourceful researcher.

12.5 INTRODUCTION TO INTERNATIONAL LAW

International law, as we stated above, is the law between or among nations. As the world has grown more complex and interrelated, some system of cooperation among the countries of the world has become increasingly necessary.

International law exists in a variety of forms. Two countries may agree on a bilateral treaty, just between them, on any of a number of subjects. Countries in a region may band together for mutual defense, or trade, or to protect the regional environment. Intergovernmental organizations such as the United Nations use their global reach to urge passage of all manner of treaties and other instruments, ranging across the entire spectrum of social, political, military and economic issues.

Often, when a nation agrees to a treaty or other international agreement, it becomes necessary for that country to change its internal domestic law to fulfill the requirements of the treaty. This new legislation is usually called implementing legislation, and may be a critical part of research on an issue of international law.

There are a number of good introductions to international legal research that go into far more detail than we will attempt here. The *Guide to International Legal Research, Germain's Transnational Law Research*, and the *International Lawyer's Deskbook* are three of the best introductory texts. There are, as you might guess, a great many titles published on more specific subjects in international law.

There are also specialized tools to help you locate journal articles about specific topics in international law. The *Index to Foreign Legal Periodicals* is similar to other periodical indexes you have examined, except that its coverage is different. *IFLP*, as it is commonly called, is an index of articles about law in systems other than the Anglo–American countries. This tool indexes legal journals regardless of where they are published (in other words, articles about French law published in U.S. journals would be indexed here) or the language in which they are written. Another useful journal index is the *Legal Journals Index*, which indexes over seven hundred periodicals having primarily to do with United Kingdom law. Both of these indexes are available in paper and in cumulative electronic formats.

12.6 SOURCES OF INTERNATIONAL LAW

By "sources" we do not mean print and electronic resources used for research. Instead, this section contains a very brief answer to the question, "Where does international law come from?" One source is obvious: treaties. In fact, treaties are what most people think of when they think of international law, but there are other sources to consider.

The treaty establishing the International Court of Justice laid out the different sources of international law. This formulation, now the classic and oft-cited statement on the subject, defines the sources of international law as including treaties, custom, general principles of law, judicial decisions, and academic writings. These five sources interrelate in such a way as to result in a fairly complex universe of material for the legal researcher to consider. What exactly, for example, is custom? Who decides what the customary practice is? There are answers, tentative and qualified though they are, to these questions, and it is the duty of the researcher to consider all of the material that could potentially be relevant when trying to determine just what the law is on any topic.

Despite the fact that there are many potential sources of international law, it is true that treaties are by far the most important single source to consider, and their centrality only increases as time passes. It is to treaty research, then, that we turn next.

12.7 TREATY RESEARCH

Much of international law stems from treaties. These treaties may be bilateral, between two countries and affecting only them, or multilateral, entered into by three or more countries. Some treaties have well over a hundred signatories. There are treaties covering every conceivable branch of human endeavor. Finding them, determining whether they are in force, locating the implementing legislation if any, and applying the terms of the treaty to your specific situation are the basic activities of treaty research. For a list of websites with good collections of treaties, **see Table 12.A**.

Bear in mind that in the United States there is a distinction between treaties and executive orders, although this distinction is not found in other jurisdictions. The difference stems from the constitutional requirement that treaties can only be entered into with the advice and consent of the Senate. Executive Orders, on the other hand, need not pass any Senatorial review. The majority of international treaties into which the United States enters in the modern era result from executive orders rather than via the Senate. In this chapter, however, we will use the term "treaty" in the broader sense, ignoring for the moment the mechanism by which the United States joined the agreement.

When the United States is a party to a treaty in which you are interested, finding that treaty becomes easier. There are a number of print and electronic sources to help. Many websites print the texts of treaties to which the U.S. is party. For official versions, the researcher can turn to *United States Treaties and Other International Agreements* (or *"UST"* as it is called). This official publication of the State Department is usually out of date by eight to ten years, however. For the initial slip form of treaties, turn to *Treaties and Other International Acts Series* (commonly called *"TIAS"*). Note, however, that this set is usually five or more years out of date. For more recent treaties, one can look in publications such as *International Legal Materials*, a journal that publishes many new treaties and similar documents, or in the websites listed in **Table 12.A**.

Finding the text of a treaty is not very difficult, even taking into account the tardy nature of official printing. What is far more difficult, and more important in many cases, is finding the status of the treaty. One needs to know whether the U.S. has ratified the treaty, or needs to. Many treaties do not go into effect until a certain number of countries have signed. Sometimes countries are signatories to a treaty, yet they draft reservations, specifying provisions to which they do not agree and by which they will not abide. Following this process, finding out whether the treaty is in force and who has agreed to which of its provisions, is the real work of treaty research.

For a treaty where the U.S. is a party, several State Department publications will help determine the status of that treaty. *Treaties in Force*, published annually, is the place to start. It lists and summarizes every treaty currently in force to which the U.S. is a party, and includes both bilateral and multilateral treaties. To update *Treaties in Force*, the State Department publishes *Treaty Actions* periodically throughout the year. Both are available on the web, as well. *Treaties in Force* can be found at http://www.state.gov/s/l/treaties/. *Treaty Actions* is found at http://www.state.gov/s/l/c3428.htm. Along with these sources, you should also consult *A Guide to the United States Treaties in Force*, the *Current Treaty Index*, and the *CCH Congressional Index*. Each of these sources contains information about the status of treaties. Doing a thorough job of updating treaty status information might require you to consult a variety of other sources, too many to discuss or even list here. Any of the good general sources discussed in Section 12.5, above, and most of the better international research guides will have more detailed instructions. The point here is to know that the information exists, but is not compiled in one convenient location.

The web is becoming an increasingly important way to research treaties. For those treaties deposited with the Secretary General of the United Nations, as an example, formerly one had to wait for the very slow publication of the print version of these treaties. Today, many of these treaties can be found very quickly, either at the United Nations website or at one of a variety of other locations, the website of one of the signatories, for example. The United Nations website, by the way, is an excellent example of the direction in which the publication of intergovernmental agency documents (and thus, research related to them) is headed. At the U.N.'s website, http://www.un.org, you can find an amazing array of information: treaties, planning documents, reports, meeting agendas, and so on. In the next few years, we may see national governments and intergovernmental organizations largely give up on the idea of trying to publish current information in print at all, and instead rely exclusively on the web. The astute researcher should, for the time being, be aware that thorough research may require both print and electronic resources. Remember, too, that any of the works in Section 12.5, above, will explain how treaty research works in far greater detail than we can here.

Table 12.A: Recommended Treaty Websites

Australian Treaties Library

http://www.austlii.edu.au/au/other/dfat/

Council of Europe, European Treaties

http://conventions.coe.int/treaty/EN/cadreprincipal.htm

European Union Treaties

http://europa.eu.int/eur-lex/en/treaties/index.htm

Hague Conventions on Private International Law

http://www.hcch.net/e/index_en.php?act=conventions.listing

International Humanitarian Law Database

http://www.icrc.org/ihl

International Labor Treaties

http://www.ilo.org/

International Treaties

http://www.law.nyu.edu/library/foreign_intl/treaties.html

Jurist International

http://www.jurisint.org/pub/

Latin American Tax Treaties

http://www.natlaw.com/treaties/taxtreat.htm

Lex Mercatoria

http://www.jus.uio.no/lm/

Multilaterals Project

http://www.fletcher.tufts.edu/multilaterals.html

Organization of American States Treaties

http://www.oas.org/DIL/treaties_and_ agreements.htm

Private International Law Database

http://www.state.gov/www/global/legal_affairs/private_intl_law.html

Project DIAL

http://www.worldlii.org/catalog/2226.html

United Nations Treaty Collection (subscription)

http://untreaty.un.org

University of Minnesota Human Rights Library

http://www.umn.edu/humanrts

WIPO Treaties

http://www.wipo.int/treaties/index.html

12.8   INTERGOVERNMENTAL ORGANIZATIONS

As important as treaty research is, there is much more to international legal research. One interesting development is the rise of the intergovernmental organization, and how the largest of them are beginning to act increasingly like governments: legislating, regulating, conducting judicial hearings, and so on. The United Nations, the European Union, the Organization of American States, and a handful of others may, in some sense, be considered to be governments or sovereigns. Conducting legal research in these "jurisdictions" is very similar to doing so in any other jurisdiction, and the patterns of publication hold as true here as in any state or national system. Let's examine one such system; the European Union. You will see that the familiar types of legal publications exist here as well.

12.9   THE EUROPEAN UNION

The European Union (or "EU") is an important example of just such an intergovernmental organization. From relatively humble beginnings as a cooperative of a few countries to deal with joint steel and coal issues, the EU by 2006 has grown into a world economic and political powerhouse comprised of twenty-five nations, regulating business, travel, citizenship, and health, and even issuing its own currency. Although the EU itself states that it is not intended to replace the nation-state, for our purposes it is helpful to think of it as its own country, its own jurisdiction.

The EU is an incredibly complex organization, involved in every aspect of European life, from the economy to defense, from environmental law to agriculture. The EU has also developed legal and governmental structures parallel to those of a sovereign nation; legislature, regulating agencies, various layers of courts with differing jurisdictions, as well as the full complement of documentary support necessary to make public its workings, its laws and rules, and its judgments.

Conducting legal research in EU law is not simple for the novice, but there is a wealth of explanatory material about the EU and specific research guides to help. You should, of course, be able to anticipate the kinds of publications you will encounter and know roughly how they are to be used. You should expect, as an example, that a wide variety of secondary sources will have been produced to help researchers navigate the complexities of EU law. Also, you should expect that the legislature will produce statutes that are first printed chronologically, and that there will be either a commercial or an official arrangement of these laws into subject order to aid in research. You should also expect that there will be something like regulation, and that the same pattern of chronological and topical printing will exist. Finally, you should not be surprised to find case law from courts, perhaps from several levels or courts or courts with different subject matter jurisdiction, and that these cases will be full-text searchable and that there will be a digest or other tool to allow subject access to opinions. Once you have these patterns firmly in your mind you will be able to approach even as complex a legal entity (or a jurisdiction, if you prefer) as the EU with confidence in your ability to find the material you need to conduct thorough and effective research.

12.10   EUROPEAN UNION— SECONDARY SOURCES

As with all international or foreign research, it would be wise to begin in the secondary literature. When approaching legal research in a novel jurisdiction, context is everything. You need to know the structure of the international body whose law you are researching in order to understand the ways in which the primary sources you will be searching fit together. Secondary sources for international legal research may be thought of as belonging to one of several categories.

Sources describing the organization generally are a good first step. For EU law, there are several informative publications and websites you can consult for help in understanding the EU's different subgroups and how they function together as interlocking branches of government. Only by beginning research with a firm command of the EU's internal structure, the limits of its power, and other basic information, can you conduct useful and accurate research. *Foreign Law: Current Sources of Codes and Legislation* (and its more frequently updated web version *Foreign Law Guide*) provide a useful discussion on the legal structure of the EU and its major publications. *Encyclopedia of the European Union* is another good source to consult for basic background. You should also know that the EU's own website, at http:// europa.eu.int/ index_ en.htm, is extremely helpful, with good explanations of the EU's basic structure, functions and documents. Most of the primary sources we will refer to below can be found at the official website. After you have gathered enough background knowledge to understand the structure of this organization, and have an idea about what kinds of primary and secondary sources to look for, you will probably find it useful to turn to another kind of secondary source, the research guide.

12.11   EUROPEAN UNION—STATUTES

EU legislation is difficult to research in part because there are at least five different bodies empowered to participate in the process; the European Commission, the European Parliament, the Council, the Economic and Social Committee and the Committee of the Regions. Each of these subgroups has their own publications and websites, their own mandates, powers and procedures, and it can be difficult even for experienced researchers to keep it all straight.

There are several major sources you should be aware of, but bear in mind that you will need to learn more about your subject matter and which body or bodies legislate on this topic before plunging into the primary sources. The *Official Journal* (or *"OJ"*) is published every business day, and is divided into two series. The L Series contains the texts of new treaties, legislation, directives and regulations. In a sense the L Series is the EU's *Statutes at Large* and the New Rules and Regulations section of the *Federal Register* rolled into one. The other series, the C Series, is the "Information and Notices" section of the *OJ*, and contains resolutions of the various subgroups, proposed regulations, minutes of meetings, notices of Court decisions, and so on. The *OJ* is the single most important source of EU legislative information. It can be found in print, online at the EU website, and on Westlaw and Lexis. The *OJ*, as you might expect, also has a number of associated indexes and other directories to help researchers gain subject access to the chronologically printed material.

The print sources available for EU statutory research are considered official, the online sources are not, not even the EU's own website. It is not practical to conduct legislative research for current EU statutes in print because they are simply not current enough. The researcher has little choice except to rely on the EU (or related) websites for the more current information. Just note that you will have to make some allowance for the unofficial nature of what you find online.

12.12   EUROPEAN UNION—CASE LAW

The European Court of Justice is the highest court in the EU structure. This court decides cases involving the founding treaties and other documents of the EU, their appropriate application, and their interpretation. There are also a series of subordinate courts with different subject matter jurisdiction as well.

The official reporter of the Court of Justice's opinions is called *Reports of Cases Before the Court* (also called *European Court Reports* or *ECR*). Like the *United States Reports*, this official reporter is always a few years out of date. For more current reports, one must turn to one of several unofficial, commercial publications; *European Community Cases* and the *European Union Law Reporter*. These offer more current coverage of EU cases. There are other print sources for opinions in addition to these two.

There are also different ways to get access to EU cases by subject. Full-text searching in one of the online databases is one way. Using the finding aids associated with the commercial version of opinions is another. There are a variety of secondary sources available that can help. These are listed and described in the research guides listed in Section 12.5, above. These opinions are also online in Westlaw and Lexis.

12.13   EUROPEAN UNION—SUMMING UP

The point of the foregoing discussion of the sources of legal information produced by the EU and available for the legal researcher is not to provide a comprehensive description of the EU's legal structure, nor to provide the researcher with a general methodology or process to employ when faced with a legal problem based on EU law. Rather, the idea here is to show that even as complex an organization as the EU produces many, if not all, of the categories of legal publication with which the US-trained law student or lawyer should be fluent. You should know how to look for and work with constitutions, legislation, regulations, case law and the like. None of these forms of publication should be new to you. All that is required before a novice can successfully undertake international law research is a clear understanding of the need to discover the source of the law to be researched, how to find secondary sources to help contextualize and explain the relevant legal structure, and how to find the underlying legal publications necessary to solve the problem. We do not mean to minimize the difficulties these tasks will occasionally present, but we believe solid legal research in foreign or international law can be conducted by any careful and persistent researcher.

Chapter 13

MUNICIPAL LAW RESEARCH

13.1 MUNICIPAL LAW: WHEN, WHY AND HOW

At the other end of the spectrum from international law lies municipal law. Some legal questions of local provenance require us to turn from focusing on the global village and instead to consider the requirements of our actual village. Preemption by legal requirements imposed by entities higher up the legal food chain need always to be considered (via all the legal research methods outlined in the previous chapters), but sometimes the governing authority will actually turn out to be a local ordinance or a village court legal decision or a city agency regulation.

When will municipal law come into play? Obviously there are local conditions and problems that would stimulate a local government to come up with its own legal strictures and remedies in order to address them. The rules about keeping poultry, for instance, are likely to vary as between a rural community and a big city within the same state. Other issues addressed by local laws are local only because there is a political will to address them locally that does not exist beyond the municipality. Both types of local concern are brought within the limited capacity of the municipality to act by a delegation of power from the state government, i.e., as a matter of state law. These delegations of power are enshrined in "home rule" statutes that can be found in the usual sources for state law: the codes and the session laws. These home rule statutes furnish (among other things) the outside limits on what the local lawgivers can legitimately undertake, and can thus provide the basis for challenging the validity of local laws.

Many of the subjects with which local laws are concerned cut quite close to the daily life of individual citizens: where they may hang out, where they may swim, what they may put out in their garbage. Accordingly, an individual's own personal rights may be more often impinged upon by these local laws than by the more lofty and institution-oriented state laws. Local ordinances that have furnished the basis for U.S. Supreme Court cases run the gamut from anti-pornography laws to ordinances concerning loitering, noise control, and the permissible size of bread loaves.

The key thing to remember about municipal or local law research is that you should analogize from state or federal law to figure out what to look for. As emphasized throughout the preceding chapters, confidence in the legal researcher comes in part from knowing what kind of material you will need to find (or not find) in order to rest easy about your legal conclusions. This principle is thrown into sharp relief in the municipal law context, where publication can be sporadic, narrowly distributed, or even non-existent. Where the published legal record peters out, you will still have to look for the things that you know must be out there. This may involve going to a tiny back office somewhere and leafing through the contents of a filing cabinet or a cardboard box; it will almost certainly involve calling on the assistance of those on the spot in the locale in question. For more on finding help from those intimately involved with a legal issue, see **section 14.14**, below, and for additional details on sources for local laws, see the research guides listed in the **Appendix**.

13.2   MUNICIPAL CHARTERS

What should you assume is out there, regardless of the nature of the municipality? And how can you find it? By analogy from larger legal systems, we would expect there to be some sort of constitutive document. In municipal law that would be two-fold: the state law delegating power to the municipality and the constitutive local document setting up the exercise of that power. In many municipalities the latter document is called the "charter". As with the federal and state systems, researching constitutional issues basically follows the path of statutory research in the same jurisdiction.

13.3   MUNICIPAL "SESSION LAWS"

The next component you would expect to find would be some sort of session law, the raw output of the local legislature. This is where the fun begins: as the fifty states' statutory publication schemes vary from each other, so, too, with the work of thousands of legislating municipalities. The distinguishing characteristic, of course, of municipal legal publishing is the relative smallness of the market. For many years, this meant that most legal information on the local level was not published by the issuing entity (too big an expense for the size of the entity's budget) and could not be published by the commercial sector (too much overhead for the size of the market). Obviously there were exceptions: for example, the New York City market contains many more people than do most of the fifty states; moreover, the place is fairly bursting with lawyers. Additionally, many people outside the city itself have legal interests there to protect. Accordingly, the New York City statutes (called Local Laws) are published in print by two different local commercial publishers. One of them even publishes the Local Laws first in "advance sheet form," in the manner of the *U.S.C.C.A.N.* advance sheets, and then subsequently reprints them in annual bound volumes. But this is far from the norm. For most municipalities, the local laws are only available from the municipality, in unpublished form.

13.4 MUNICIPAL STATUTORY CODES

Session laws are not where the legal researcher starts out anyway, so the absence of a browsable collection of them is not a huge problem. As you well know by now, the starting point for statutory legal research in primary sources is the code, the subject arrangement and compilation of the laws that originally appeared individually as session laws. While municipal codes were always at least marginally more available than session laws, the big difference today is the internet. Now that the overhead costs of publishing the codes has plummeted, more and more municipalities have taken the plunge of putting their codes out there for public perusal. Many of them have subcontracted the preparation of their web codes out to specialists in this function, and the resulting collocation of multiple codes on the web sites of the contractors has been a boon for comparativists in the municipal area (see **section 13.6**, below). The Seattle Public Library, an early collector of these electronic codes, maintains a useful web portal devoted to accessing these materials, at http://www.spl.org/default.asp?pageID=collection_municodes. Lexis and Westlaw also have accumulated collections of this type.

13.5 MUNICIPAL DECISIONAL LAW

All this local law making, as might be expected, generates a certain amount of need for clarification when those laws get applied to individuals' circumstances. In addition to identifying any local statute that applies to your case, you will also want to ascertain whether there is any history of relevant decisions. Arrangements for seeking to apply local laws vary from jurisdiction to jurisdiction. Sometimes there is a regular court involved, sometimes a special court specifically charged with enforcing local ordinances. As a preliminary step towards discovering where the relevant decisions would have been generated, you can consult a court organization chart. These charts, featured in commercially-published national court directories such as *Want's Federal–State Court Directory*, give rough summaries of the structure of local courts within the schematic layout of the courts for each state. However, these charts are not supported by statutory citations, so you will need to verify their accuracy by doing regular statutory research in the jurisdictional statutes of the state.

As discussed above with respect to the output of federal district courts, the value of reading through previous decisions from the relevant local courts will mostly reside in their predictive value. The precedential clout of decisions at this level is much less significant than is simply trying to figure out what this particular judge or this particular court are likely to do in your case, based on their past track record. Note that since these local courts are part of the regular appeals structure, you should research any and all local law issues in the regular state and federal case law universe, to account for the outcome of previous appeals in similar cases.

Finding the actual local decisions, however, can take you outside the sources familiar to you from state and federal research. Only a minute proportion of local court decisions are selected for publication in the regular state reporters or in local legal newspapers. Those that are part of the ordinary world of published decisional law can be located in a number of familiar ways, including the use of state Shepard's citators in print. Many of the print Shepard's volumes for statutory citations include a section listing case and law review citations to local laws within that state. Some of these volumes also include a subject index to the local laws covered, so that comparison between laws in different locales may be easily accomplished. As noted above (**section 5.23)**, certain unusually remunerative jurisdictions and subject matters have supported the development of local reporters and/or digests that include cases not reported in the larger structure of state law case reporting.

In many instances, however, local courts may be statutorily or constitutionally designated as courts not of record, meaning that a permanent record of their proceedings is not legally mandated. But even these ''inferior'' courts usually are required to keep certain records of their activities, and you may find yourself obliged to prevail on someone working with these records to dig them out for you. Some case records can be consultable as a matter of public record, while others may be sealed to the general public for privacy reasons. Seek guidance in these matters from the clerk in charge of records for the jurisdiction. If you already know what jurisdiction is involved, the information about who to contact is usually only a Google away. If you are not sure of the jurisdiction, you may get some ideas about where to start calling by consulting a directory of court clerks like the *Directory of State Court Clerks and County Courthouses* (Want Publishing, annual).

13.6 DOING COMPARATIVE RESEARCH ON MUNICIPAL LAW

In the state law context, the practitioner is likely to undertake comparative statutory research in order to choose a favorable venue for a client's undertaking, or in order to look as far afield as necessary for favorably persuasive interpretation of a statute similar to that in the client's own jurisdiction. Both of these purposes can also, of course, motivate the local law researcher. The latter purpose, the search for analogous and persuasive judicial interpretation can be particularly crucial for the local law researcher because of the relative thinness of an interpretive record for statutes at this level.

However, there is a third reason that many lawyers find themselves interested in finding out about the ordinances of other localities. Each and every community that undertakes this kind of lawgiving is likely to consult with a lawyer as to the fitness and properness of what they want to do. Not to do so would be to court challenge from state or federal law, or merely to suffer ineffectuality from a poorly drafted and thus unenforceable statute. Thus, drafting and revising of of local ordinances is something that many lawyers will encounter in their practice. Accordingly, the legal information market has provided them with several sources of comparative information that enables them readily to compare statutes of many jurisdictions.

One of these sources, mentioned in **section 13.4** above, is the swarm of websites produced by commercial contractors of municipal code production. In addition to singing the praises of codification of ordinances and promoting their own services to that end, these websites serve as the residence for many of the codes of their respective client municipalities. In most cases each code is separate, and they are generally grouped by state. But the uniform format for each code produced by a given publisher and the simplicity of arrangement born out of long and repeated experience with what makes these codes work combine to make dipping into these codes to check out the experiences of other municipalities a relatively straightforward task. The issue of variant nomenclature, however, still exists, since the commercial codifiers are working in each instance with locally-produced ordinance language.

There is, however, a singular tool that draws together references to municipal codes by subject, regardless of the local terminology used: *Municipal Ordinance Annotations* (formerly the crusty old standby titled *Shepard's Municipal Ordinance Annotations*, currently receiving a facelift from its new owners Thomson/West). This digest-like multivolume compilation collects citations to published decisions (and summaries of the same) which construe or apply municipal ordinances on a particular topic. Despite its limitations (only those laws interpreted in regularly published cases are mentioned, and no actual code or law citations are actually given), this set offers a good jumping off point for comparative analysis of local law topics from Laundries to Libraries, from Ice to Junk, from "Adult Businesses" to Weed Abatement.

13.7 ADMINISTRATIVE REGULATIONS AND DECISIONS ON THE MUNICIPAL LEVEL

As with states and the federal government, the agencies and departments of the executive branch of municipal entities may engage in both delegated legislating via agency rules and regulations and in delegated judicial activity in administrative decisions. In New York City this output is captured in a commercially-published multi-volume annotated set, *The Official Compilation of the Rules of the City of New York*, as well as being available on both Lexis and Westlaw. This easy accessibility, however, is the exception to the rule: for the most part, research in these materials will involve extensive exploration of byways of the internet, and/or personal contact with the individual agencies.

Chapter 14

WHERE THE LAW IS

14.1 GENERAL PRINCIPLES

As suggested in the first chapter, research on any legal issue should always consider whether there are statutes, cases, regulations, or administrative decisions (or materials analogous to any of these) that have any bearing on the situation. The subsequent chapters, we hope, have led you to explore the circle of information that surrounds each of these four types of legal authority, and to think about when the search for any of them should become a high research priority for you. Any legal authority might have historical background, commentary, or subsequent applications which either strengthen or undercut it for your purposes. This galaxy of interrelated sources defines, for the legal researcher, where the law is.

We hope, also, that you have come to appreciate how certain principles of legal research come into play over and over again, in many different contexts. Conscious application of these principles can come to your aid whenever you find yourself thrust into a legal area you have never encountered before. Soon enough, the initially bewildering sources you need to use in such an area will become trusted allies; remembering these general rules will help to make it so.

14.2 LOOK FOR BASIC STRUCTURES

Thinking about what type of material you need to look for can get you oriented even in a totally alien jurisdiction or legal subculture. There's always going to be something like a statute (official entities telling people what to do), even if only a constitutional document, and something like a case (official decisions as to the legality of what people did in certain circumstances). For finding both of these types of material, there's always going to be something **chronological**, something **subject–based**, and something **name–based**.

Many publications appear first in **chronological** order, then are arranged by someone into **subject** order. All branches of government act in real time, performing work in chronological order. Chronicling this work results in a record that is official and accurate, but very difficult to use for research. After the chronological record is captured, then, someone has to arrange all that material in subject order as an aid to practitioners and researchers. Remember the analogies we have seen:

Chronological Order	Subject Order
Session laws	*Codes*
United States Statutes at Large	United States Code
USCCAN	USCA
State session law	State code
Reporter	*Digest*
Texas Reports	Texas Digest
Pacific Reporter	Pacific Digest
Administrative Register	*Administrative Code*
Federal Register	Code of Federal Regulations
State administrative register	State administrative code

Remember, too, that even though electronic publication has lessened the time gap between appearance of the chronological record and appearance of the subject–arranged tool, the former is usually still the more official authority.

One of the first steps in bringing the chronological record under control is to create an alphabetical index of its contents. A case **name**, boiled down to a condensed form A v. B, will be filed alphabetically in a Table of Cases. Some statutes and cases also receive or develop popular names or even nicknames, and these can be found in a number of ways. Some of these ways we have discussed specifically in the preceding chapters (the indexing to session laws and codes, *Shepard's Acts and Cases by Popular Names*, full text searching, especially in law review articles). Other ways to go fishing for nicknames of cases or statutes include keyword searching in law library online catalogs, or simply on the web (where, however, you will of course face the problems of too many false drops and lots of erroneous information).

14.3   ESTIMATE WHAT FORM YOUR ANSWER WILL COME IN

As you begin your research, ask yourself what form the answer may take. Is your answer likely to be a statute, a regulation, an article, a definition in a dictionary, a line of cases, or something else? You might have to revise your estimate as you go along (in many instances it is nearly impossible, for example, to predict whether any particular state issue is addressed in the statutes or the regulations) but there's no harm in that. By focusing on what form your answer will likely take, it will help you choose your approach and to think clearly about your research strategy. On the other hand, making a guess as to the ultimate, substantive outcome of your research before you begin is almost never helpful, and in fact, can prejudice your search. Don't let hunches about the outcome cloud your thinking about the research process.

14.4   YOUR STRATEGY WILL DEPEND UPON YOUR STARTING POINT. WHAT DO YOU KNOW NOW?

You should know how to start from a known case, or statute, or article, or issue, and move from your starting point to gather all the rest of the relevant material on your topic. As an example, starting with a known case you can use a citator to update it, use its headnotes to find its place (and other similar cases) in a digest, use the tables of cases in secondary sources to find where in a treatise or encyclopedia or law review article your issue is discussed. The finding aids and other tools in law books allow you to start anywhere and move forward or backward in time, or laterally to encircle all the sources relevant to your issue in your jurisdiction. There is a real art to framing the issue, imagining the possible arguments, etc., but there are simple mechanical procedures to follow once that is done to gather all the material that is relevant.

14.5   THE LESS YOU KNOW, THE MORE CERTAINLY YOU NEED SECONDARY SOURCES

Context is king in legal research. When faced with a new area of law or a new concept, begin your research in the secondary sources, using them to help you understand the general framework in which your issue can be placed. If you get an assignment related to admiralty law, and you don't know the first thing about admiralty law, you need to start with secondary sources. After you understand a little about your area, then you can proceed to the primary sources you need to solve your problem. Just jumping straight into primary sources with no context is dangerous.

14.6   SECONDARY LEADS TO PRIMARY, BUT THERE ARE OTHER WAYS AROUND THE CIRCLE

The main use for secondary sources is to steer you to primary sources. Sometimes, though, secondary sources lead to other secondary sources. Or you might use a primary source (say, a known case) as a way into a secondary source (looking up that case in the table of cases in a well-respected treatise or maybe a Restatement) which will then lead you to further primary sources. You often have to use a variety of sources in different combinations to get from where you are to where you need to be. The more you know about the kinds of finding aids that exist, the better the odds that your work will be thorough, accurate and timely.

14.7 OFFICIAL PUBLICATIONS OFTEN LESS USEFUL

This isn't very complicated. Official publications often come with two distinct disadvantages: first, they are usually not current, and, second, they are not annotated. A good example is the official *United States Statutes at Large*, compared with both *U.S.C.C.A.N.* and the government-posted materials on Thomas.

14.8 HUMAN ORDERING vs. MACHINE RECALL

As you know, keyword searching is very powerful, allowing you to search for specific factual situations, names or phrases. The ability to search through full-text databases using keywords has changed legal research profoundly. The dangers in this power stem from the fact that the success of this method of searching depends upon your understanding and control of vocabulary.

The literal nature of machine recall (i.e., the keyword search) means that you sometimes sacrifice recall in favor of precision. Precision means getting a narrowly defined, specific result, and running the risk of missing some relevant material. Using human ordering, such as an index, a table, a table of contents, or especially a digest or other assigned subject headings, the opposite is true: you get improved recall at the expense of precision. Recall means getting a large, inclusive result, including some hits that may not be relevant (for example, you have to wade through all the warrantless search cases to find the ones that were searches of car interiors).

Every technique, every source, every approach you take involves a trade-off between these two. Ask yourself what compromise you can afford to make at any particular point in your research, and what you might do to minimize the risk, then pick your source. If you have the luxury of a little time, you should use both kinds of technique. For example, as discussed in Chapter Five above, when searching for cases you might begin with a keyword search in Lexis or Westlaw, then gather the key number(s) from the cases you find, and check the completeness of your result in a digest to see if there is anything you missed. You won't always have the time to do that, of course.

14.9 IT IS VERY DIFFICULT TO DO EFFECTIVE STATUTORY RESEARCH ONLINE

Typically, statutory research involves using a variety of tabular or columnar material. This material, tables of contents, conversion tables of various kinds, indexes, outlines of titles, etc., are available in the online databases, but they are cumbersome to use in electronic form. Also, codes are arranged in outline form, with titles, chapters, sections, and subsections, with notes and appendices added. This structure can be very hard to visualize online. If you start your statutory research with a search for a particular term or phrase, click on the likeliest looking hit, and determine whether this section is relevant. If it appears to be relevant, you need to place that section in its larger context to ensure that language in other, related sections doesn't control or alter the interpretation of what you've found in the section your search turned up. Extra caution is called for when you do this online because of the more restrictive window that frames what you see at any one time.

14.10 KNOW EXACTLY WHAT LEGISLATIVE HISTORIES ARE, AND WHAT THEY ARE FOR

A legislative history is an attempt to determine the intent of the legislature. The intent of the legislature is one of the arguments you can use when arguing how a facially ambiguous statute should be interpreted. It is not controlling or binding on a court. A legislative history is compiled from all of the published evidence of legislative deliberation. In the federal setting, much of what Congress does is published. Understand, though, that the importance of the major committee report (reprinted in *U.S.C.C.A.N.*) dwarfs the importance of everything else you might find. Remember, too, that many courts and many judges are hostile to legislative intent arguments.

14.11 LET SOMEONE ELSE DO THE WORK FOR YOU

There is nothing more satisfying than finding out that some scholar or publisher has already compiled the information you need. Before you dig in to a long research problem, try to think whether it is likely that someone has already done this for you. Federal legislative histories for the past 20 years are easy if you know about the CIS volumes, for example. Digests gather many of the cases on a particular issue together in one place. Many treatises are filled with information that would be very time consuming to gather from scratch. Always try to find the easiest way to do a thorough and accurate job. Librarians can help you find out if someone has done your work for you. Make use of them.

14.12 BUT DON'T BE AFRAID TO BE THE FIRST, IF NECESSARY!

Stare decisis and binding precedent are, in some sense, fairy tales. You must be able to make an argument, even in the seemingly hopeless case. Remember, nothing is binding, nothing is controlling, there is always an argument. You have to train yourself to step up to the plate: make the distinction, resist the temptation to say there's nothing out there, work to craft an argument even where the case seems hopeless. And remember, novel arguments are successfully put forward all the time. Just because nobody has made an argument or a distinction before doesn't mean that it's a loser argument or baseless distinction.

14.13 EVALUATING SOURCES

In legal research, evaluating sources involves balancing what you need and want in terms of **authenticity**, **currency**, and **editorial work** (human-provided connections in and out from the source). Look at the organization of the source, the publisher, the date, the table of contents, the finding aids and tables. If there is an instructional preface, read it. Even if you've never seen this source before, you'll find that it falls into one of a very few types. You're ready to discern what the source has to offer you in your current situation.

Authenticity can be gauged by the publisher, and its relationship with the originator of the material. When dealing with primary sources, is the publisher the originating government entity itself? Is publication of the material specifically delegated to the publisher by that originating government entity? If there is no connection between the publisher and the originating government entity, be alert for motivations that might lead to either biased or sloppy publishing of inaccurately reproduced primary sources, especially in the case of material freely available on the Web.

Currency should be appropriate for your needs. One characteristic to look for is specific and accurate indication of how current the information is. Strangely enough, that information is often more unambiguously available for print resources than for online material, even though the latter may actually be more up to date.

Evaluating the **editorial** component of a source can involve assaying the authoritativeness of its commentary, the care with which the information has been indexed, or such elements as the clarity of the graphical layout. One factor to consider is the nature and reputability of the publisher. American legal publishing was dominated for many years by two large companies, West and Lawyers' Cooperative. These both published a full range of legal materials, starting with law reports and branching out into statutes, secondary works, and other practitioners' tools. Other publishers or imprints concentrated on the legal education area, sometimes branching out from there into more general legal works. Specialist publishers developed works designed for practitioners in areas like tax or criminal law, or catered to a local market. Today, American legal publishing, both online and in print, is even more dominated by two large companies, Thomson and Reed Elsevier. Comparatively few independent legal print publishers still function in the United States, but of course independent entrepreneurs aplenty are trying to gain a toehold in the market via the internet.

What are the implications of these industry developments for the researcher? Traditional publishers got involved in evaluation of the material they published because of the capital that would be tied up in producing and distributing that material, and because their reputations were on the line. West, in deciding to publish this book, considered the credentials, education, position, and experience of the two authors, as well as the characteristics of the proposed book itself: i.e., some moderate level of vetting went on. A potential reader of this book is entitled to rely to some extent on West's track record of such judgements in the past. The most respected law reviews have a long history of vetting the articles submitted to them: you would expect an article published in one of them to be by an important writer, a famous writer, or at least a good writer.

By contrast, a publishing company without such a track record puts the entire onus of evaluation onto the researcher. Such is the case with many online sources, including such mainstays as Westlaw and Lexis. Free portals on the Web (like Findlaw, the Legal Information Institute, LLRX, the 'Lectronic Law Library, etc.) have varying criteria for choosing links to sources of legal information, but ultimately they do not control the accuracy or the currency of that information. The commercial vendors or consolidators (e.g., Westlaw, Lexis, Lois) historically have taken some responsibility (not to be confused with legal liability!) for the completeness of their principal database components. If the information was not "out there" electronically from its producer, the consolidator would undertake to get it into electronic form themselves. This expansive undertaking paid off with a legal industry more and more inclined to focus on those resources available to them on Westlaw and Lexis.

Now that more and more data is becoming available without charge from its originators via the Web, researchers need to compare the merits of conducting research on Westlaw and Lexis with doing more piecemeal research via the free sources on the Web. Time efficiencies and the greater confidence that comes from familiarity are Westlaw/Lexis advantages, due to the more or less uniform interfaces within their respective databases. Theoretically, the data available on either Westlaw or Lexis is more complete. However, since the data does come from a variety of sources and was added to the database in accordance with a great number of different contracts with providers, you cannot rely absolutely on the commercial databases to be complete or accurate. You need, as with all research, to use your professional estimation of what should be available, not abdicate responsibility and limit yourself to what is available on one or even both services.

This matter of using your professional judgment when conducting research on Westlaw and Lexis needs to be underscored. Both services have instituted elaborate advisory services, available over the phone, by e-mail, or in live chat over the internet. These services can usefully help you zero in on where a particular kind of information is located within that system, or verify the date of currency or non-inclusion of certain data, but that's all. Again, the research is your responsibility. Anything you get from the research advisors you must be able to reconstruct or verify using your own logic and your own review of the sources.

14.14   AN AFTERWARD: THE WORLD OF UNPUBLISHED INFORMATION

The chapters prior to this one have emphasized the use of information that is published, whether electronically or in print, to the world at large. But sometimes the information you want is not circulated to the world on a "push" model. The task at hand can turn out to involve the extraction of information which is only made available by its originators on an "as needed" basis. This may involve presenting your "need to know" credentials to someone who is acting as a gatekeeper. Or the information may be freely available to all, but so time sensitive that it is generated fresh for every postulant (e.g., has there been any action on this bill in the last 6 hours?) When you need to rely on working with personal contacts in order to get needed information, the first step is finding someone who can help you.

Websites of entities like legislative committees, government agencies, courts, and law firms usually provide telephone numbers and e-mail addresses for public inquiries. Although directories of these web addresses exist (and indeed are touted over the air in radio advertising!), the best and most convenient way to find them is simply to use a search engine like Google. Put in as much detail as you know about the name of the sub-entity for which you are looking. Unlike print directories of web addresses, print directories of names and phone numbers can still be handy because they pull together a lot of such information into one handy list **(see Table 14.A)**. For more specific guidance than can be teased out of the titles people are given in such directories, the individual state guides to legal research **(Appendix)** usually go into detail about which government office is the appropriate target for different sorts of queries.

When calling a government entity for information, arm yourself in advance with the docket number of the case or the chapter (or bill) number of the law you are calling about. If you don't know the docket number of a case, at least know the official parties' names under which the case would be filed in the court records (e.g., ask for the records from "California v. Powell," not "the Rodney King case").

Table 14.A: Selected Directories of Helpful Phone Numbers

1. *Want's Federal–State Court Directory*. Washington, D.C.: WANT Pub. Co., c1984–

   This annual includes charts showing the organization of the different court systems, and lists useful phone numbers for each individual court. Try this book when you have to call around to a bunch of courts.

2. The "Yellow Books": a series of directories published by Leadership Directories, Inc. The most useful ones for the legal researcher are the *Federal Yellow Book* (executive agencies), the *Congressional Yellow Book*, and the *Judicial Yellow Book*. These are also available via the Web: see http://www. leadershipdirectories. com for details.

3. *The Martindale–Hubbell Law Directory*. New York: Martindale–Hubbell Law Directory, Inc.

   This annual listing of firms requires that you know the city in which the person or firm you seek is located in order to use the print version. The listings are also available on Lexis in a single file (Library and File = **MARHUB;ALL-DIR**), which eliminates this problem.

4. West Legal Directory. This directory permits you to search specifically for government or corporate counsel lawyers as well as lawyers in law firms. On Westlaw, the path is All Databases > Directories & Reference Materials > West Legal Directories (there is a variety of Databases, because you can also look for such supporting players as court reporters and process servers, each in their own file). Information from the Directory is also available without charge at Findlaw (http://lawyers.findlaw.com/).

If no public entity can or will provide you with the information you need, the private sector may be able to oblige. Figure out from case reports or from newspaper accounts whether a law firm or a particular lawyer is involved in the matter. You can then try and locate that firm or practitioner through a legal directory. Legal directories fall into two basic categories: directories where you pay to be included, and directories that are based on bar licensure records. Specialized directories also exist for particular types of practice. Many directories are subdivided by city, so get as much information as you can from your original source about where the firm or practitioner is located.

Now go out, do good, and have fun!

Appendix

SELECTED LEGAL RESEARCH
GUIDES FOR EACH OF THE
FIFTY STATES

Alabama:

Gary Orlando Lewis, *Legal Research in Alabama: How to Find and Understand the Law in Alabama.* Montgomery, Ala.: Gary Orlando Lewis, c2001.

University of Alabama School of Law, Bounds Law Library:
http://www.library.law.ua.edu/links/bama.htm [annotated links to web sources]

Alaska:

Alaska Court System page on Legal Research: Alaska Resources
http://www. state.ak. us/courts/ aklegal.htm [covers print as well as web sources]

Arizona:

Kathy Shimpock–Vieweg and Marianne Sidorski Alcorn, *Arizona Legal Research Guide.* Buffalo, N.Y.: W.S. Hein, 1992.

Arizona State University, Ross–Blakley Law Library: Research Guides: Arizona
http://www. law.asu. edu/?id=8551#Arizona [detailed guides on Arizona legal research]

Arizona State Library, Archives, and Public Records: Law and Research Library Division Guide to Arizona Legislative History at Arizona's Capitol
http://www.lib. az.us/ is/lr/ leghist.cfm

Arkansas:

Arkansas Judiciary website: Arkansas Resources
http://courts.state. ar.us/ courts/ links.html [links to online information]

California:

John K. Hanft, *Legal Research in California.* 5th ed. [St. Paul, Minn.]: Thomson/West Group, 2004.

Daniel W. Martin, *Henke's California Law Guide.* 7th ed. Newark, N.J.: LexisNexis/Matthew Bender, 2004

University of California, Berkeley, Boalt Hall School of Law, Law Library: Research Guides: California
http://www.law.berkeley. edu/library/ online/guides/ california.html [includes link to "A Guide to Finding California Legislative History"]

University of California, Los Angeles, School of Law, Hugh and Hazel Darling Law Library: California Research Guides
http:// www. law.ucla.edu/home/ index.asp?page=1435 [a collection of detailed guides in .pdf format]

Colorado:

Gary Alexander, *Colorado Legal Resources: An Annotated Bibliography.* [Chicago, Ill.]: American Association of Law Libraries, c1987.

University of Denver College of Law, Westminster Law Library: Research Handouts
http://www. law.du.edu/library/ handouts/ colorado.cfm [a collection of guides in .pdf format, with links]

Connecticut:

Lawrence G. Cheeseman and Arlene C. Bielefield, *The Connecticut Legal Research Handbook.* Guilford, CT: Connecticut Law Book Co., 1992.

Connecticut State Library: Guide to Connecticut Legislative History
http://www.cslib.org/leghis.asp

Connecticut State Library: Frequently Asked Questions
http://www.cslib.org/faq.htm [click on Law and Legislation]

Connecticut Judicial Branch Law Libraries: Research Guides
http://www.jud.state.ct.us/LawLib/selfguides.htm

Delaware:

Widener University School of Law, Law Library and Legal Information Center: Delaware: Legal and Non Legal Online Resources
http://www. law.widener. edu/Law–Library/ new/research/ de.shtml

District of Columbia:

Leah F. Chanin, Pamela J. Gregory, Sarah K. Wiant, *Legal Research in the District of Columbia, Maryland and Virginia.* 2nd ed. Buffalo, N.Y.: W.S. Hein, 2000–

University of the District of Columbia, School of Law Library: Legal Resources on the Internet: The District of Columbia (D.C.), by Rick

Apgood, April 2002:
http:// www.law.udc.edu/ library/ reference.htm

Florida:

Barbara J. Busharis and Suzanne E. Rowe, *Florida Legal Research: Sources, Process, and Analysis*. 2nd ed. Durham, N.C.: Carolina Academic Press, c2002.

University of Florida Levin College of Law, Legal Information Center: Florida Research Guides
http://www.law. ufl. edu/lic/ guides/ [includes annotated links on legislative history]

Georgia:

Leah F. Chanin and Suzanne L. Cassidy, *Guide to Georgia Legal Research and Legal History*. Norcross, GA: Harrison Co., c1990–

Emory School of Law, Macmillan Law Library: Internet Legal Research: Georgia Law
http://www. law. emory.edu/ erd/subject/ ilrga.html

Mercer University, Walter F. George School of Law, Furman Smith Law Library: Georgia Resources
http:// www.law.mercer. edu/library/ GeorgiaResources/ GeorgiaResources.cfm

Hawaii:

Richard F. Kahle, *How to Research Constitutional, Legislative, and Statutory History in Hawaii*. 3rd ed. Honolulu, Hawaii: Legislative Reference Bureau, [2001]. Available as .pdf file at
http:// www. state.hi.us/lrb/ reports/ pams.html

University of Hawaii at Manoa, William S. Richardson School of Law Library: Hawaii Internet Legal Resources
http:// library.law. hawaii.edu/ refres/ legal_resources /hawaii.php

Idaho:

University of Idaho College of Law Library: Legal Research Guides
http:// www.law. uidaho.edu/ default. aspx?pid=66157 [links to guides on various aspects of Idaho legal research]

Illinois:

Mark E. Wojcik, *Illinois Legal Research*. Durham, N.C.: Carolina Academic Press, c2003.

University of Illinois College of Law, Albert E. Jenner, Jr. Memorial Law Library: Illinois Legislative History
http:// library.law. uiuc.edu/sub/ leghistory.htm [detailed guide dealing with print, fiche, and audio sources only]

Illinois General Assembly, Legislative Reference Bureau
http:// www. ilga.gov/ commission/ lrb_home.html [includes link to
Researching Legislative History, by Richard C. Edwards]

Indiana:

Indiana University Law Library: Where to Locate Indiana Legislative History Sources
http://www. law.indiana.edu /lib/netres/govt/inleghis.pdf

AccessIndiana: Law and Justice
http://www. in.gov/ai/ law/ [official site of the State of Indiana: links
to legal resources]

Iowa:

John Edwards, *Iowa Legal Research Guide*. Buffalo, N.Y.: William S.
Hein, 2003.

Iowa Legislature, General Assembly: Track Legislation
http:// www.legis. state.ia.us/Legislation.html

State of Iowa, Judicial Branch
http://www.judicial.state.ia.us/

Kansas:

Joseph A. Custer and Fritz Snyder, *Kansas Legal Research and
Reference Guide*. 3rd ed. Topeka, Kansas: Kansas Bar Association,
c2003–

University of Kansas School of Law, Wheat Law Library: Legal
Research Links—Kansas
http://www.law.ku.edu/library/research/kansas.shtml

Kentucky:

Kurt X. Metzmeier, Amy Beckham Osborne, Shaun Esposito, *Kentucky Legal Research Manual*. 3rd ed. Lexington, Ky.: University of
Kentucky College of Law, Office of Continuing Legal Education,
c2005.

University of Louisville, Louis D. Brandeis School of Law Library:
Kentucky Jump Zone
http:// library.louisville. edu/law/Research/kyjump.htm [detailed
guides and lists of links]

Louisiana:

Win–Shin S. Chiang, *Louisiana Legal Research*. 2nd ed. Austin,
Tex.: Butterworth Legal Publishers, c1990.

Law Library of Louisiana
http:// www.lasc.org/law_library/ library_information. asp [links, at
the bottom of the page, to pathfinders]

Maine:

William W.Wells, *Maine Legal Research Guide*. Portland, Me.: Tower Pub. Co., c1989.

Maine State Law and Legislative Reference Library: Compiling a Legislative History
http:// www.state.me.us/ legis/lawlib/leghist.htm

Maryland:

Leah F. Chanin, Pamela J. Gregory, Sarah K. Wiant, *LegalResearch in the District of Columbia, Maryland and Virginia*. 2nd ed. Buffalo, N.Y.: W.S. Hein, 2000–

University of Maryland School of Law, Thurgood Marshall Law Library: Maryland Resources
http://www.law. umaryland.edu/marshall/researchguides/specialtypages/ marylandresources. asp [includes links to very detailed research guides]

Massachusetts:

Mary Ann Neary, editor, *Handbook of Legal Research in Massachusetts*. 2nd ed. Boston, MA: Massachusetts Continuing Legal Education, 2002–

The State Library of Massachusetts: Guide to Massachusetts Law and Legal Resources
http://www. mass.gov/lib/ guides/ masslaw.htm [includes link to detailed Legislative History page]

Michigan:

Richard L. Beer and Judith J. Field, *Michigan Legal Literature: An Annotated Guide*. 2nd ed. Buffalo, NY: W.S. Hein, 1991.

Michigan State Law Library:
http:// www.michigan.gov/hal/ [click on Resources for Law Research, then Law Library: Research Guides]

Minnesota:

John Tessner, Brenda Wolfe, George R. Jackson, Arlette M. Soderberg, *Minnesota Legal Research Guide*. 2nd ed. Buffalo, N.Y.: W.S. Hein, 2002.

Minnesota State Legislature: Minnesota Legislative History Step by Step
http://www.leg.state.mn.us/leg/leghist/histstep.asp

University of Minnesota Law Library: Basic Minnesota Legal Research
http:// www.law.umn.edu/ library/tools/pathfinders/minnresearch.html

Mississippi:

University of Mississippi Law Library: Mississippi Law
http://library.law.olemiss.edu/library/state/ms.shtml

Missouri:

Missouri House of Representatives
http://www.house.mo.gov [Click on Legislative Information]

Montana:

Stephen R. Jordan, *A Guide to Montana Legal Research*.7th ed.,
updated by Meredith Hoffman. Helena, MT: State Law Library of
Montana, c2002.

State Law Library of Montana: Montana Legal Information
http://www. lawlibrary.state. mt.us/ [then click on "Montana Legal
Information"; includes the Jordan and Hoffman work in .pdf]

Nebraska:

Kay L. Andrus, et al, *Research Guide to Nebraska Law, 2005*.
[United States]: LexisNexis.

University of Nebraska–Lincoln, College of Law, Schmid Law Library: Legal Research Guides
http:// www.unl. edu/lawcoll/ schmid/guides.html [includes guides on
Nebraska Cases, Numbering System for Nebraska Revised Statutes,
and Using Nebraska Statutes]

Nevada:

Nevada Legislature: Nevada Law Library
http://www.leg.state.nv.us/law1.cfm [links to primary sources on the
Web]

University of Nevada Las Vegas, William S. Boyd School of Law,
Wiener–Rogers Law Library: Research: Nevada Legal Resources
http:// www.law.unlv.edu/ library/libraryResearch_ nevada_law.html
[links to sources on the Web]

New Hampshire:

Franklin Pierce Law Center Library: New Hampshire Legislative
History, by Cynthia R. Landau
http://www.library.piercelaw.edu/LWP–New/Research/Guides/NH_
Legislative-History.htm

New Jersey:

Paul Axel–Lute, *New Jersey Legal Research Handbook*. 4th ed. New
Brunswick, N.J.: New Jersey Institute for Continuing Legal Education, 1998.

Rutgers–Newark Law Library: Library Pathfinders
http:// law-library.rutgers.edu/resources/ pathfinders.php [includes guides to N.J. legal materials and legislative history]

New Jersey State Library: Legislative Histories
http:// www.njstatelib. org/NJLH

New Mexico:

New Mexico Supreme Court Library
http:// fscll.org/ [links to sources on the Web]

New York:

William H. Manz, *Gibson's New York Legal Research Guide*, 3rd ed. Buffalo, N.Y.: W.S. Hein, 2004.

New York State Library: The Legislative History of a New York State Law
http://www.nysl.nysed.gov/leghist/

> Legislative Intent
> http://www.nysl.nysed.gov/legint.htm

New York Law School Library: Guide to New York Legal Research in the Mendik Library
http://www.nyls.edu/miscdownloads/ny_research.pdf

North Carolina:

Jean Sinclair McKnight, *North Carolina Legal Research Guide*. Littleton, Colo.: F.B. Rothman, 1994.

University of North Carolina at Chapel Hill, Kathrine R. Everett Law Library: North Carolina Law Sites
http:// library.law.unc.edu/ research/nc_legal_databases. html [links to sources on Web and to research guides]

North Carolina Supreme Court Library: Legislative History in North Carolina
http:// www.aoc. state.nc.us/www/copyright/ library/liblegh.html

North Dakota:

North Dakota Supreme Court: Legal Research: North Dakota Legal Resources
http:// www.court.state. nd.us/ Research/ [links to sources on Web]

Ohio:

Melanie K. Putnam and Susan M. Schaefgen, *Ohio Legal Research Guide*. Buffalo,N.Y.: W.S. Hein, 1997.

Ohio State University, Michael E. Moritz Law Library: Introduction to the State Materials of Ohio
http:// moritzlaw.osu.edu/ library/researchguides/ohio.html

Ohio Legislative Service Commission: A Guide to Legislative History in Ohio
http:// www.lsc.state.oh. us/membersonly/history.pdf

Oklahoma:

Oklahoma Department of Libraries: Resources Regarding Oklahoma's Legislative Measures
http:// www.odl.state.ok. us/lawinfo/billinfo.htm [information about legislative history]

State of Oklahoma, Office of the Attorney General: Oklahoma Public Legal Research System
http://oklegal.onenet.net/

Oregon:

Suzanne E. Rowe, *Oregon Legal Research*. Durham, N.C.: Carolina Academic Press, 2003.

Northwestern School of Law of Lewis and Clark College, Paul L. Bole Law Library: Oregon Legal Research
http:// lawlib.lclark.edu/ research/ oregonlaw.php [extensive collection of links and guides]

Pennsylvania:

Frank Y. Liu, et al, *Pennsylvania Legal Research Handbook*. 2001 ed. Philadelphia, PA: American Lawyer Media, c2001.

Jenkins Law Library: Research Guides
http:// www.jenkinslaw.org/ collection/ researchguides/ index.php [includes "How to Compile a Pennsylvania Legislative History"]

University of Pittsburgh School of Law, Barco Law Library: Pennsylvania Legal Research, by Marc Silverman
http:// www. law.pitt.edu/ library/legal/paresearch.html [extensive guide, with links]

Rhode Island:

University of Rhode Island, University Libraries: Rhode Island Legal Sources
http:// www.uri.edu/ library/guides/subject/govlaw/rilegal.html#leghist

South Carolina:

Paula G. Benson and Deborah A. Davis, *A Guide to South Carolina Legal Research and Citation*. [Columbia, S.C.]: South Carolina Bar, Continuing Legal Education Division, 1991.

University of South Carolina, School of Law, Coleman Karesh Law Library: South Carolina Reference Desk
http:// www.law.sc.edu/ library/online/scref.shtml [links to sources on Web]

South Dakota:

Delores A. Jorgensen, *South Dakota Legal Research Guide*. 2nd ed. Buffalo, N.Y.: W.S. Hein & Co., 1999.

South Dakota Legislature, Legislative Research Council
http:// legis.state.sd.us/ index.aspx [main page]

South Dakota Legislature, Legislative Research Council: How to Compile Legislative History Using the Legislative Research Council Web Site
http://legis.state.sd.us/general/index.htm

Tennessee:

Lewis L. Laska, *Tennessee Legal Research Handbook*. Buffalo, N.Y.: W. S. Hein, 1977.

University of Tennessee, University Libraries: Tennessee Legislative Materials
http:// www.lib.utk.edu/ gpo/tnlegs.html [annotated bibliographic guide with links]

Texas:

Brandon D. Quarles and Matthew C. Cordon, *Legal Research for the Texas Practitioner*. Buffalo, N.Y.: William S. Hein, 2003.

Matthew C. Cordon and Brandon D. Quarles, *Specialized Topics in Texas Legal Research*. Buffalo, N.Y.: W.S. Hein, 2005.

Southern Methodist University, Underwood Law Library: Legal Research Guides
http:// library.law.smu.edu/ resguide/ [many detailed guides to Texas topics, with links]

Utah:

Utah State Records and Archives Service: Legislative Intent and Legislative History
http:// www.archives.state.ut.us/ referenc/leghist.htm

State of Utah, Office of the Attorney General: Legal Research Tools: Utah Legal Resources
http:// attorneygeneral.utah.gov/ legalresearch.html [Links to Web sources]

Vermont:

Vermont Judiciary: Vermont Legal Research
http://www.vermontjudiciary.org/Resources/Links/LinksLegal.htm
[links to Web sources]

Virginia:

Leah F. Chanin, Pamela J.Gregory, and Sarah K. Wiant, *Legal Research in the District of Columbia, Maryland and Virginia.*2nd ed. Buffalo, N.Y.: W.S. Hein, 2000–

John D. Eure and Gail F. Zwirner, editors, *A Guide to Legal Research in Virginia.* 5th ed. [Virginia]: Virginia CLE Publications, 2005.

University of Virginia Law Library: Virginia Legal Research
http:// www.law.virginia. edu/main/virginia + research [covers print and Web sources]

Washington:

Penny A. Hazelton, et al, *Washington Legal Researcher's Deskbook, 3d.* Seattle, Wash.: Marian Gould Gallagher Law Library, 2002.

University of Washington, Marian Gould Gallagher Law Library: Washington State Legislative History, by Peggy Jarrett and Cheryl Nyberg
http://lib.law. washington. edu/ref/washleghis.html [detailed guide with links]

Washington State Law Library: Informational Brochures
http:// www.courts.wa.gov/library/ [topics include administrative law research; no links]

West Virginia:

West Virginia College of Law, George R. Farmer, Jr. College of Law Library: West Virginia Guides
http://www.wvu.edu/=law/library/Guides_wv.htm

Wisconsin:

Richard A. Danner, *Legal Research in Wisconsin.* Madison: University of Wisconsin, Extension Law Dept., c1980.

Wisconsin Legislative Reference Bureau: Guide to Researching Wisconsin Legislation
http:// www.legis.state.wi.us/ lrb/pubs/ [click on "Wisconsin Briefs" and then on No.98–8]

Wisconsin State Law Library: Legal Research Guides
http://wsll.state.wi.us/legalresearch.html [links to research guides, including "Finding Administrative Intent in the Wisconsin Administrative Register"]

Wyoming:

Wyoming State Law Library: Wyoming Legal Materials
http:// www.courts.state. wy.us/wylegal.htm [links to Web sources]

*

Index

D

E

F

G

H

Supreme Court,
  see United States Supreme Court
Supreme Court Reporter (West), 122–123

T

Terms and connectors searching,
  see Boolean searching
Terms of art, 8
THOMAS (website)
  bills, 50–52, 83
  committee reports, 69, 70, 73, 75
  Congressional Record, 84, 86
  Public Laws, 35, 39
Treaties and International Law (website),
  215
Treaties and Other International Acts Series
  (GPO), 213
Treaties in Force (GPO), 214
  Treaty Actions (website), 214
Treatises, 53, 137–140
Treaty research, 213–214

U

Uniform Laws Annotated, 57–58, 199
Uniform acts, 88, 199
Uniform System of Citation, A
  see *Bluebook, The*
Union List of Appellate Court Records and
  Briefs (Whiteman and Campbell), 129
United Nations, 207, 212–214, 215, 216
  United Nations Treaty Collection (web-
    site), 215
United States Code, 5, 14–26, 28–31, 43, 46,
  148, 149, 165–170, 179
United States Code Annotated, 5, 14, 16–23,
  25–29, 45–46, 54–57, 68, 70, 95, 141,
  192, 193
United States Code Congressional and Ad-
  ministrative News, 5–6, 32–39, 64,
  68–70, 73, 74, 76, 85
United States Code Service, 14–20, 23,
  25–30, 32–36, 38, 39, 45–46, 54–57,
  95, 141, 192, 193
United States Congressional Serial Set,
  69, 74, 81
United States Congressional Serial Set Ca-
  talog, 74
United States Courts of Appeals, 124,
  127–129
  records and briefs, 129
United States District Courts, 124–126
United States Law Week (BNA), 123, 181,
  188
United States Patent Quarterly, 124
United States Reports, 123, 195
United States Statutes at Large, 5, 28,
  31–33, 35–38, 39, 40–44, 46, 64, 73,
  74, 76, 85, 148, 163, 169, 227
United States Supreme Court, 107, 119,
  121–126, 181, 195

United States Supreme Court—Cont'd
  oral arguments, 124
  records and briefs, 124, 125
United States Supreme Court Digest (West),
  109, 114, 119, 193, 194
United States Supreme Court Reports, Law-
  yers' Edition (Lexis), 122–123
  Quick Case Table, 119
United States Tax Cases (CCH), 183
United States Treaties and Other Interna-
  tional Agreements (GPO), 213
Universal citations, 4
University of Minnesota Human Rights Library (website), 215
Updating,
  cases, 134–136
  code annotations, 55–56
  Code of Federal Regulations, 171–174
  codes, 25–27, 31–33
  court rules, 195–197
  session laws, 41–42

V

Virtual Chase (website), 206

W

Want's Federal–State Court Directory, 131,
  222
Weekly Compilation of Presidential Docu-
  ments, 169
Westlaw,
  bills, 50–51, 83
  cases, 106–133
  Congressional committee reports, 69, 73,
    75
  Congressional hearings, 78
  Congressional Record, 84, 86
  court rules, 193
  Keysearch, 104
  law review indexes, 91–102 *passim*
  legal ethics, 202, 203, 205
  legislative histories, compiled, 65
  municipal ordinances, 222
  Public Laws, 33, 35, 36, 39
  state statutes compared, 62
  Supreme Court
    records and briefs, 125
    transcripts, 126
  USCA, 16, 45–46, 70
  USCCAN, 70, 73
West's Federal Forms, 146
West's Legal Desk Reference (Statsky), 140
West's Legal Forms, 146
West's Texas Forms, 147
White House (website), 169
WilsonWeb, 91
WIPO Treaties (website), 215
"Words and phrases", 2
World Dictionary of Legal Abbreviations
  (Kavass and Prince), 103

Z

†